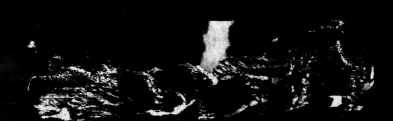

WITCHBLADE

SHADES OF GRAY

WITCHBLADE
SHADES OF GRAY

Written by
LEAH MOORE
& JOHN REPPION

Art by
STEPHEN SEGOVIA Issues 1 and 2
WALTER GEOVANI Issues 3 and 4

Lettering by
SIMON BOWLAND

Coloring by
ROMULO FAJARDO JR.

Cover by
STEPHEN SEGOVIA

Collects issues 1 through 4 of the Dynamite Entertainment
and Top Cow mini-series, Witchblade: Shades of Gray.

Trade Design by Jason Ullmeyer

FOR TOP COW PRODUCTIONS, INC.

MARC SILVESTRI • CHIEF EXECUTIVE OFFICER
MATT HAWKINS • PRESIDENT AND CHIEF OPERATING OFFICER
FILIP SABLIK • PUBLISHER
ROB LEVIN • VICE PRESIDENT - EDITORIAL
MEL CAYLO • VICE PRESIDENT - MARKETING & SALES
CHAZ RIGGS • GRAPHIC DESIGN
PHIL SMITH • MANAGING EDITOR
JOSHUA COZINE • ASSISTANT EDITOR

FOR DYNAMITE ENTERTAINMENT
NICK BARRUCCI • PRESIDENT
JUAN COLLADO • CHIEF OPERATING OFFICER
JOSEPH RYBANDT • DIRECTOR OF MARKETING
JOSH JOHNSON • CREATIVE DIRECTOR
JASON ULLMEYER • GRAPHIC DESIGNER

First Edition
ISBN-10: 1-933305-72-X   ISBN-13: 9-781933-305721
10 9 8 7 6 5 4 3 2 1

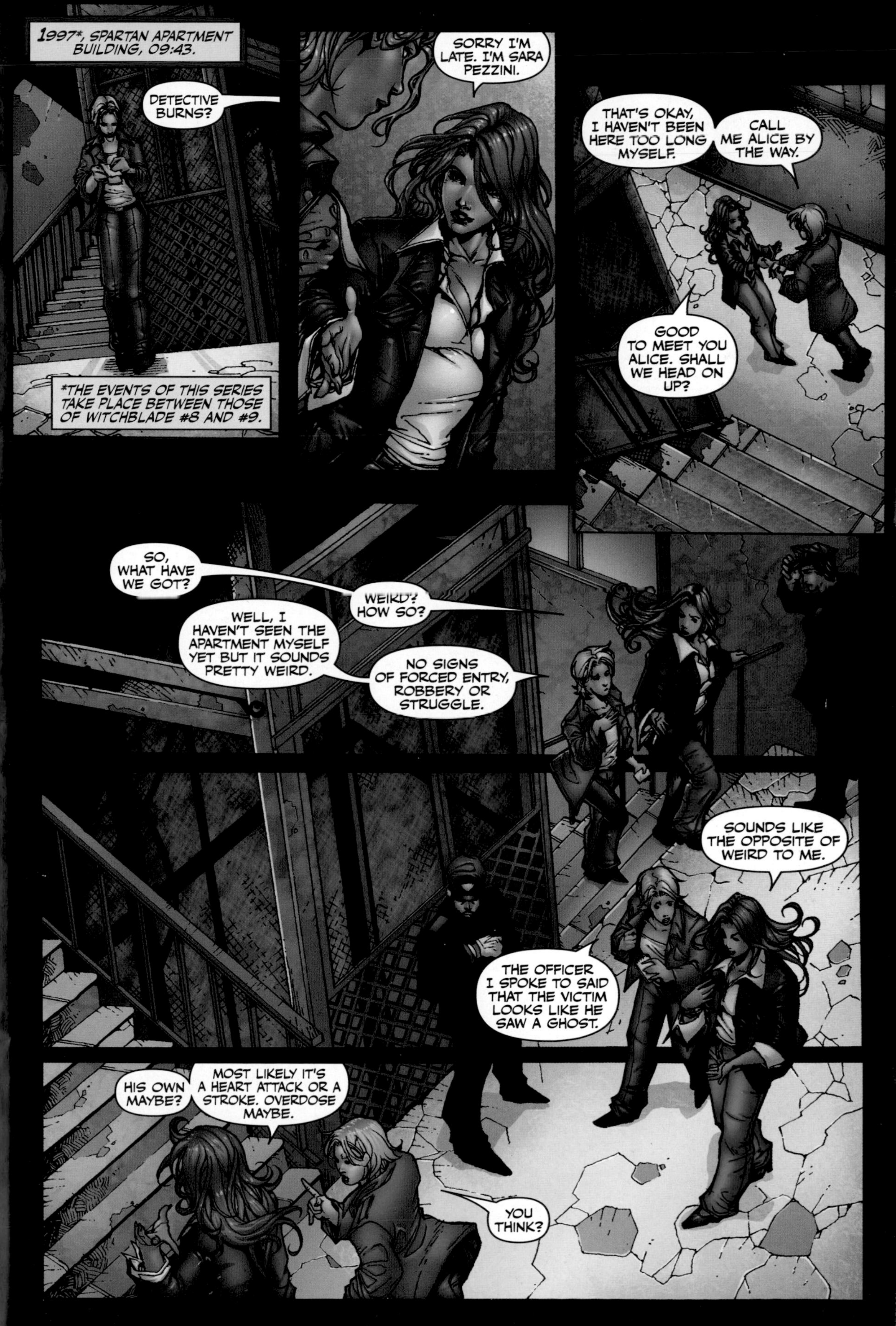
1997*, SPARTAN APARTMENT BUILDING, 09:43.
DETECTIVE BURNS?
*THE EVENTS OF THIS SERIES TAKE PLACE BETWEEN THOSE OF WITCHBLADE #8 AND #9.
SORRY I'M LATE. I'M SARA PEZZINI.
THAT'S OKAY, I HAVEN'T BEEN HERE TOO LONG MYSELF.
CALL ME ALICE BY THE WAY.
GOOD TO MEET YOU ALICE. SHALL WE HEAD ON UP?
SO, WHAT HAVE WE GOT?
WELL, I HAVEN'T SEEN THE APARTMENT MYSELF YET BUT IT SOUNDS PRETTY WEIRD.
WEIRD? HOW SO?
NO SIGNS OF FORCED ENTRY, ROBBERY OR STRUGGLE.
SOUNDS LIKE THE OPPOSITE OF WEIRD TO ME.
THE OFFICER I SPOKE TO SAID THAT THE VICTIM LOOKS LIKE HE SAW A GHOST.
HIS OWN MAYBE?
MOST LIKELY IT'S A HEART ATTACK OR A STROKE. OVERDOSE MAYBE.
YOU THINK?

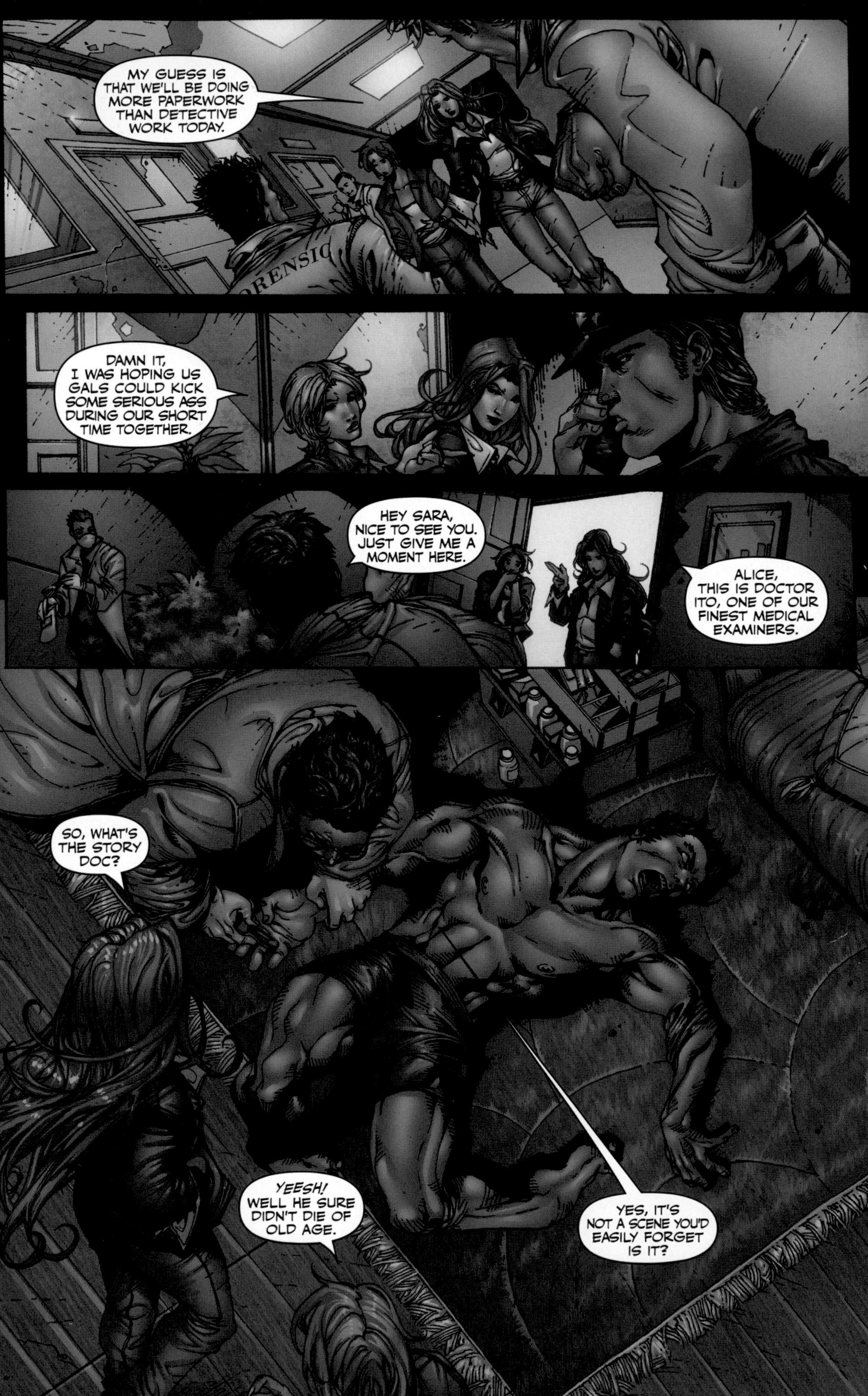

MY GUESS IS THAT WE'LL BE DOING MORE PAPERWORK THAN DETECTIVE WORK TODAY.
FORENSIC
DAMN IT, I WAS HOPING US GALS COULD KICK SOME SERIOUS ASS DURING OUR SHORT TIME TOGETHER.
HEY SARA, NICE TO SEE YOU. JUST GIVE ME A MOMENT HERE.
ALICE, THIS IS DOCTOR ITO, ONE OF OUR FINEST MEDICAL EXAMINERS.
SO, WHAT'S THE STORY DOC?
YEESH! WELL HE SURE DIDN'T DIE OF OLD AGE.
YES, IT'S NOT A SCENE YOU'D EASILY FORGET IS IT?

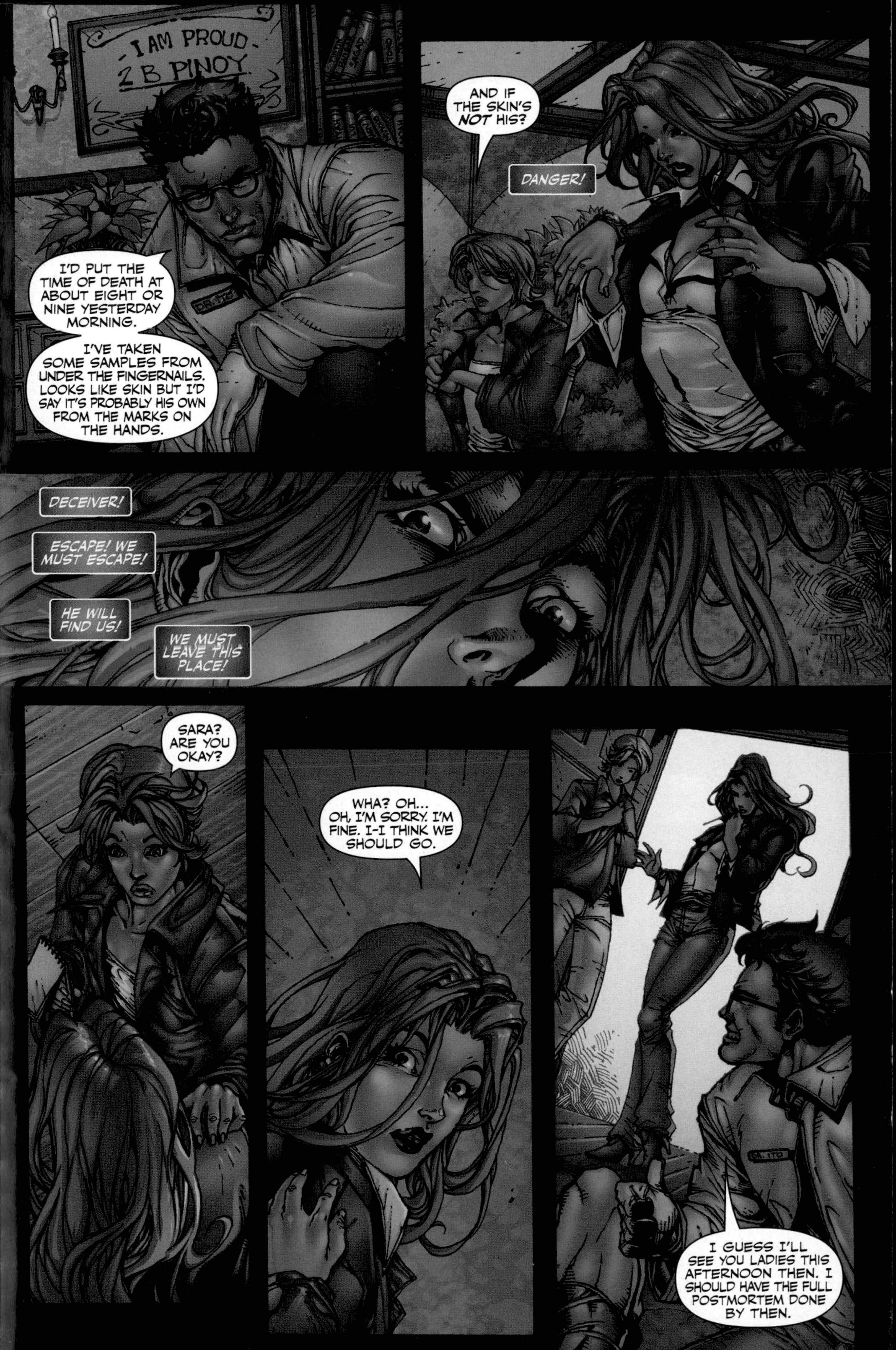
I AM PROUD 2 B PINOY
I'D PUT THE TIME OF DEATH AT ABOUT EIGHT OR NINE YESTERDAY MORNING.
I'VE TAKEN SOME SAMPLES FROM UNDER THE FINGERNAILS. LOOKS LIKE SKIN BUT I'D SAY IT'S PROBABLY HIS OWN FROM THE MARKS ON THE HANDS.
AND IF THE SKIN'S *NOT* HIS?
DANGER!
DECEIVER!
ESCAPE! WE MUST ESCAPE!
HE WILL FIND US!
WE MUST LEAVE THIS PLACE!
SARA? ARE YOU OKAY?
WHA? OH... OH, I'M SORRY. I'M FINE. I-I THINK WE SHOULD GO.
I GUESS I'LL SEE YOU LADIES THIS AFTERNOON THEN. I SHOULD HAVE THE FULL POSTMORTEM DONE BY THEN.

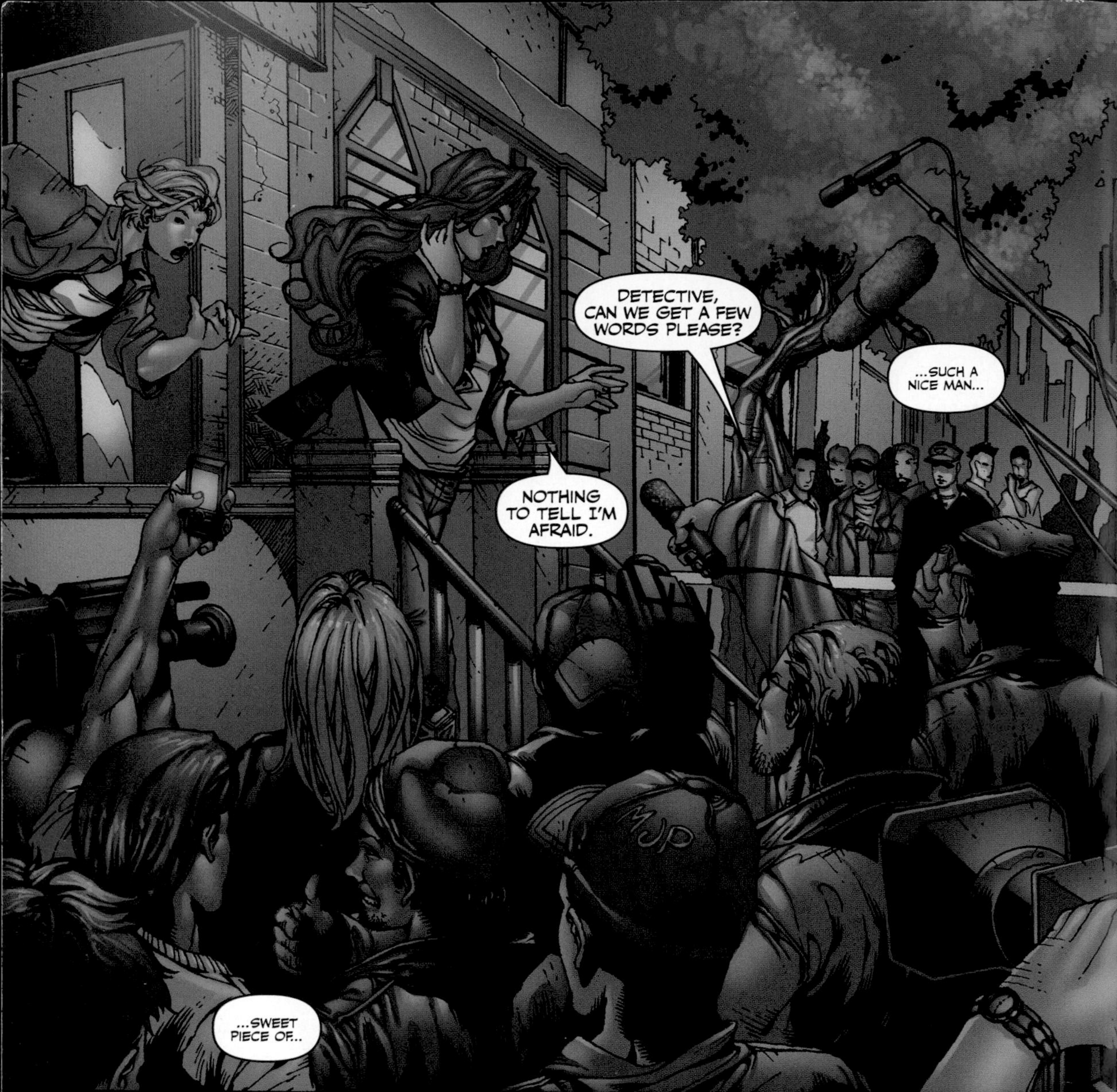
DETECTIVE, CAN WE GET A FEW WORDS PLEASE?
...SUCH A NICE MAN...
NOTHING TO TELL I'M AFRAID.
...SWEET PIECE OF...

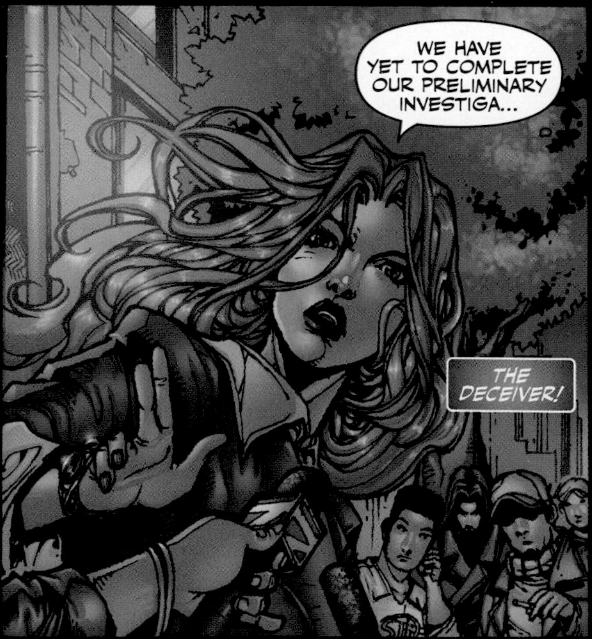
WE HAVE YET TO COMPLETE OUR PRELIMINARY INVESTIGA...
THE DECEIVER!

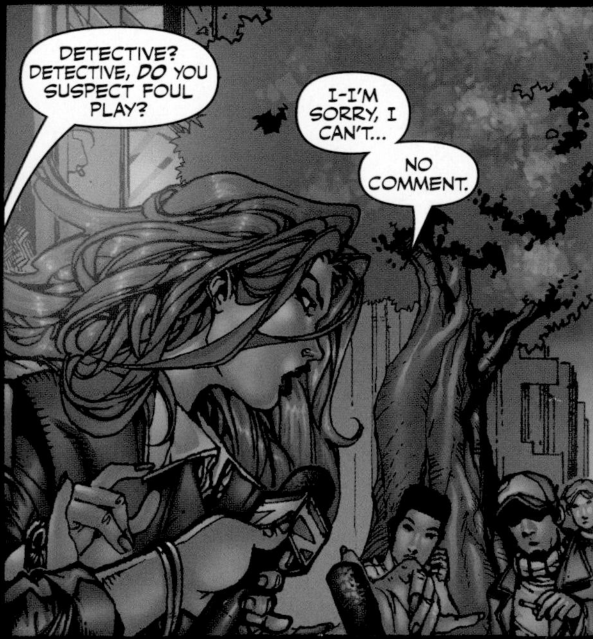
DETECTIVE? DETECTIVE, DO YOU SUSPECT FOUL PLAY?
I-I'M SORRY, I CAN'T...
NO COMMENT.

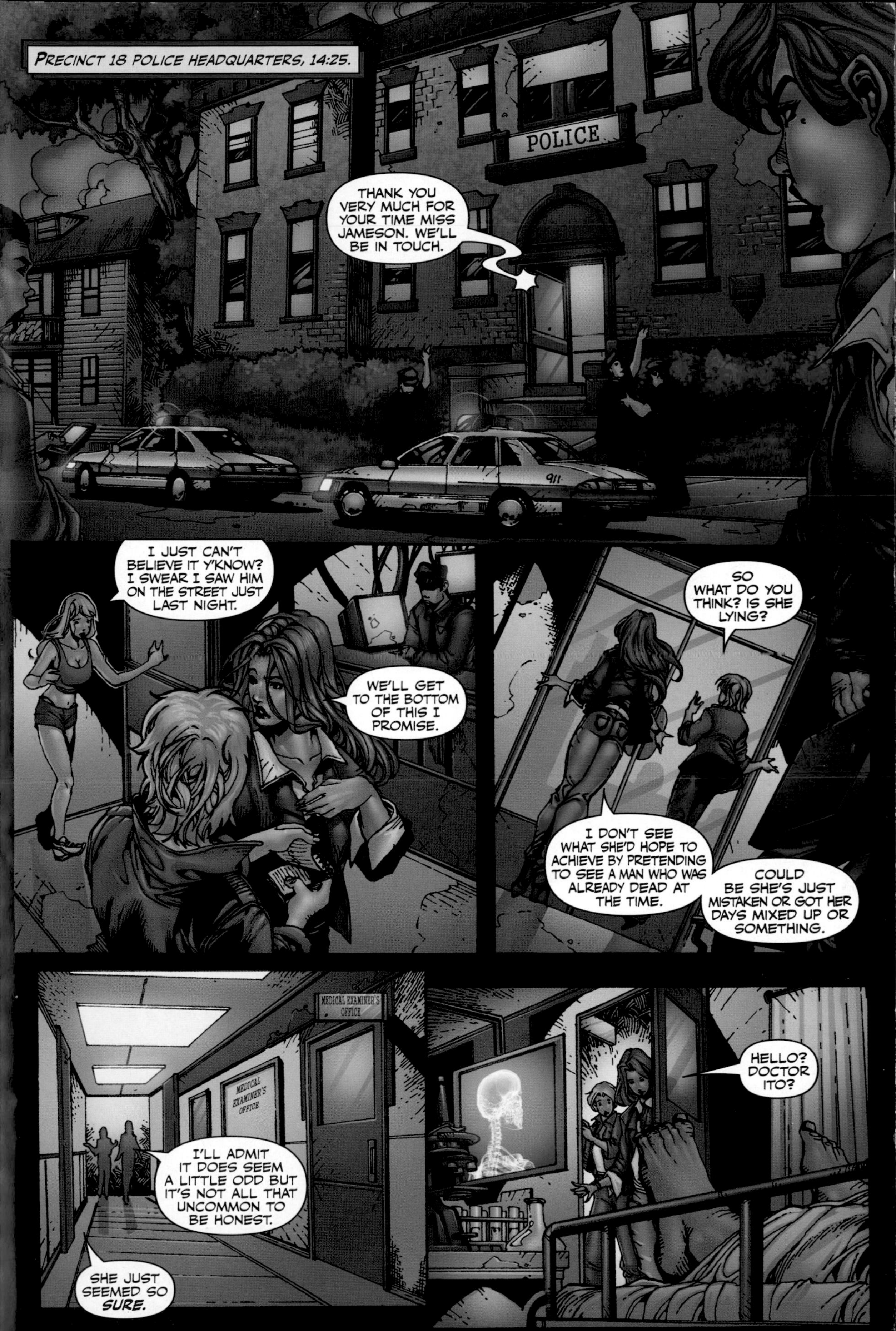
PRECINCT 18 POLICE HEADQUARTERS, 14:25.
POLICE
THANK YOU VERY MUCH FOR YOUR TIME MISS JAMESON. WE'LL BE IN TOUCH.
I JUST CAN'T BELIEVE IT Y'KNOW? I SWEAR I SAW HIM ON THE STREET JUST LAST NIGHT.
WE'LL GET TO THE BOTTOM OF THIS I PROMISE.
SO WHAT DO YOU THINK? IS SHE LYING?
I DON'T SEE WHAT SHE'D HOPE TO ACHIEVE BY PRETENDING TO SEE A MAN WHO WAS ALREADY DEAD AT THE TIME.
COULD BE SHE'S JUST MISTAKEN OR GOT HER DAYS MIXED UP OR SOMETHING.
MEDICAL EXAMINER'S OFFICE
MEDICAL EXAMINER'S OFFICE
I'LL ADMIT IT DOES SEEM A LITTLE ODD BUT IT'S NOT ALL THAT UNCOMMON TO BE HONEST.
SHE JUST SEEMED SO *SURE.*
HELLO? DOCTOR ITO?

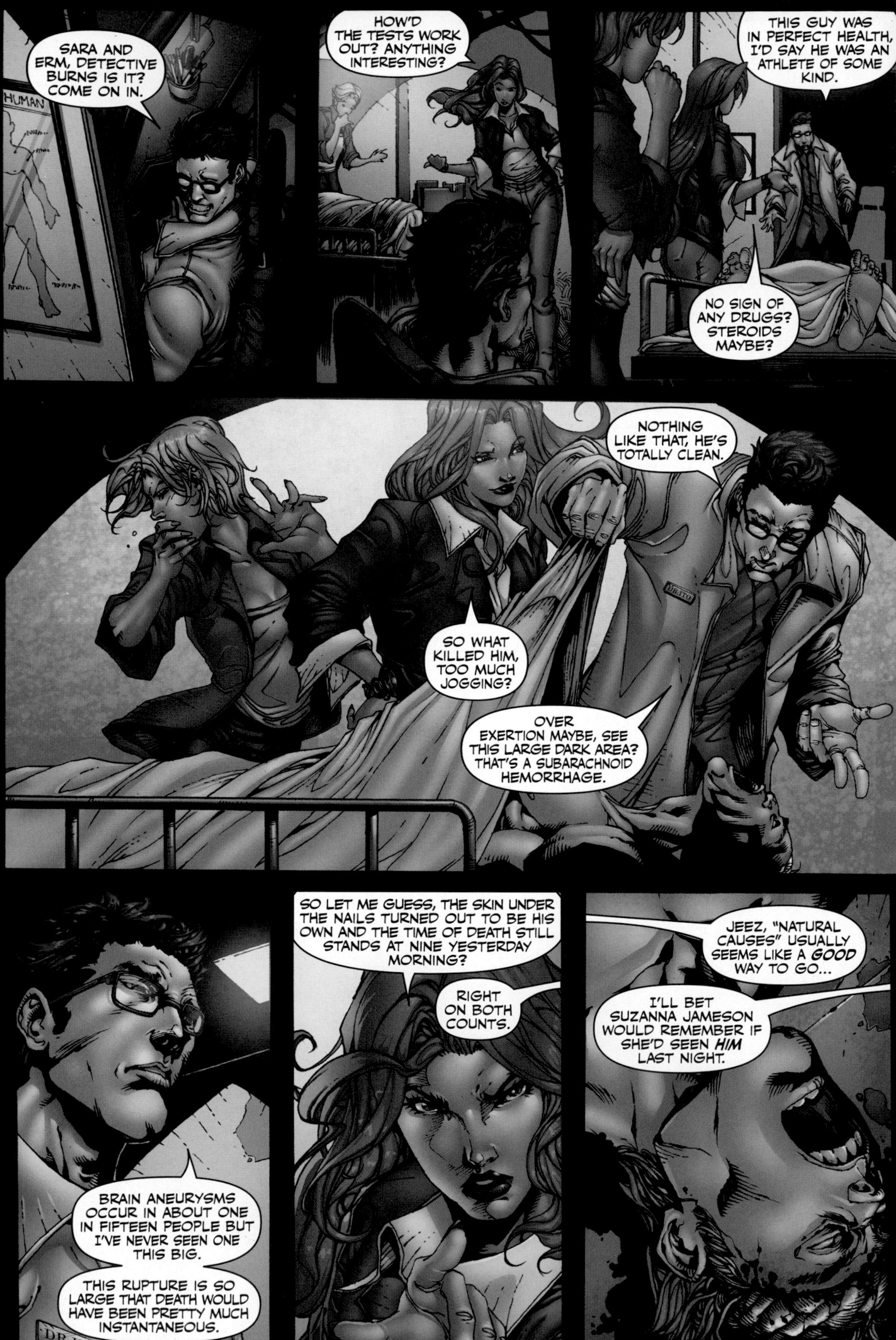
SARA AND ERM, DETECTIVE BURNS IS IT? COME ON IN.
HUMAN
HOW'D THE TESTS WORK OUT? ANYTHING INTERESTING?
THIS GUY WAS IN PERFECT HEALTH, I'D SAY HE WAS AN ATHLETE OF SOME KIND.
NO SIGN OF ANY DRUGS? STEROIDS MAYBE?
NOTHING LIKE THAT, HE'S TOTALLY CLEAN.
SO WHAT KILLED HIM, TOO MUCH JOGGING?
OVER EXERTION MAYBE, SEE THIS LARGE DARK AREA? THAT'S A SUBARACHNOID HEMORRHAGE.
DR. ITO
BRAIN ANEURYSMS OCCUR IN ABOUT ONE IN FIFTEEN PEOPLE BUT I'VE NEVER SEEN ONE THIS BIG.
THIS RUPTURE IS SO LARGE THAT DEATH WOULD HAVE BEEN PRETTY MUCH INSTANTANEOUS.
DR. ITO
SO LET ME GUESS, THE SKIN UNDER THE NAILS TURNED OUT TO BE HIS OWN AND THE TIME OF DEATH STILL STANDS AT NINE YESTERDAY MORNING?
RIGHT ON BOTH COUNTS.
JEEZ, "NATURAL CAUSES" USUALLY SEEMS LIKE A *GOOD* WAY TO GO...
I'LL BET SUZANNA JAMESON WOULD REMEMBER IF SHE'D SEEN *HIM* LAST NIGHT.

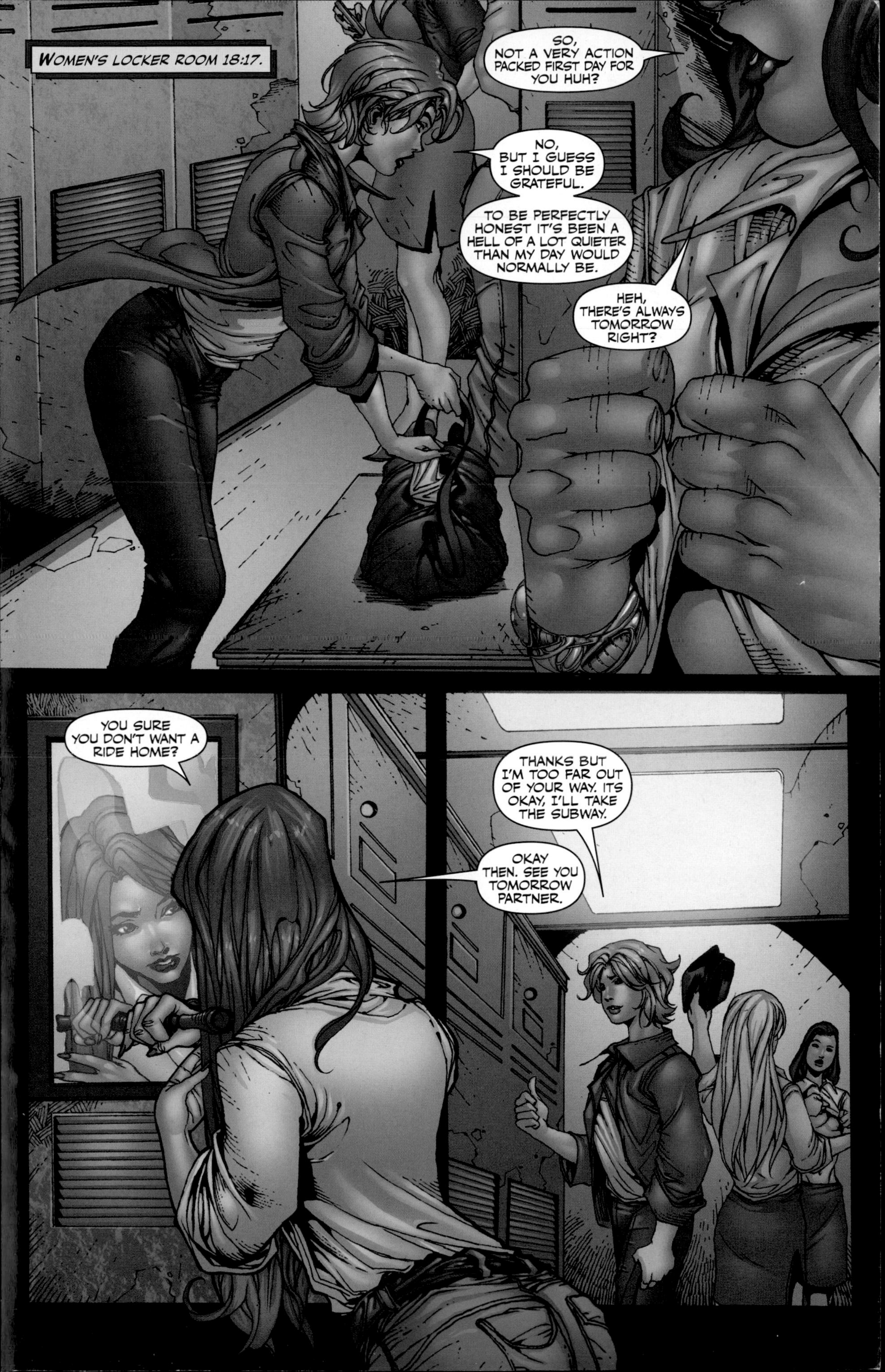
WOMEN'S LOCKER ROOM 18:17.
SO, NOT A VERY ACTION PACKED FIRST DAY FOR YOU HUH?
NO, BUT I GUESS I SHOULD BE GRATEFUL.
TO BE PERFECTLY HONEST IT'S BEEN A HELL OF A LOT QUIETER THAN MY DAY WOULD NORMALLY BE.
HEH, THERE'S ALWAYS TOMORROW RIGHT?
YOU SURE YOU DON'T WANT A RIDE HOME?
THANKS BUT I'M TOO FAR OUT OF YOUR WAY. ITS OKAY, I'LL TAKE THE SUBWAY.
OKAY THEN. SEE YOU TOMORROW PARTNER.

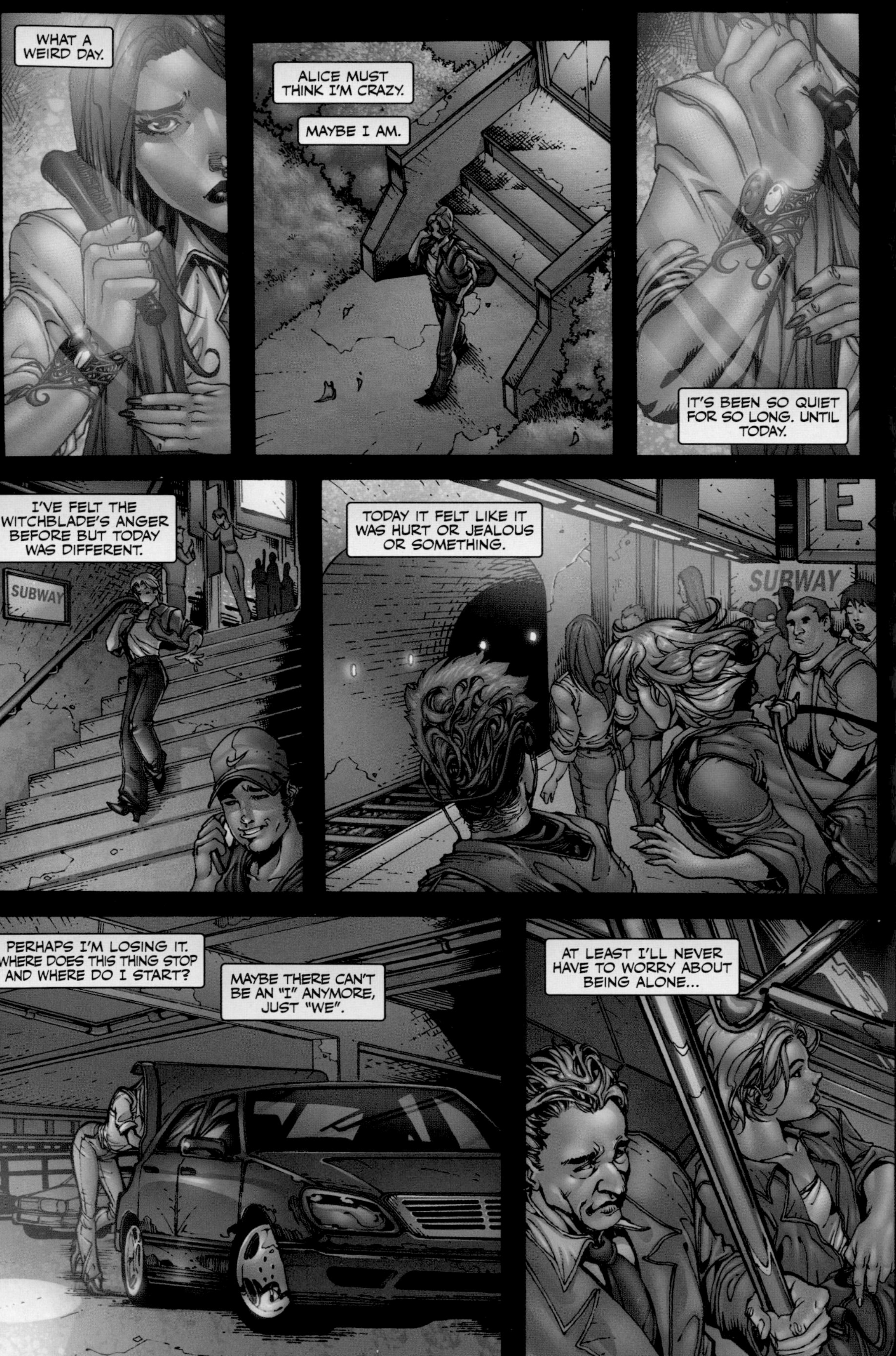
WHAT A WEIRD DAY.
ALICE MUST THINK I'M CRAZY.
MAYBE I AM.
IT'S BEEN SO QUIET FOR SO LONG. UNTIL TODAY.
I'VE FELT THE WITCHBLADE'S ANGER BEFORE BUT TODAY WAS DIFFERENT.
SUBWAY
TODAY IT FELT LIKE IT WAS HURT OR JEALOUS OR SOMETHING.
E
SUBWAY
PERHAPS I'M LOSING IT. WHERE DOES THIS THING STOP AND WHERE DO I START?
MAYBE THERE CAN'T BE AN "I" ANYMORE, JUST "WE".
AT LEAST I'LL NEVER HAVE TO WORRY ABOUT BEING ALONE...

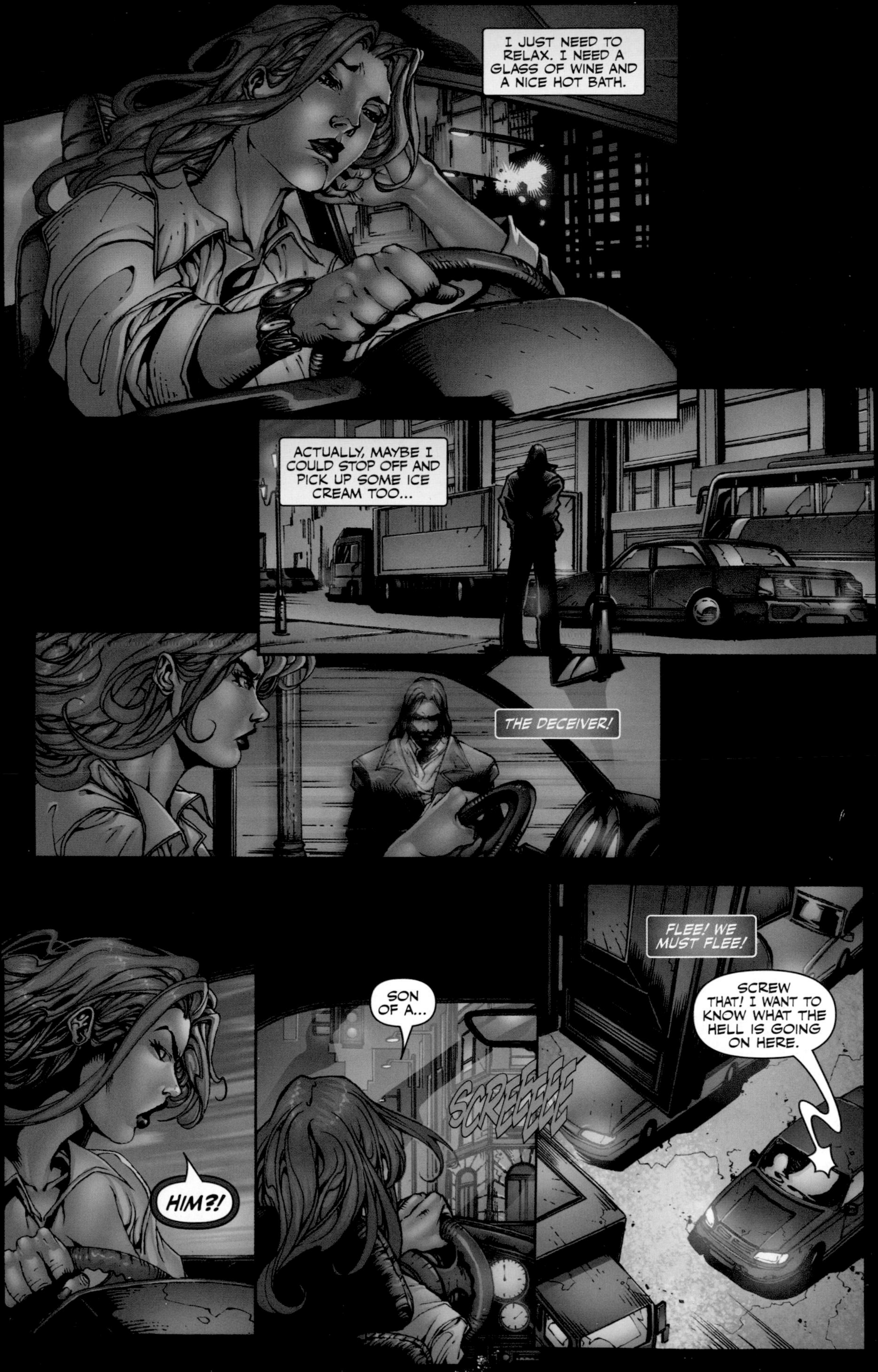
I JUST NEED TO RELAX. I NEED A GLASS OF WINE AND A NICE HOT BATH.
ACTUALLY, MAYBE I COULD STOP OFF AND PICK UP SOME ICE CREAM TOO...
THE DECEIVER!
HIM?!
SON OF A...
SCREEEEE
FLEE! WE MUST FLEE!
SCREW THAT! I WANT TO KNOW WHAT THE HELL IS GOING ON HERE.

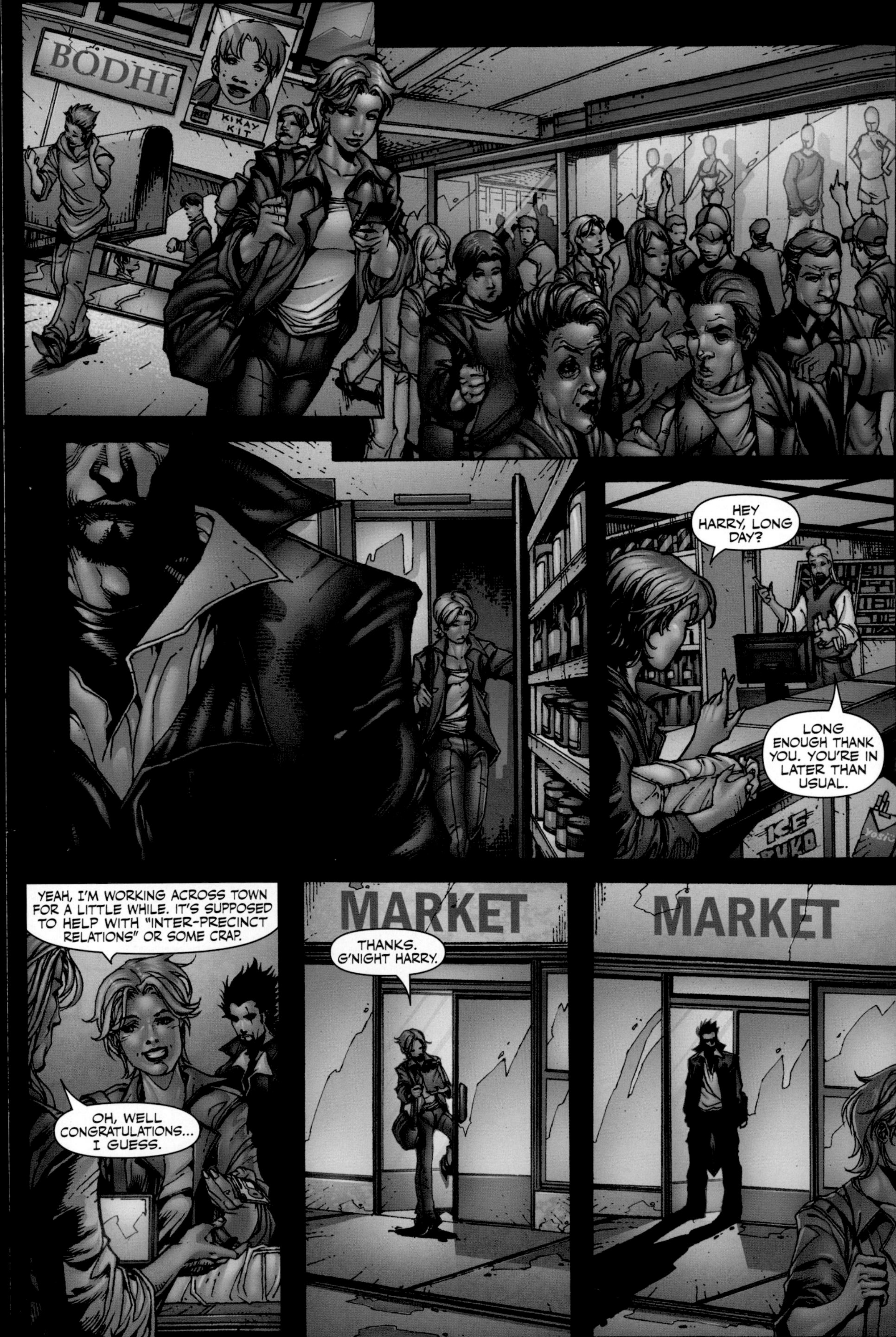
BODHI
KIKAY KIT
HEY HARRY, LONG DAY?
LONG ENOUGH THANK YOU. YOU'RE IN LATER THAN USUAL.
YEAH, I'M WORKING ACROSS TOWN FOR A LITTLE WHILE. IT'S SUPPOSED TO HELP WITH "INTER-PRECINCT RELATIONS" OR SOME CRAP.
OH, WELL CONGRATULATIONS... I GUESS.
MARKET
THANKS. G'NIGHT HARRY.
MARKET

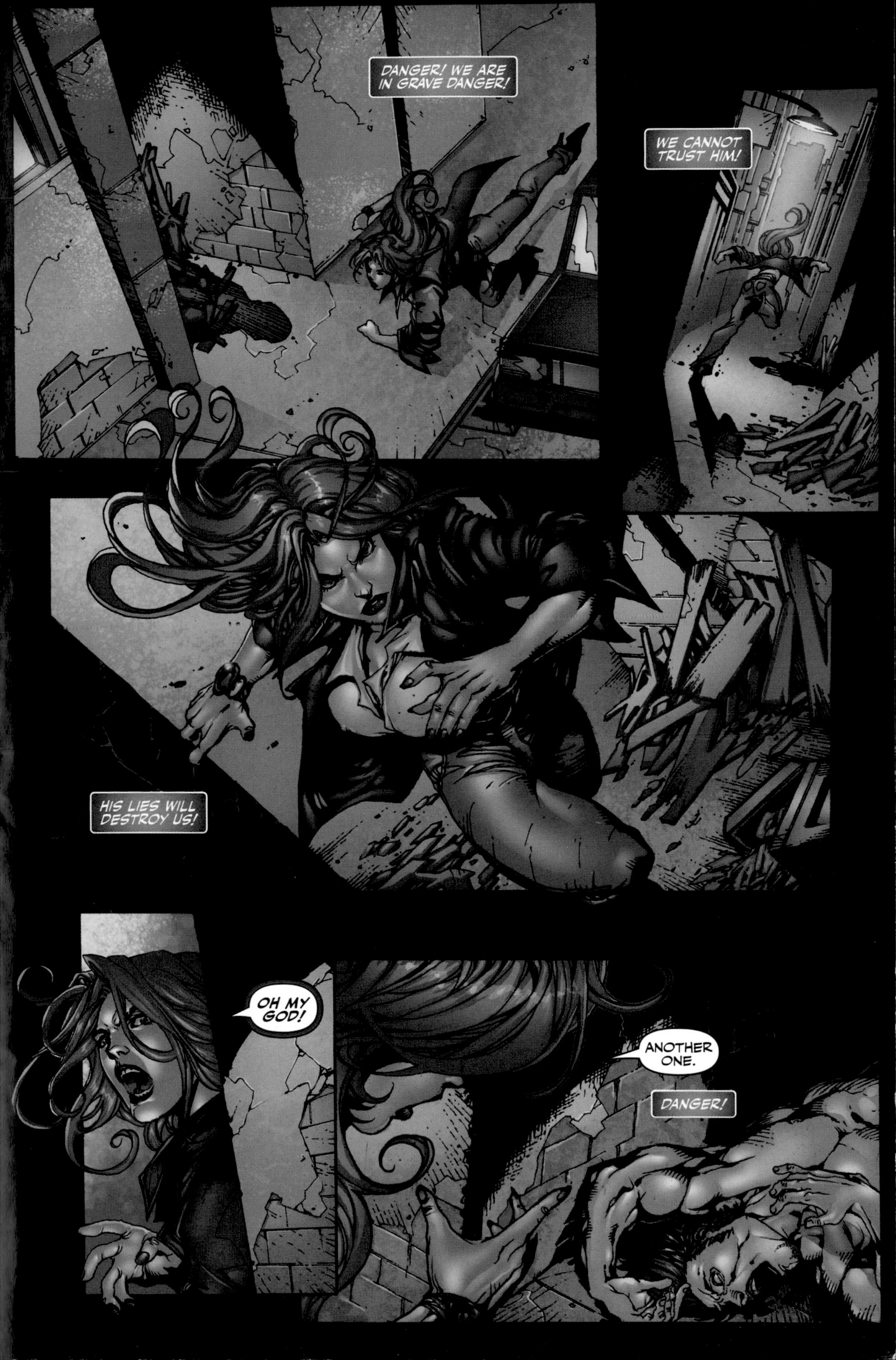
DANGER! WE ARE IN GRAVE DANGER!
WE CANNOT TRUST HIM!
HIS LIES WILL DESTROY US!
OH MY GOD!
ANOTHER ONE.
DANGER!

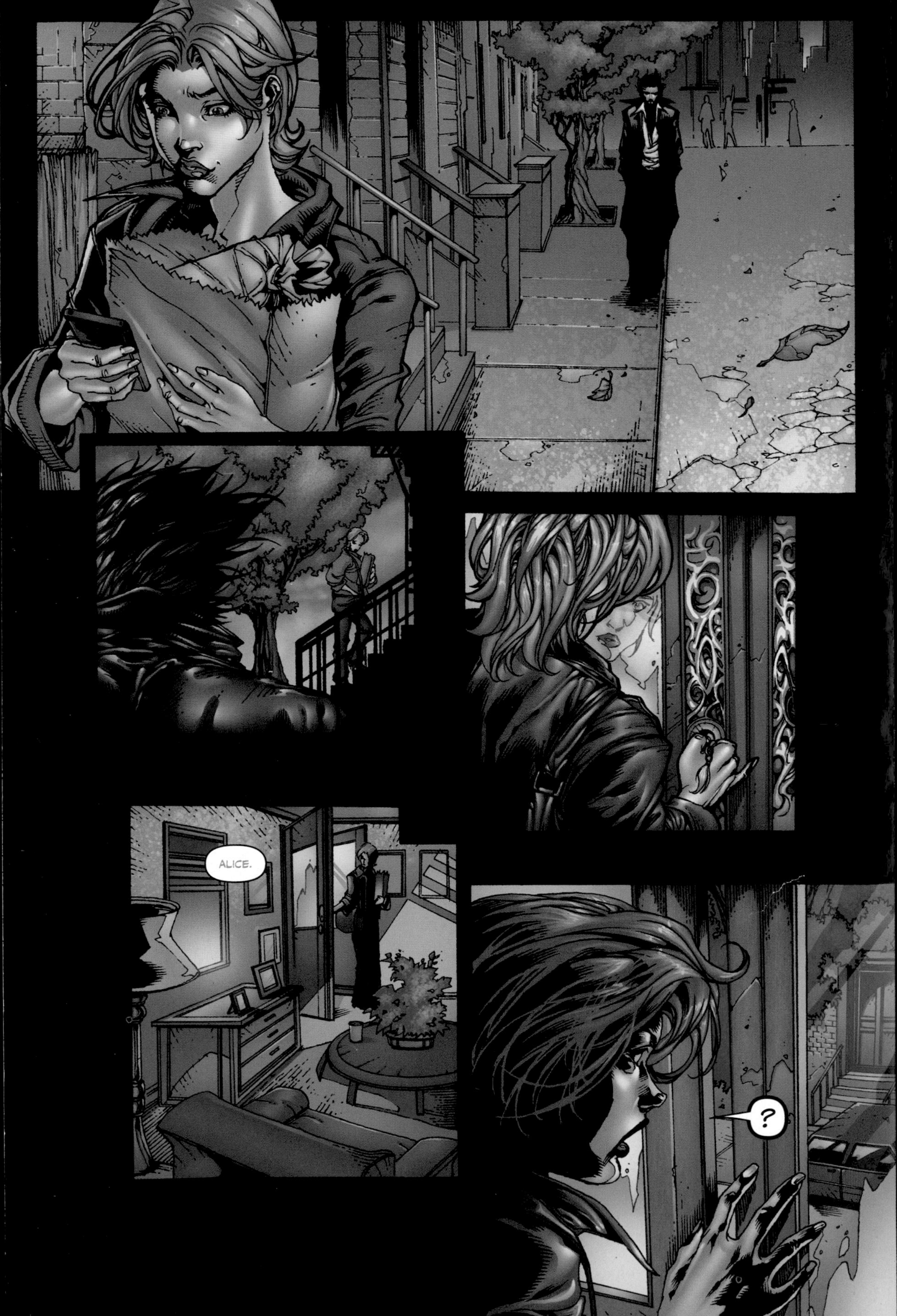
ALICE.
?

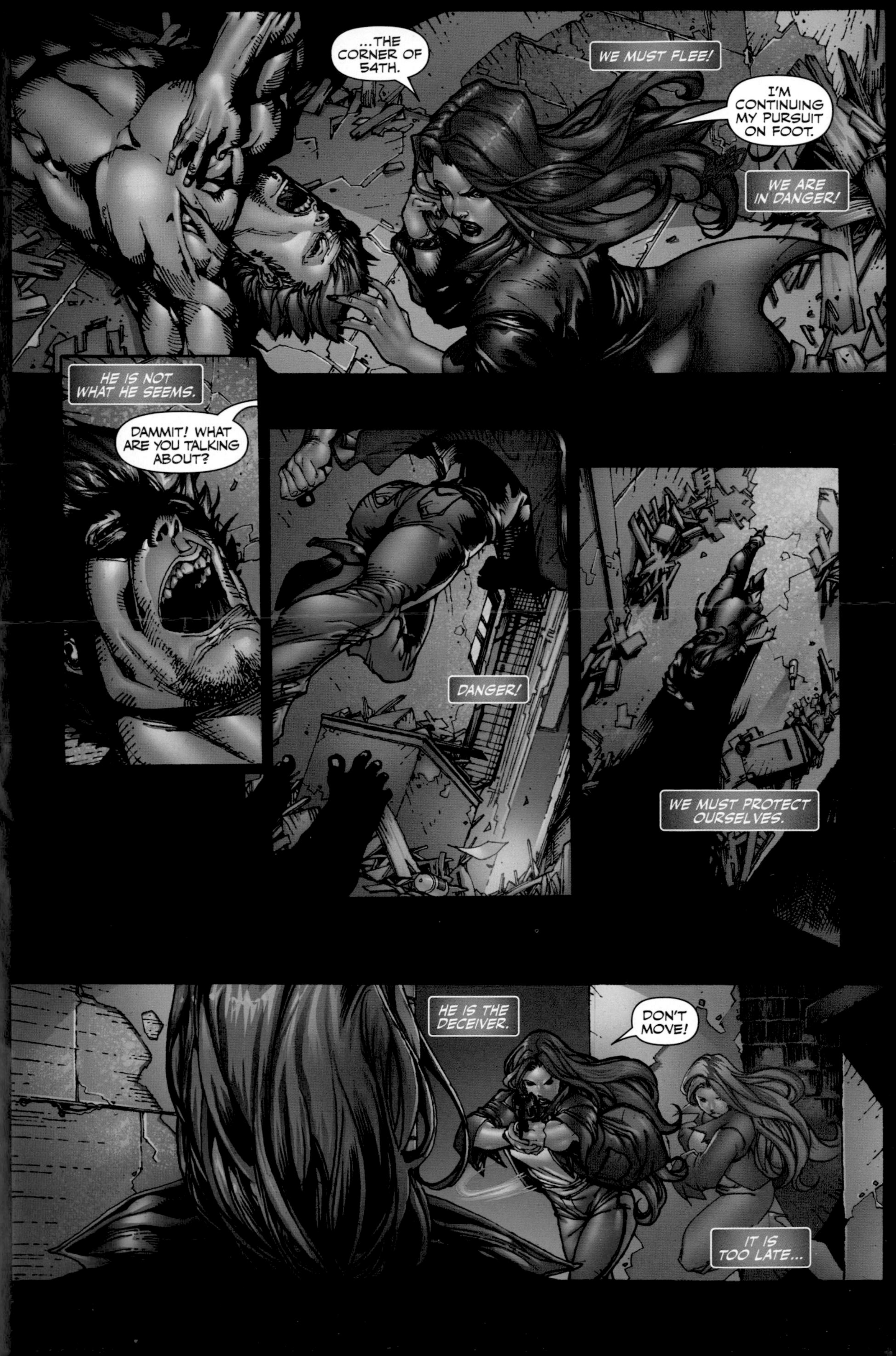
...THE CORNER OF 54TH.
WE MUST FLEE!
I'M CONTINUING MY PURSUIT ON FOOT.
WE ARE IN DANGER!
HE IS NOT WHAT HE SEEMS.
DAMMIT! WHAT ARE YOU TALKING ABOUT?
DANGER!
WE MUST PROTECT OURSELVES.
HE IS THE DECEIVER.
DON'T MOVE!
IT IS TOO LATE...

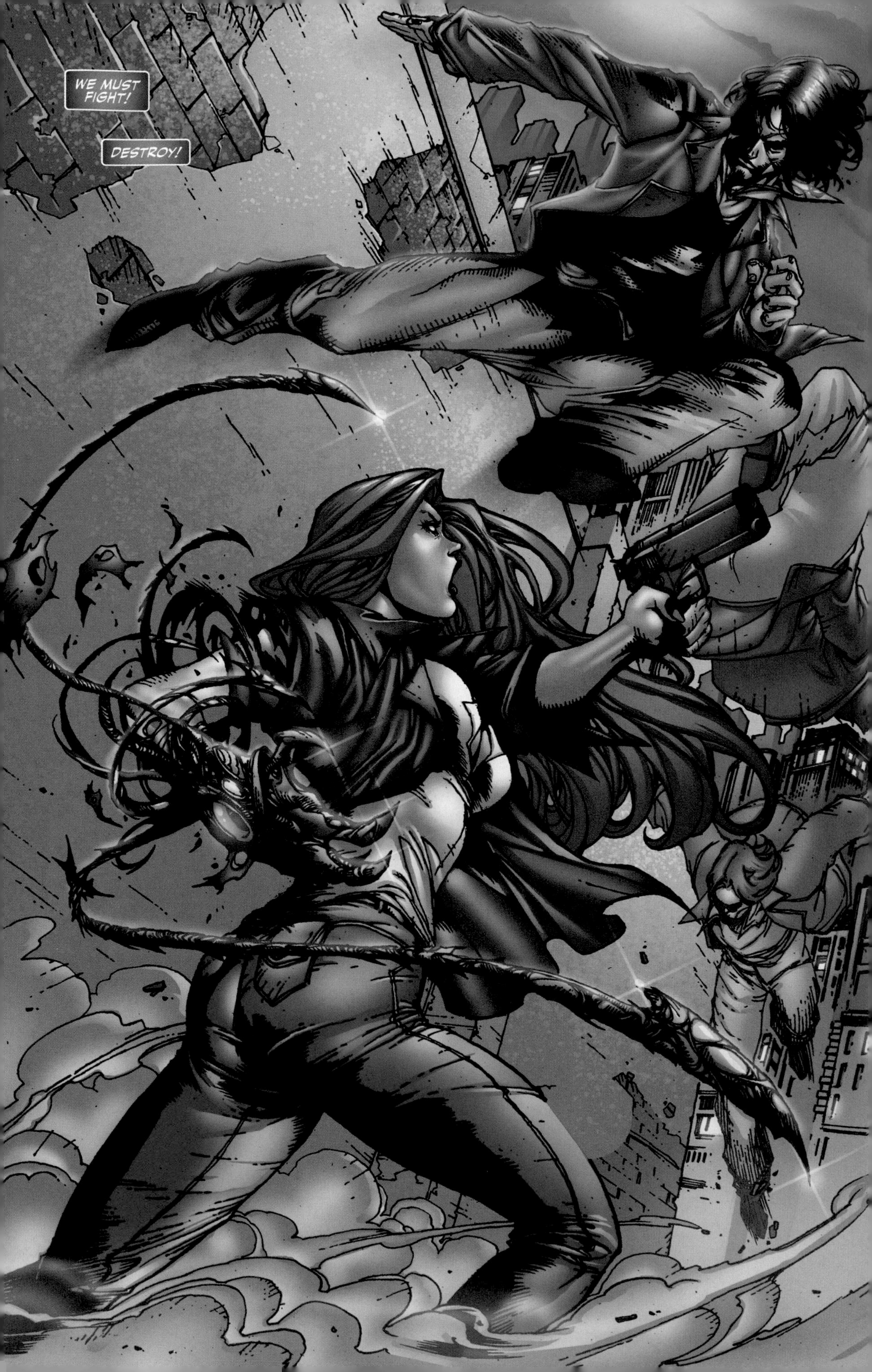
WE MUST FIGHT!
DESTROY!

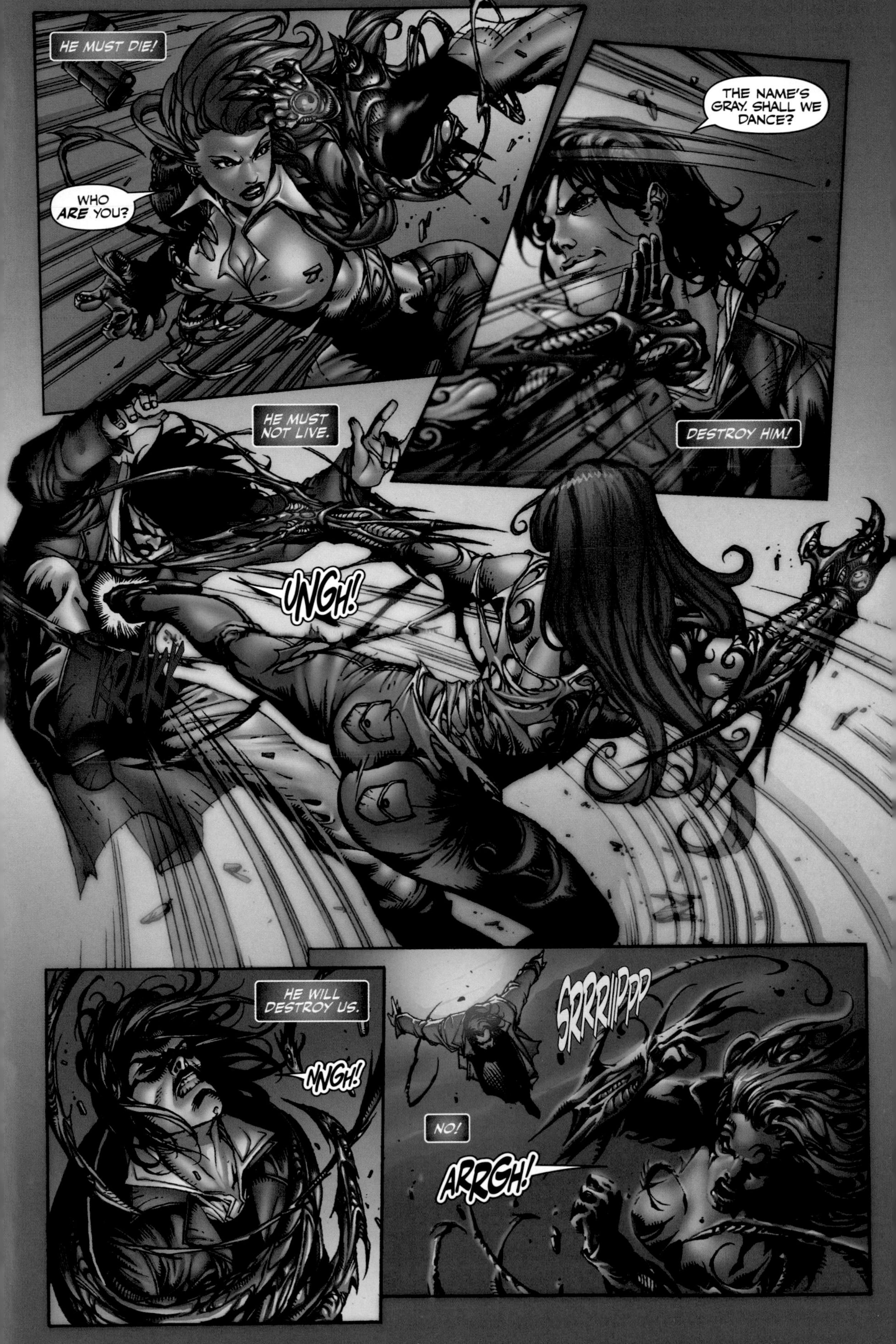
HE MUST DIE!
WHO ARE YOU?
THE NAME'S GRAY. SHALL WE DANCE?
HE MUST NOT LIVE.
DESTROY HIM!
UNGH!
KRAKK
HE WILL DESTROY US.
NNGH!
SRRRIIPPP
NO!
ARRGH!

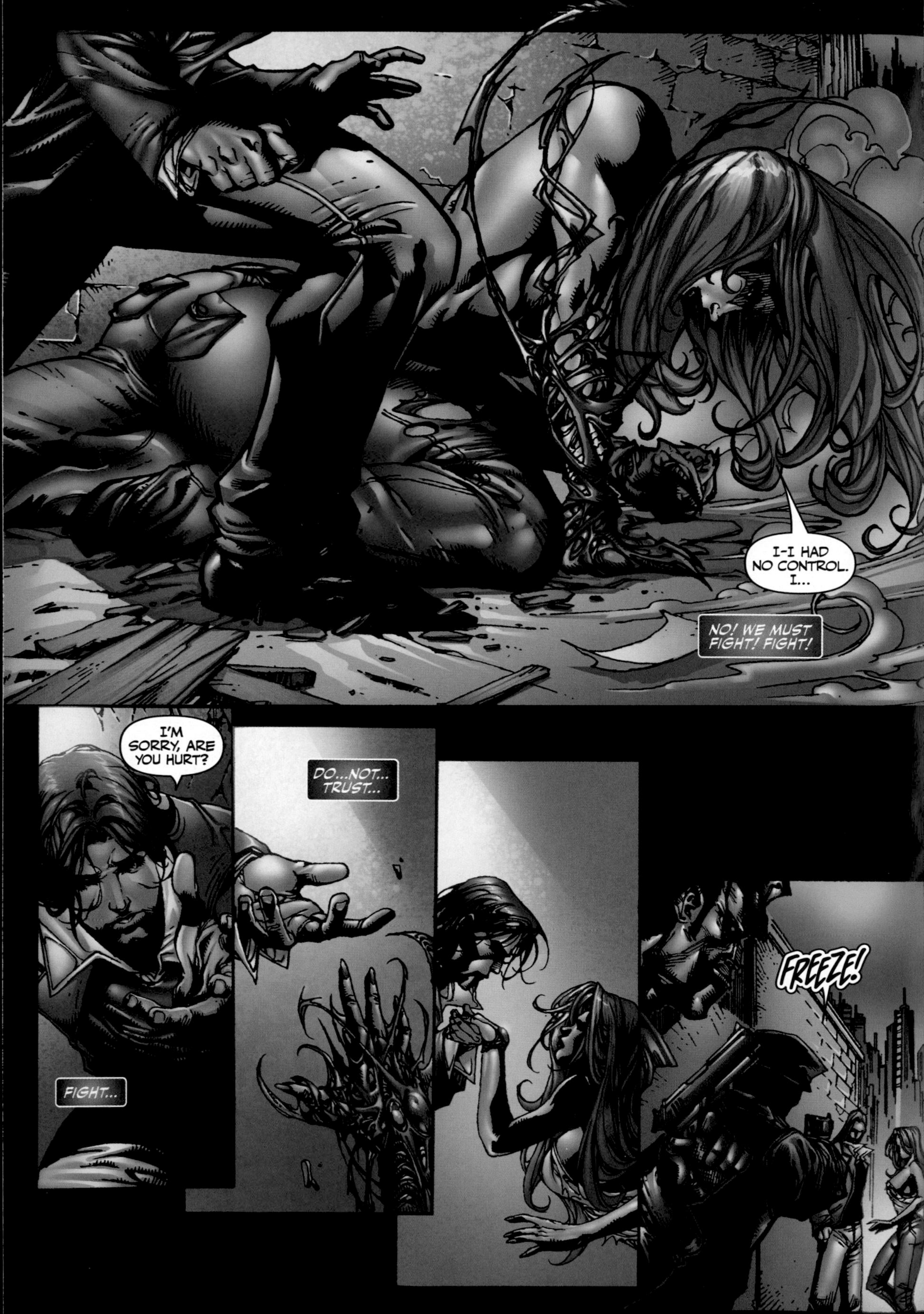
I-I HAD NO CONTROL. I...
NO! WE MUST FIGHT! FIGHT!
I'M SORRY, ARE YOU HURT?
FIGHT...
DO...NOT... TRUST...
FREEZE!

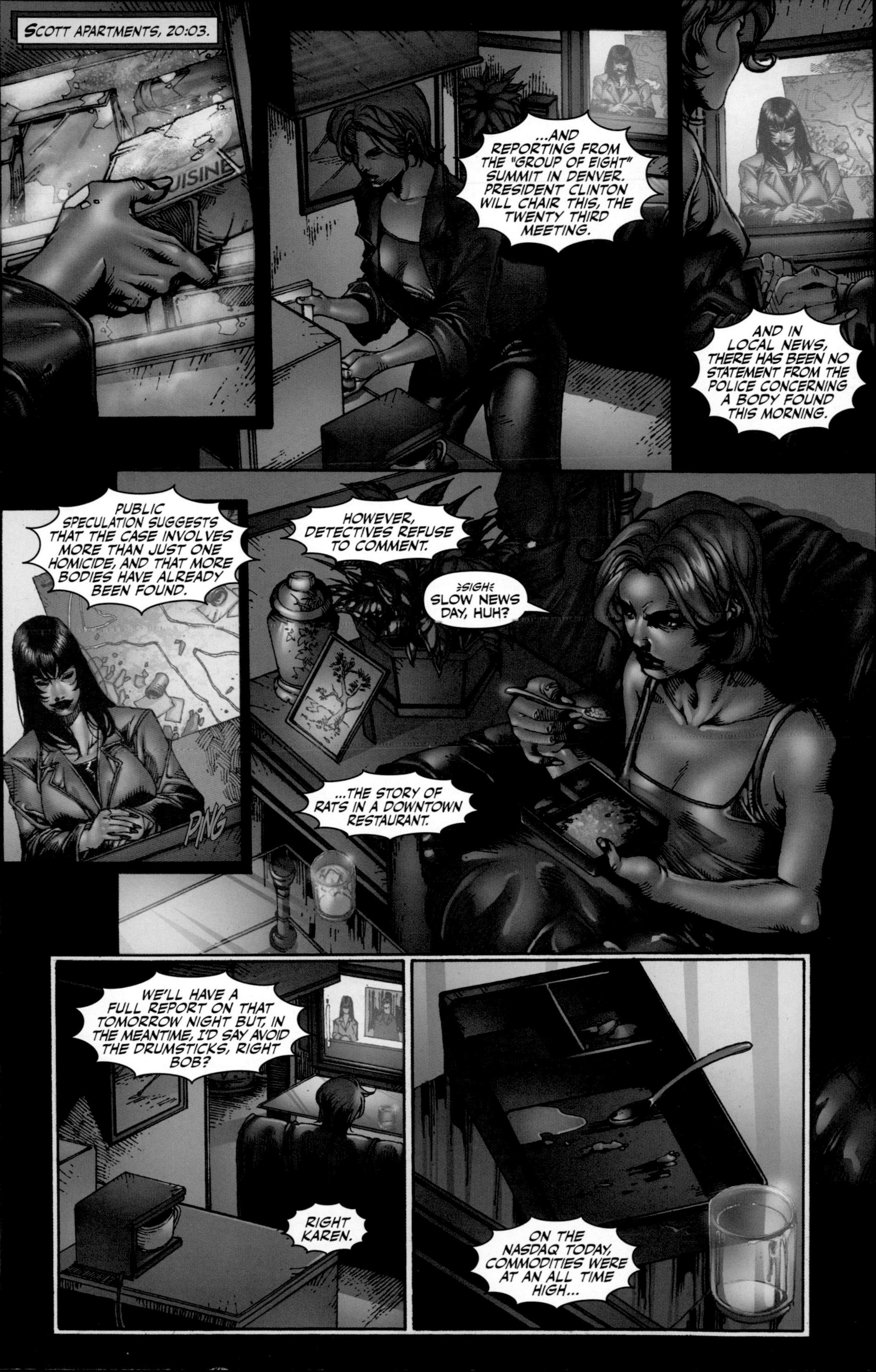
SCOTT APARTMENTS, 20:03.
CUISINE
...AND REPORTING FROM THE "GROUP OF EIGHT" SUMMIT IN DENVER. PRESIDENT CLINTON WILL CHAIR THIS, THE TWENTY THIRD MEETING.
AND IN LOCAL NEWS, THERE HAS BEEN NO STATEMENT FROM THE POLICE CONCERNING A BODY FOUND THIS MORNING.
PUBLIC SPECULATION SUGGESTS THAT THE CASE INVOLVES MORE THAN JUST ONE HOMICIDE, AND THAT MORE BODIES HAVE ALREADY BEEN FOUND.
HOWEVER, DETECTIVES REFUSE TO COMMENT.
SIGH
SLOW NEWS DAY, HUH?
...THE STORY OF RATS IN A DOWNTOWN RESTAURANT.
PING
WE'LL HAVE A FULL REPORT ON THAT TOMORROW NIGHT BUT, IN THE MEANTIME, I'D SAY AVOID THE DRUMSTICKS, RIGHT BOB?
RIGHT KAREN.
ON THE NASDAQ TODAY, COMMODITIES WERE AT AN ALL TIME HIGH...

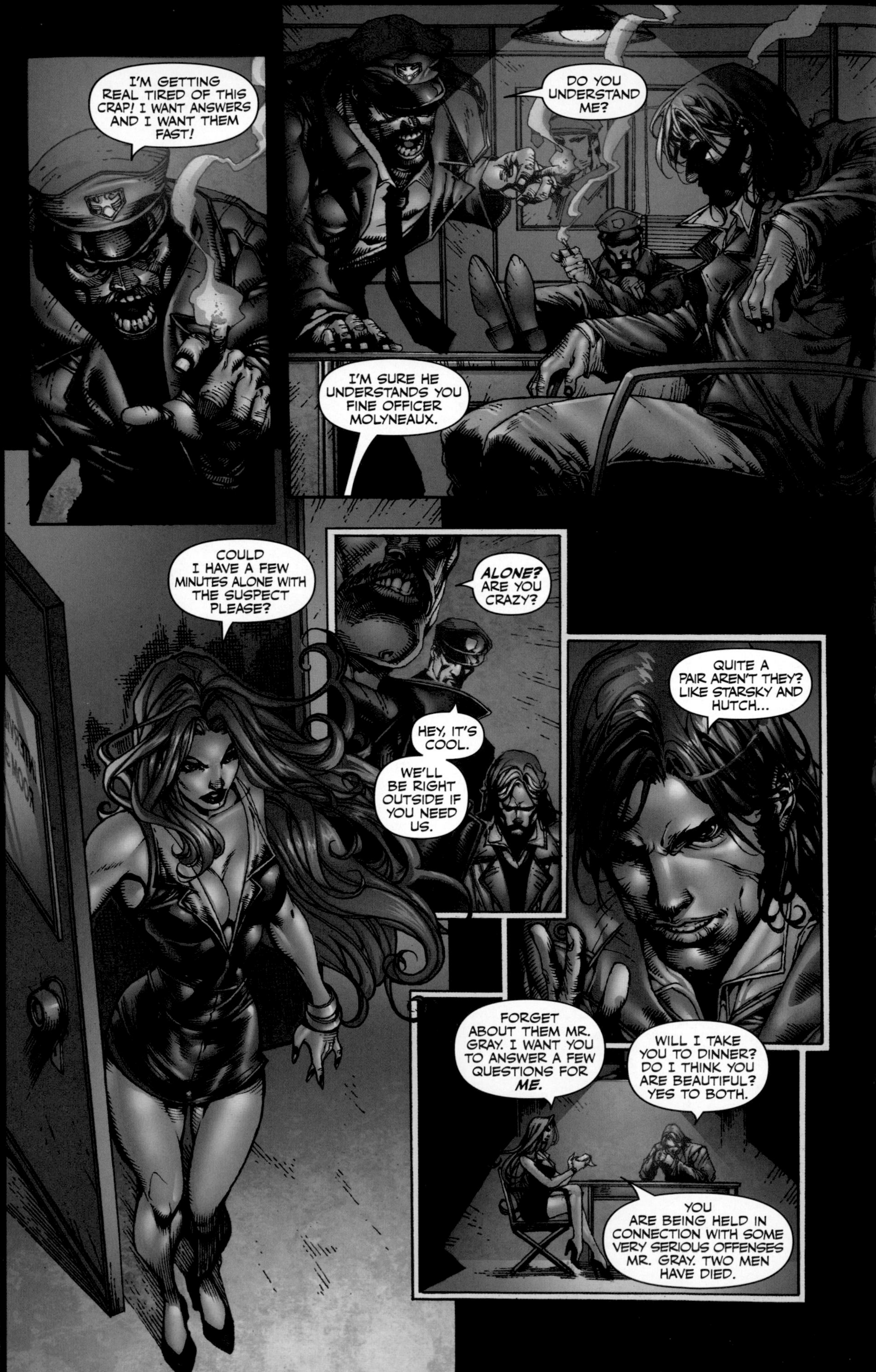
I'M GETTING REAL TIRED OF THIS CRAP! I WANT ANSWERS AND I WANT THEM FAST!
DO YOU UNDERSTAND ME?
I'M SURE HE UNDERSTANDS YOU FINE OFFICER MOLYNEAUX.
COULD I HAVE A FEW MINUTES ALONE WITH THE SUSPECT PLEASE?
ALONE? ARE YOU CRAZY?
HEY, IT'S COOL.
WE'LL BE RIGHT OUTSIDE IF YOU NEED US.
QUITE A PAIR AREN'T THEY? LIKE STARSKY AND HUTCH...
FORGET ABOUT THEM MR. GRAY. I WANT YOU TO ANSWER A FEW QUESTIONS FOR ME.
WILL I TAKE YOU TO DINNER? DO I THINK YOU ARE BEAUTIFUL? YES TO BOTH.
YOU ARE BEING HELD IN CONNECTION WITH SOME VERY SERIOUS OFFENSES MR. GRAY. TWO MEN HAVE DIED.

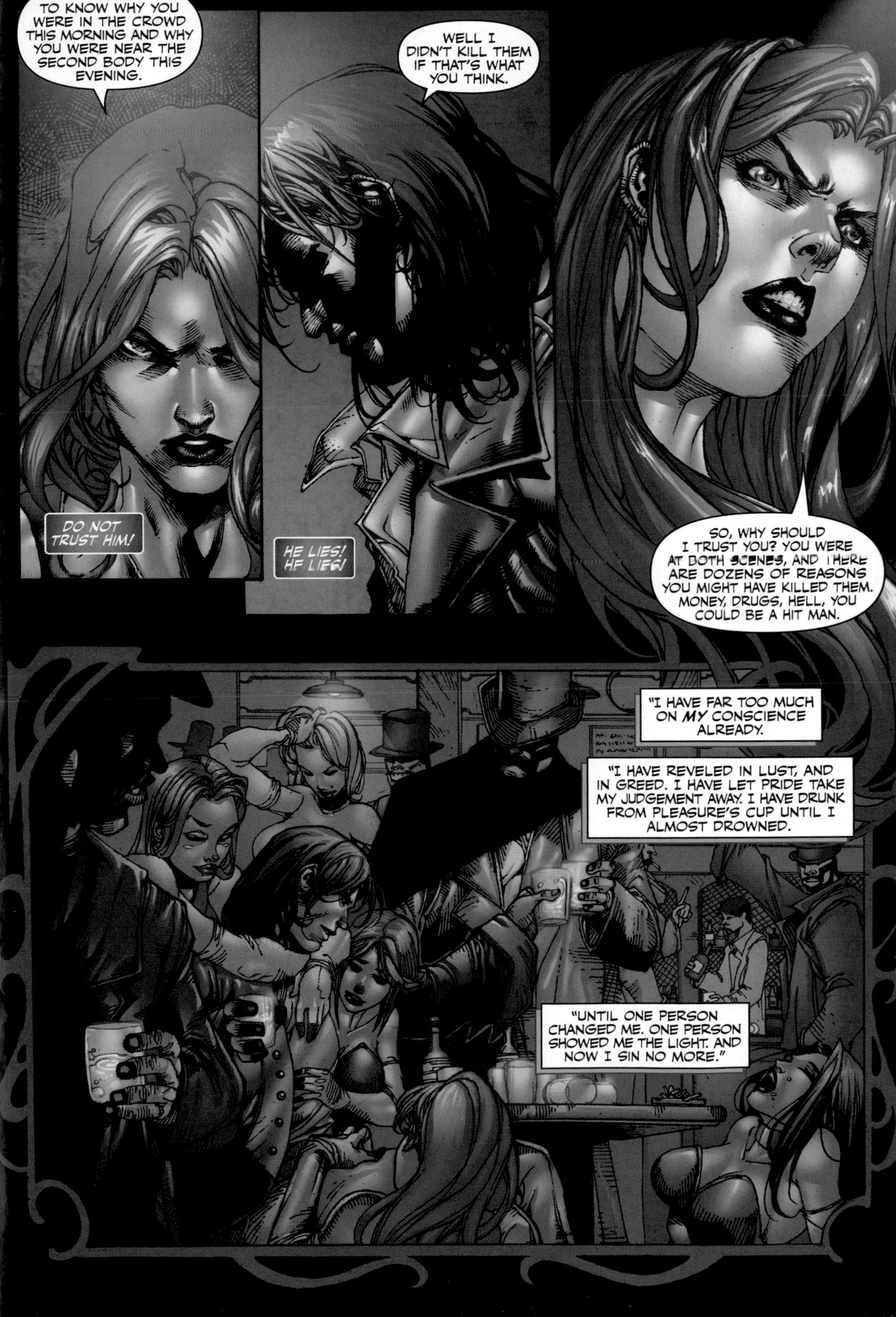
I WANT TO KNOW WHY YOU WERE IN THE CROWD THIS MORNING AND WHY YOU WERE NEAR THE SECOND BODY THIS EVENING.
DO NOT TRUST HIM!
WELL I DIDN'T KILL THEM IF THAT'S WHAT YOU THINK.
HE LIES! HE LIES!
SO, WHY SHOULD I TRUST YOU? YOU WERE AT BOTH SCENES, AND THERE ARE DOZENS OF REASONS YOU MIGHT HAVE KILLED THEM. MONEY, DRUGS, HELL, YOU COULD BE A HIT MAN.
"I HAVE FAR TOO MUCH ON *MY* CONSCIENCE ALREADY.
"I HAVE REVELED IN LUST, AND IN GREED. I HAVE LET PRIDE TAKE MY JUDGEMENT AWAY. I HAVE DRUNK FROM PLEASURE'S CUP UNTIL I ALMOST DROWNED.
"UNTIL ONE PERSON CHANGED ME. ONE PERSON SHOWED ME THE LIGHT. AND NOW I SIN NO MORE."

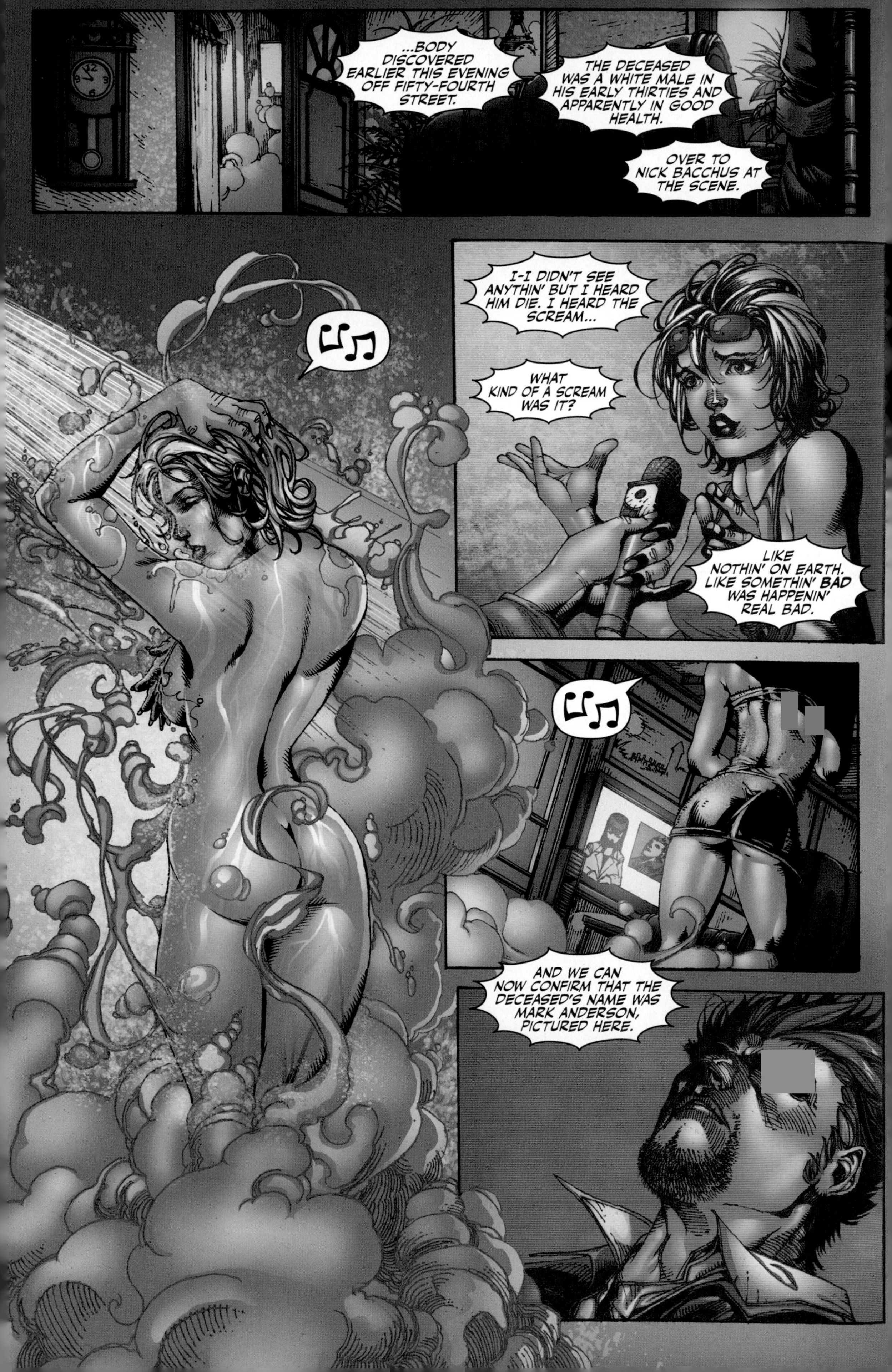
...BODY DISCOVERED EARLIER THIS EVENING OFF FIFTY-FOURTH STREET.
THE DECEASED WAS A WHITE MALE IN HIS EARLY THIRTIES AND APPARENTLY IN GOOD HEALTH.
OVER TO NICK BACCHUS AT THE SCENE.
I-I DIDN'T SEE ANYTHIN' BUT I HEARD HIM DIE. I HEARD THE SCREAM...
WHAT KIND OF A SCREAM WAS IT?
LIKE NOTHIN' ON EARTH. LIKE SOMETHIN' BAD WAS HAPPENIN' REAL BAD.
AND WE CAN NOW CONFIRM THAT THE DECEASED'S NAME WAS MARK ANDERSON, PICTURED HERE.

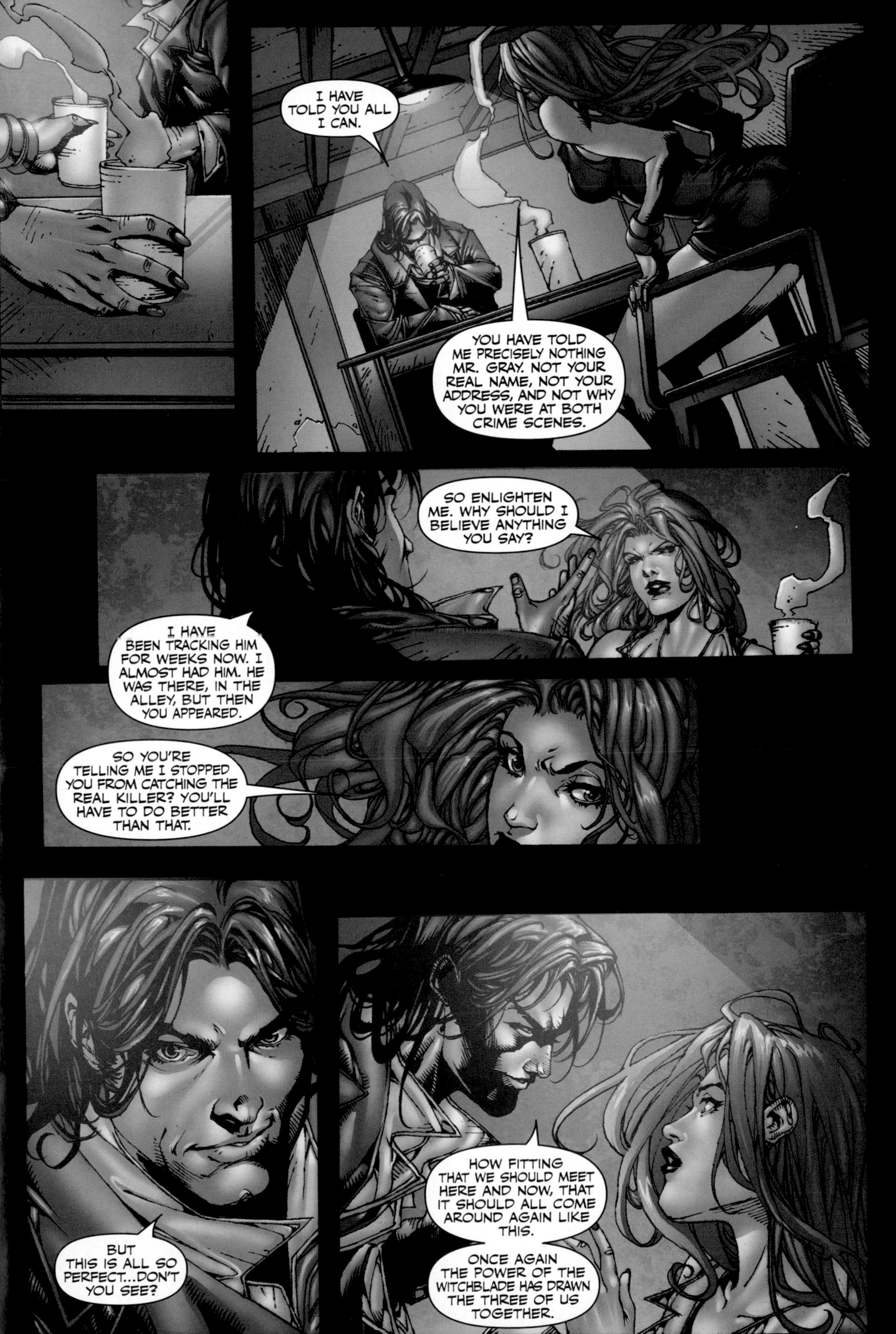

I HAVE TOLD YOU ALL I CAN.
YOU HAVE TOLD ME PRECISELY NOTHING MR. GRAY. NOT YOUR REAL NAME, NOT YOUR ADDRESS, AND NOT WHY YOU WERE AT BOTH CRIME SCENES.
SO ENLIGHTEN ME. WHY SHOULD I BELIEVE ANYTHING YOU SAY?
I HAVE BEEN TRACKING HIM FOR WEEKS NOW. I ALMOST HAD HIM. HE WAS THERE, IN THE ALLEY, BUT THEN YOU APPEARED.
SO YOU'RE TELLING ME I STOPPED YOU FROM CATCHING THE REAL KILLER? YOU'LL HAVE TO DO BETTER THAN THAT.
BUT THIS IS ALL SO PERFECT...DON'T YOU SEE?
HOW FITTING THAT WE SHOULD MEET HERE AND NOW, THAT IT SHOULD ALL COME AROUND AGAIN LIKE THIS.
ONCE AGAIN THE POWER OF THE WITCHBLADE HAS DRAWN THE THREE OF US TOGETHER.

RRRRUUMMMBBLE

"THREE?"

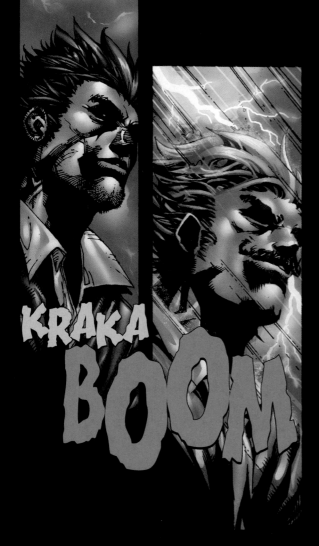

KRAKA
BOOM

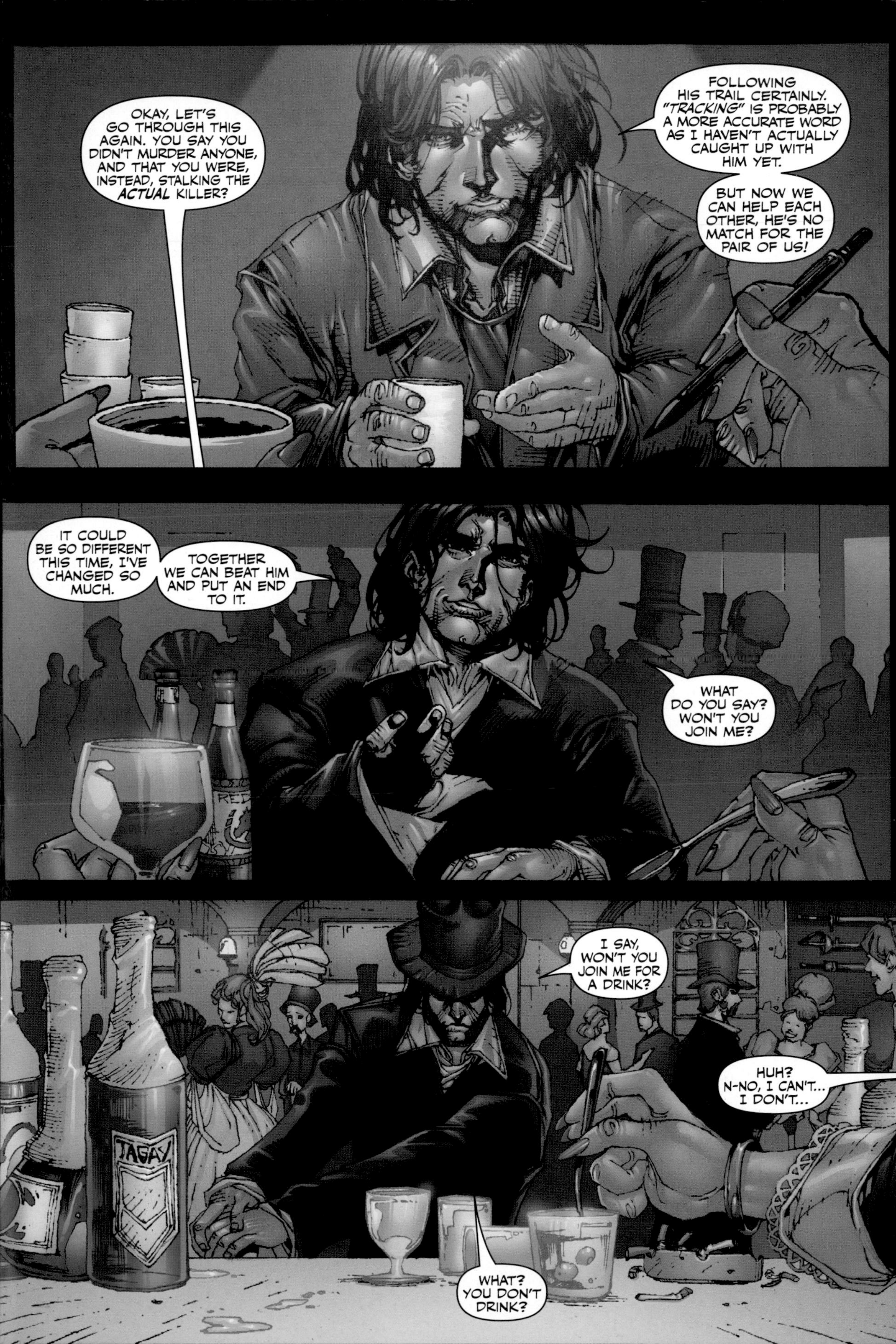
OKAY, LET'S GO THROUGH THIS AGAIN. YOU SAY YOU DIDN'T MURDER ANYONE, AND THAT YOU WERE, INSTEAD, STALKING THE *ACTUAL* KILLER?
FOLLOWING HIS TRAIL CERTAINLY. *"TRACKING"* IS PROBABLY A MORE ACCURATE WORD AS I HAVEN'T ACTUALLY CAUGHT UP WITH HIM YET.
BUT NOW WE CAN HELP EACH OTHER, HE'S NO MATCH FOR THE PAIR OF US!
IT COULD BE SO DIFFERENT THIS TIME, I'VE CHANGED SO MUCH.
TOGETHER WE CAN BEAT HIM AND PUT AN END TO IT.
WHAT DO YOU SAY? WON'T YOU JOIN ME?
I SAY, WON'T YOU JOIN ME FOR A DRINK?
HUH? N-NO, I CAN'T... I DON'T...
TAGAY
WHAT? YOU DON'T DRINK?

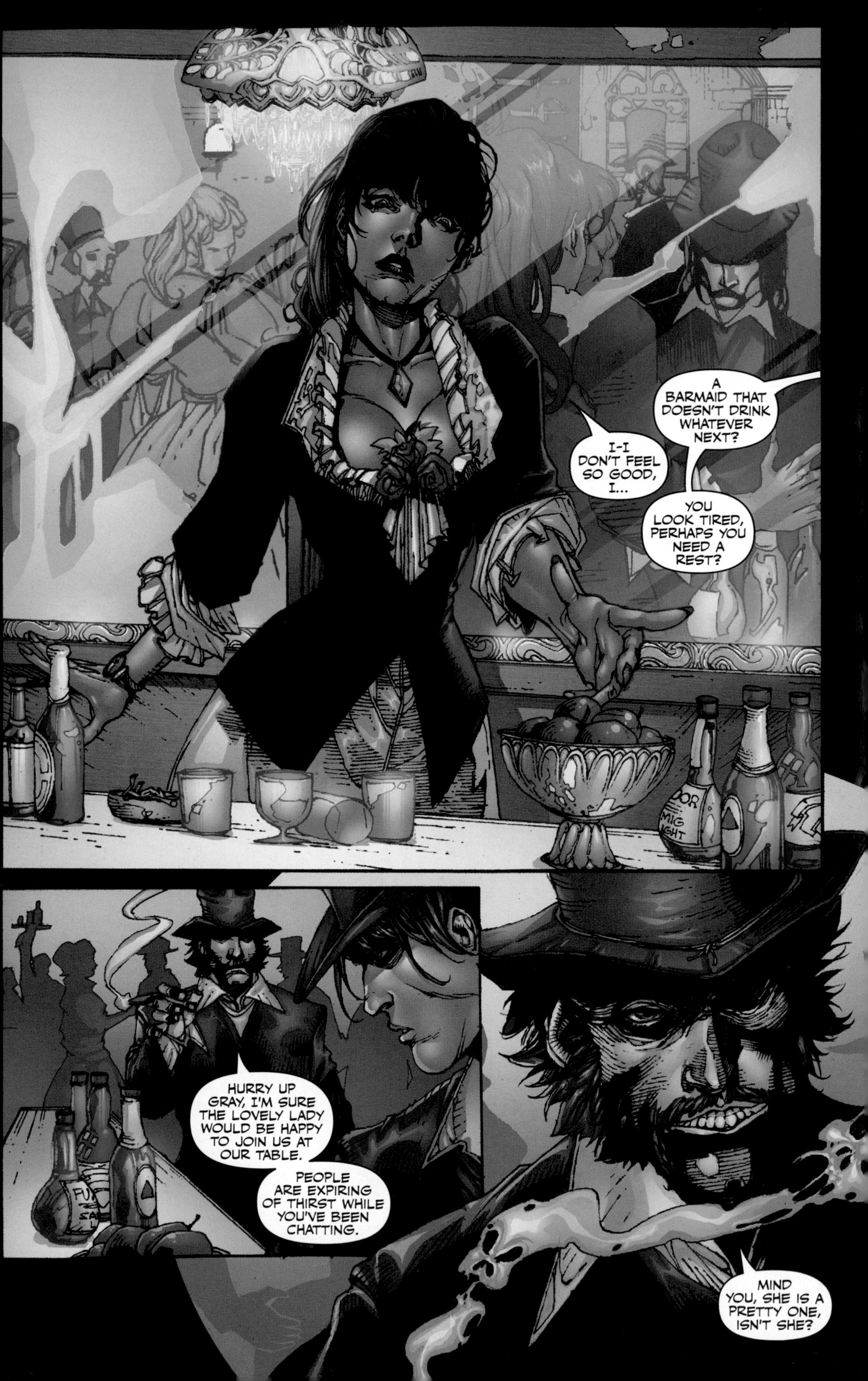
A BARMAID THAT DOESN'T DRINK WHATEVER NEXT?
I-I DON'T FEEL SO GOOD, I...
YOU LOOK TIRED, PERHAPS YOU NEED A REST?
HURRY UP GRAY, I'M SURE THE LOVELY LADY WOULD BE HAPPY TO JOIN US AT OUR TABLE.
PEOPLE ARE EXPIRING OF THIRST WHILE YOU'VE BEEN CHATTING.
MIND YOU, SHE IS A PRETTY ONE, ISN'T SHE?

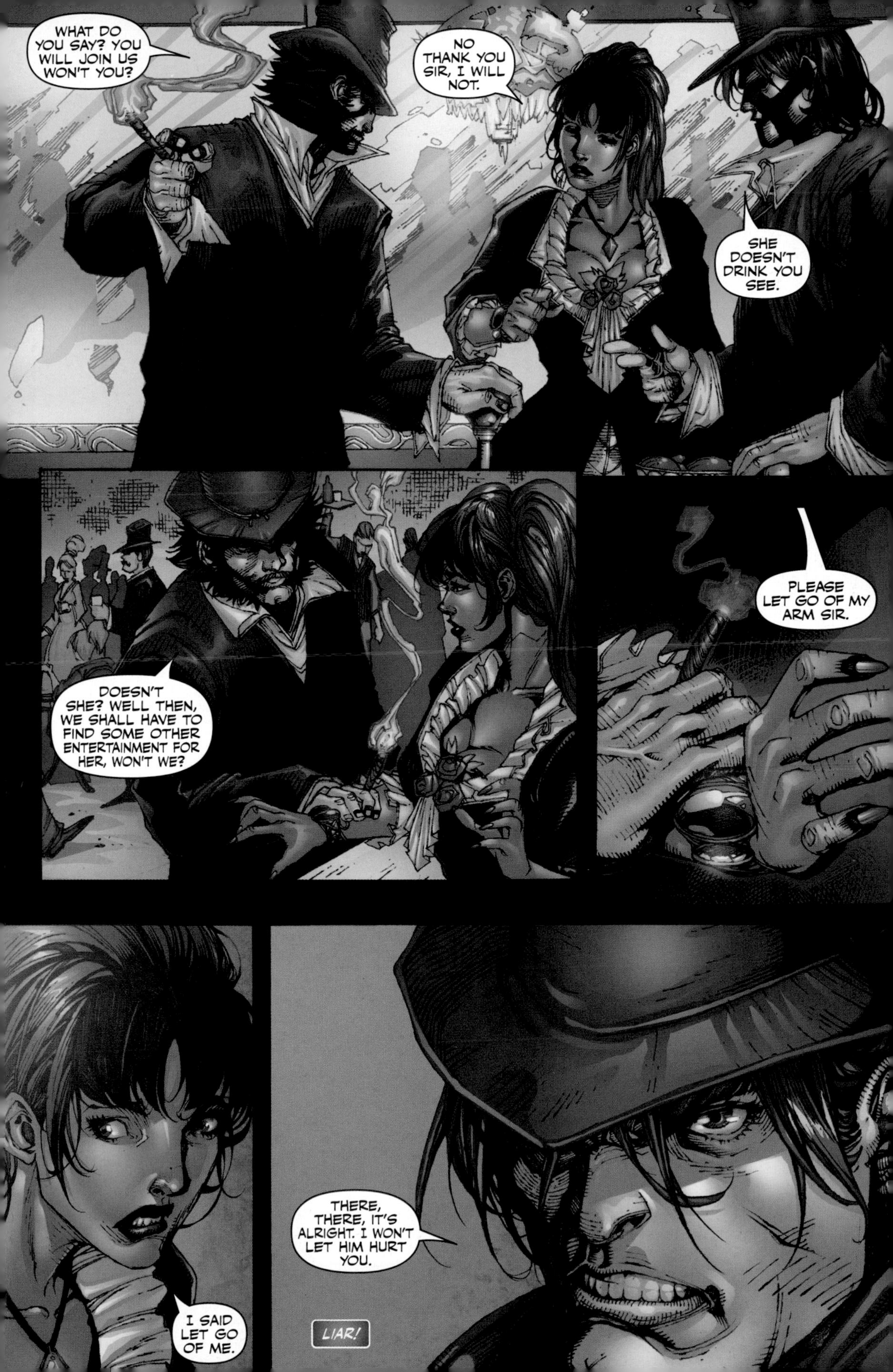
WHAT DO YOU SAY? YOU WILL JOIN US WON'T YOU?
NO THANK YOU SIR, I WILL NOT.
SHE DOESN'T DRINK YOU SEE.
DOESN'T SHE? WELL THEN, WE SHALL HAVE TO FIND SOME OTHER ENTERTAINMENT FOR HER, WON'T WE?
PLEASE LET GO OF MY ARM SIR.
I SAID LET GO OF ME.
THERE, THERE, IT'S ALRIGHT. I WON'T LET HIM HURT YOU.
LIAR!

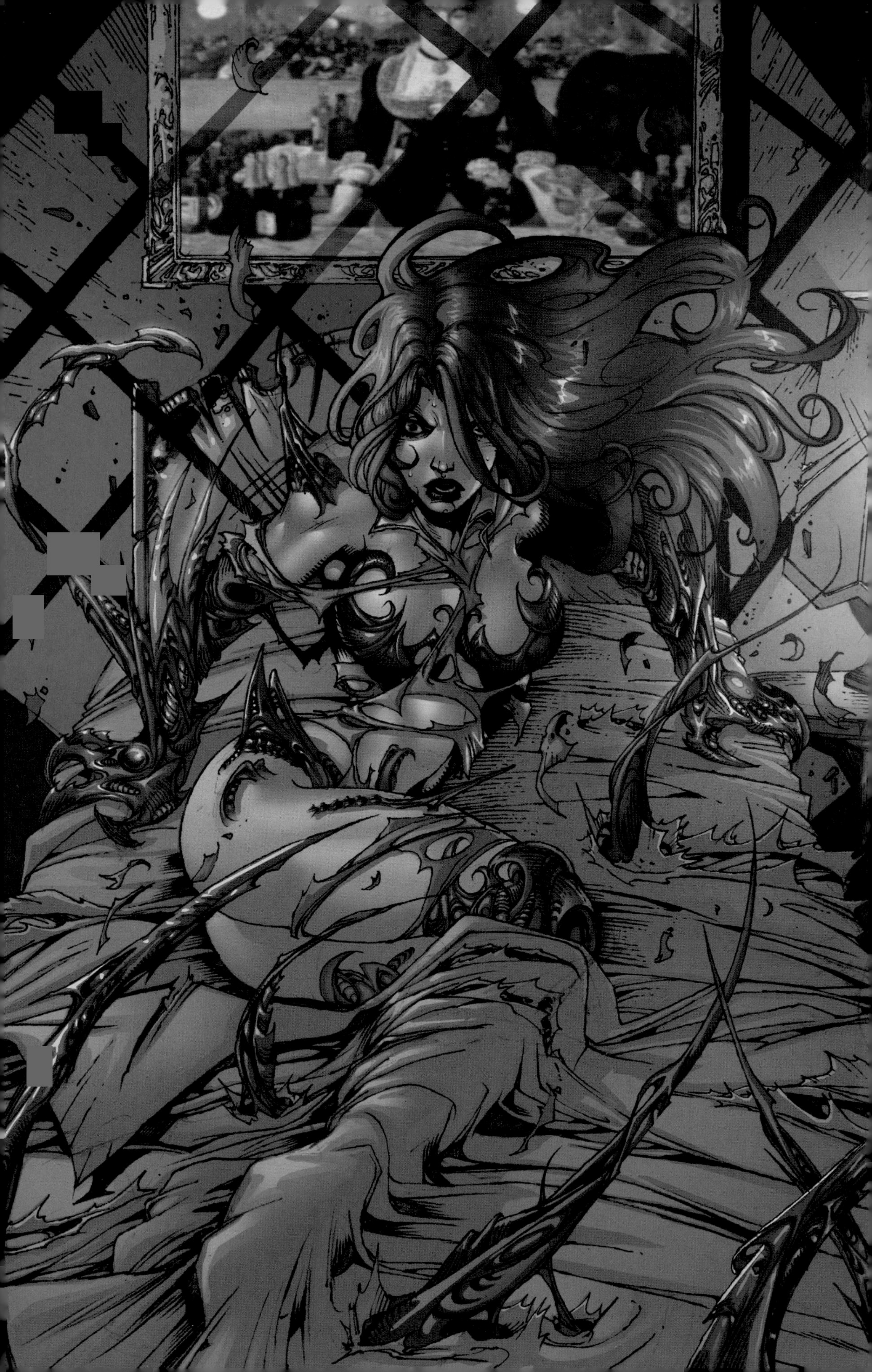

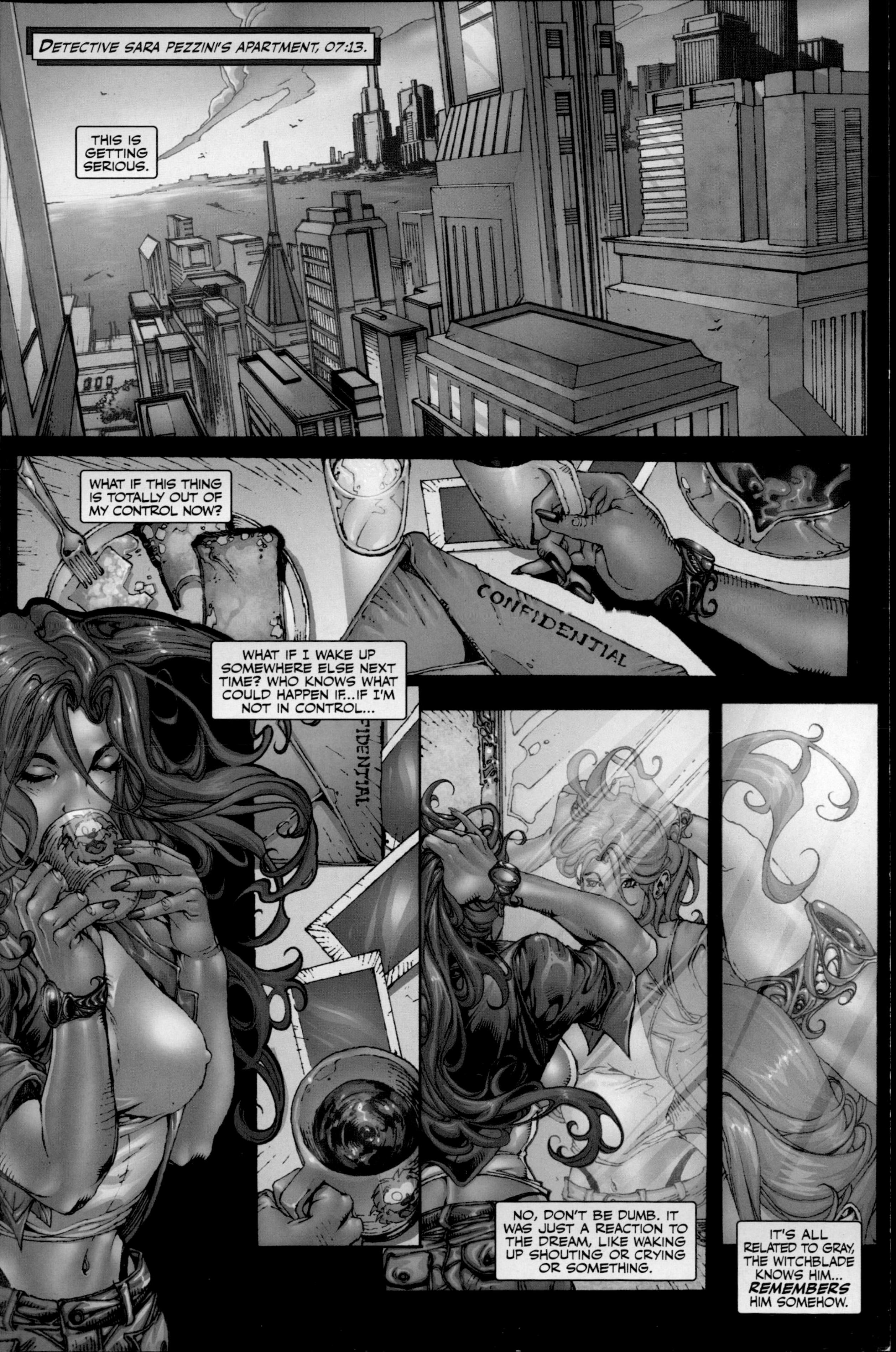
Detective sara pezzini's apartment, 07:13.
THIS IS GETTING SERIOUS.
WHAT IF THIS THING IS TOTALLY OUT OF MY CONTROL NOW?
CONFIDENTIAL
WHAT IF I WAKE UP SOMEWHERE ELSE NEXT TIME? WHO KNOWS WHAT COULD HAPPEN IF...IF I'M NOT IN CONTROL...
NO, DON'T BE DUMB. IT WAS JUST A REACTION TO THE DREAM, LIKE WAKING UP SHOUTING OR CRYING OR SOMETHING.
IT'S ALL RELATED TO GRAY, THE WITCHBLADE KNOWS HIM... REMEMBERS HIM SOMEHOW.

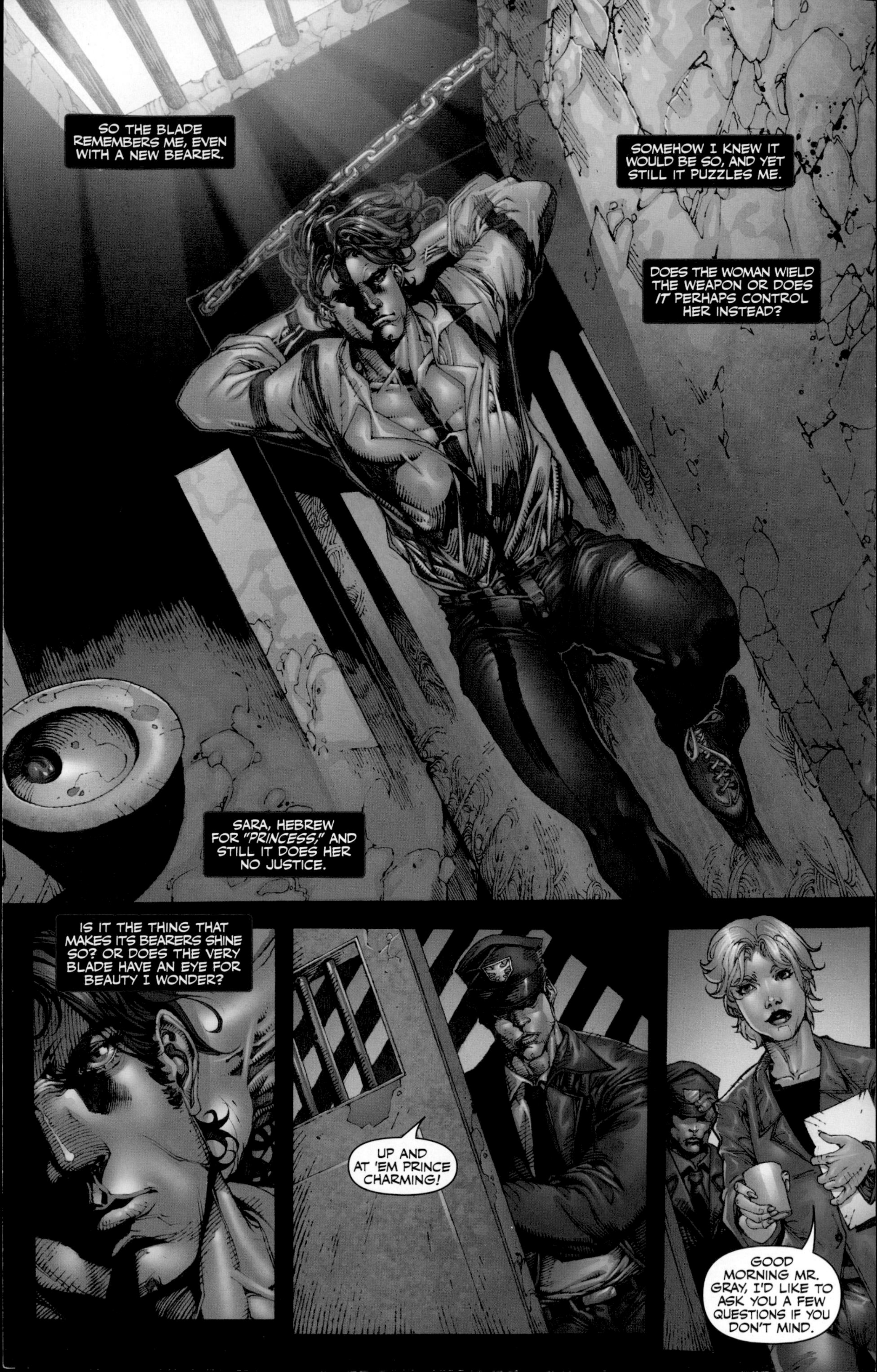
SO THE BLADE REMEMBERS ME, EVEN WITH A NEW BEARER.
SOMEHOW I KNEW IT WOULD BE SO, AND YET STILL IT PUZZLES ME.
DOES THE WOMAN WIELD THE WEAPON OR DOES *IT* PERHAPS CONTROL HER INSTEAD?
SARA, HEBREW FOR *"PRINCESS,"* AND STILL IT DOES HER NO JUSTICE.
IS IT THE THING THAT MAKES ITS BEARERS SHINE SO? OR DOES THE VERY BLADE HAVE AN EYE FOR BEAUTY I WONDER?
UP AND AT 'EM PRINCE CHARMING!
GOOD MORNING MR. GRAY, I'D LIKE TO ASK YOU A FEW QUESTIONS IF YOU DON'T MIND.

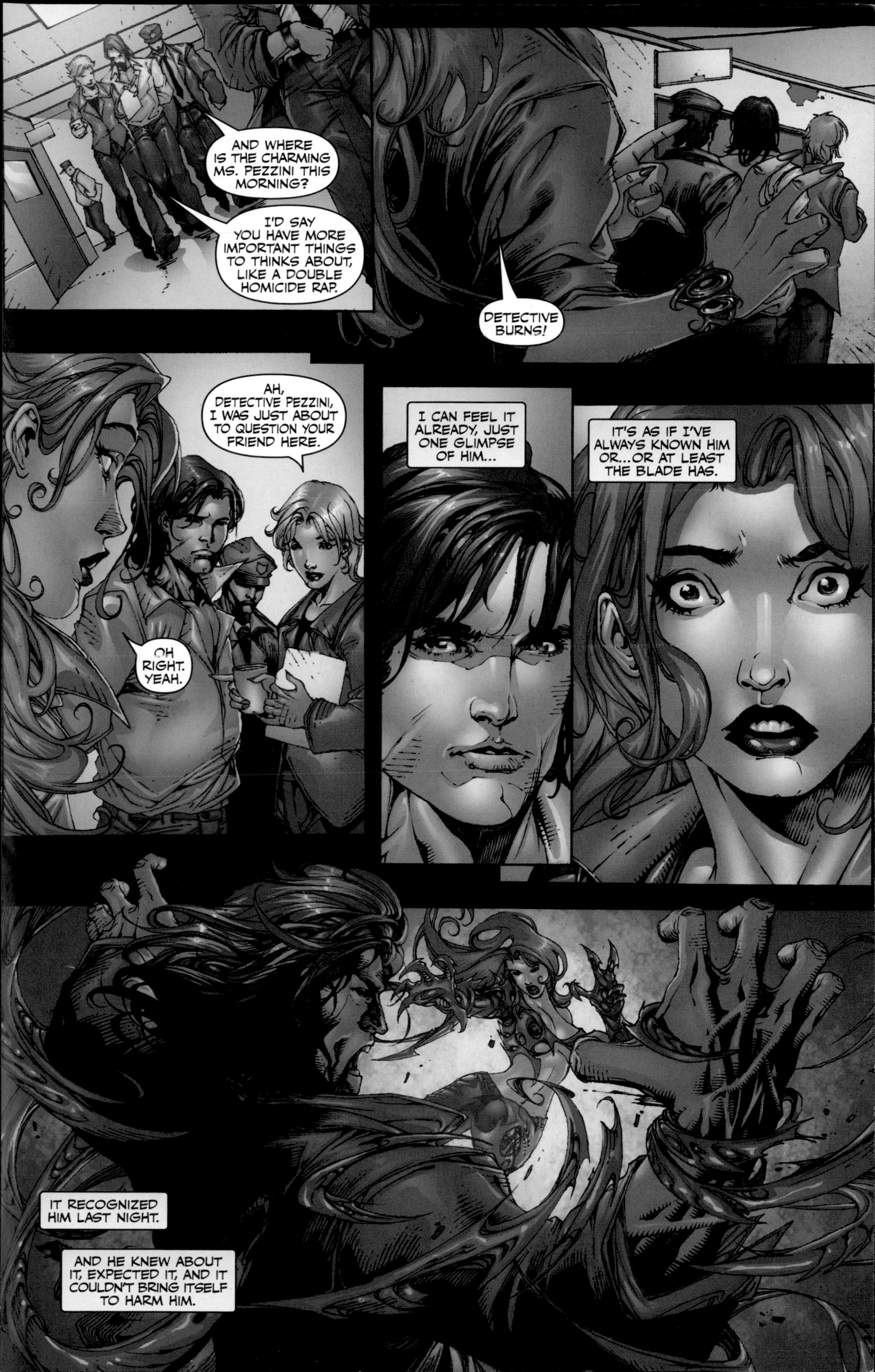
AND WHERE IS THE CHARMING MS. PEZZINI THIS MORNING?
I'D SAY YOU HAVE MORE IMPORTANT THINGS TO THINKS ABOUT, LIKE A DOUBLE HOMICIDE RAP.
DETECTIVE BURNS!
AH, DETECTIVE PEZZINI, I WAS JUST ABOUT TO QUESTION YOUR FRIEND HERE.
OH RIGHT. YEAH.
I CAN FEEL IT ALREADY, JUST ONE GLIMPSE OF HIM...
IT'S AS IF I'VE ALWAYS KNOWN HIM OR...OR AT LEAST THE BLADE HAS.
IT RECOGNIZED HIM LAST NIGHT.
AND HE KNEW ABOUT IT, EXPECTED IT, AND IT COULDN'T BRING ITSELF TO HARM HIM.

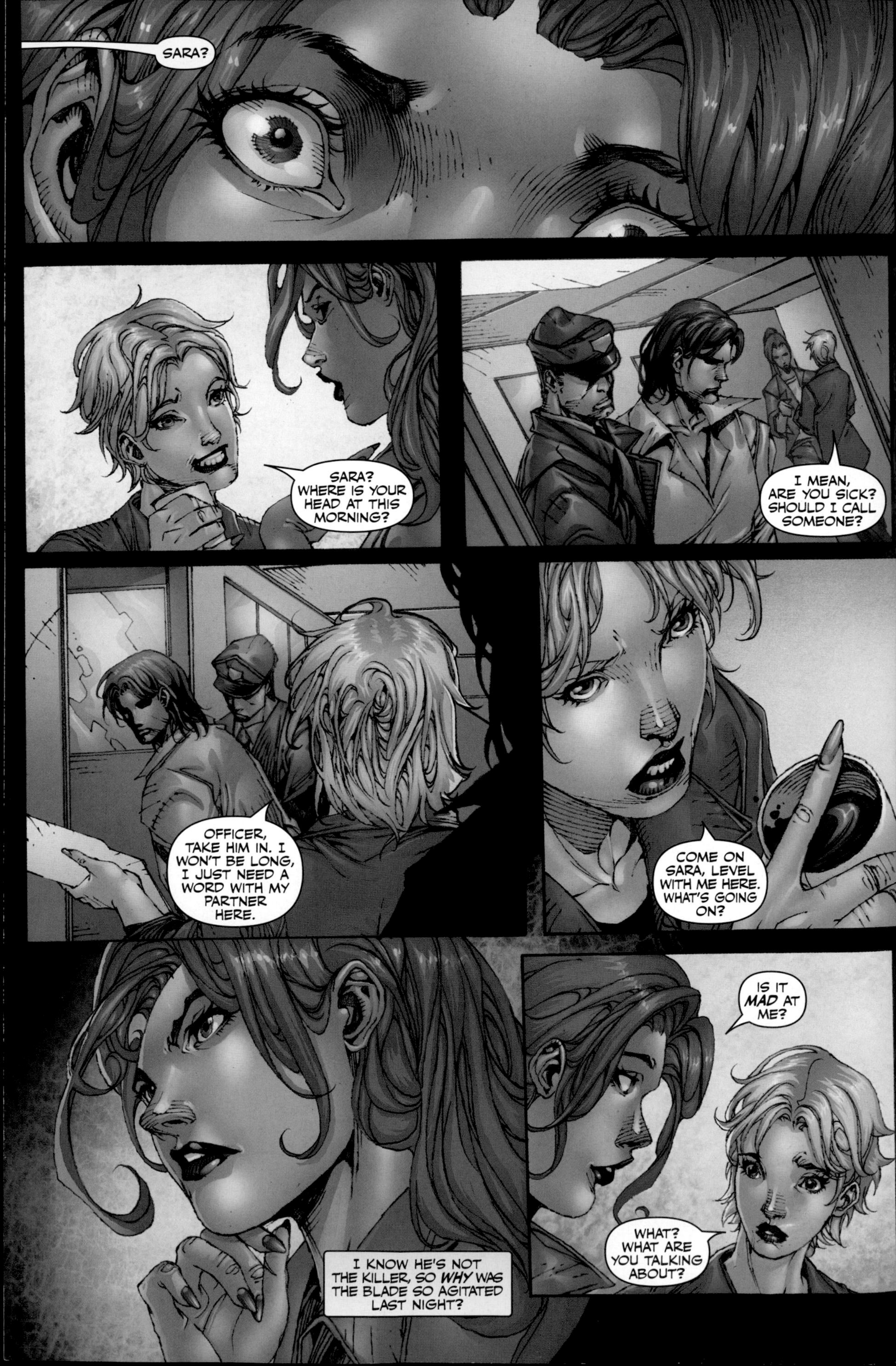
SARA?
SARA? WHERE IS YOUR HEAD AT THIS MORNING?
I MEAN, ARE YOU SICK? SHOULD I CALL SOMEONE?
OFFICER, TAKE HIM IN. I WON'T BE LONG, I JUST NEED A WORD WITH MY PARTNER HERE.
COME ON SARA, LEVEL WITH ME HERE. WHAT'S GOING ON?
I KNOW HE'S NOT THE KILLER, SO WHY WAS THE BLADE SO AGITATED LAST NIGHT?
IS IT MAD AT ME?
WHAT? WHAT ARE YOU TALKING ABOUT?

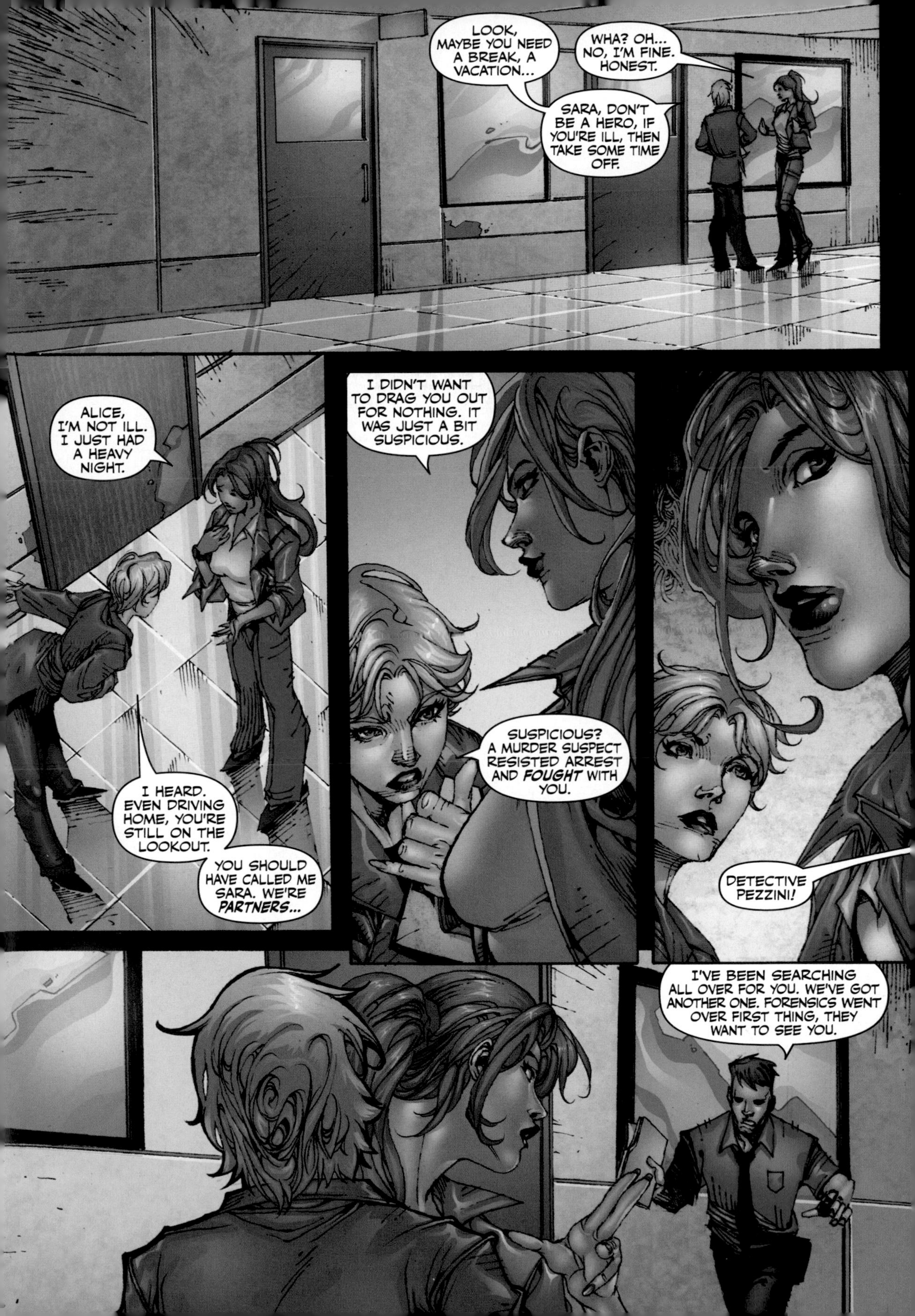
LOOK, MAYBE YOU NEED A BREAK, A VACATION...
WHA? OH... NO, I'M FINE. HONEST.
SARA, DON'T BE A HERO, IF YOU'RE ILL, THEN TAKE SOME TIME OFF.
ALICE, I'M NOT ILL. I JUST HAD A HEAVY NIGHT.
I HEARD. EVEN DRIVING HOME, YOU'RE STILL ON THE LOOKOUT.
YOU SHOULD HAVE CALLED ME SARA. WE'RE *PARTNERS...*
I DIDN'T WANT TO DRAG YOU OUT FOR NOTHING. IT WAS JUST A BIT SUSPICIOUS.
SUSPICIOUS? A MURDER SUSPECT RESISTED ARREST AND *FOUGHT* WITH YOU.
DETECTIVE PEZZINI!
I'VE BEEN SEARCHING ALL OVER FOR YOU. WE'VE GOT ANOTHER ONE. FORENSICS WENT OVER FIRST THING, THEY WANT TO SEE YOU.

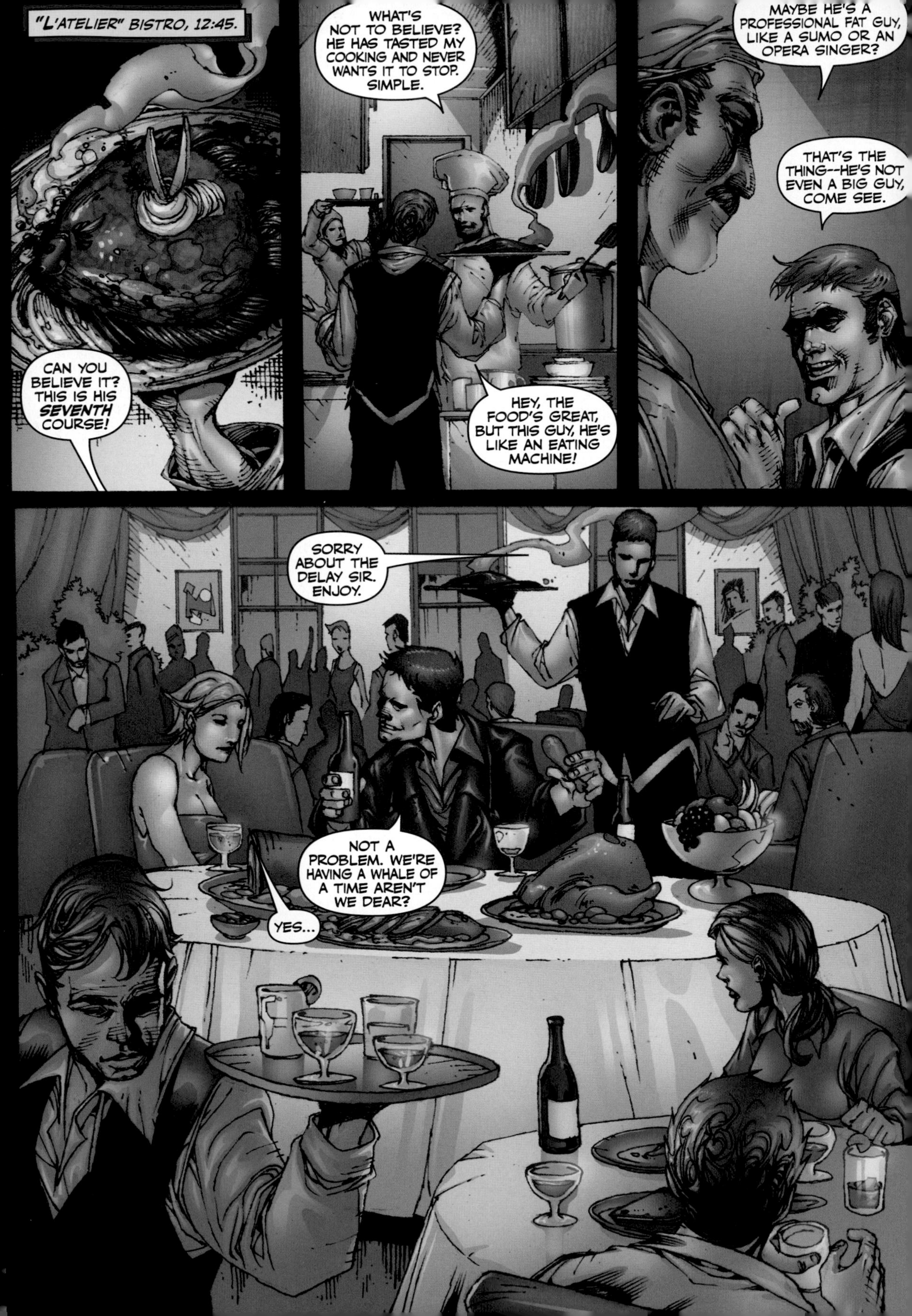
"L'ATELIER" BISTRO, 12:45.
CAN YOU BELIEVE IT? THIS IS HIS SEVENTH COURSE!
WHAT'S NOT TO BELIEVE? HE HAS TASTED MY COOKING AND NEVER WANTS IT TO STOP. SIMPLE.
HEY, THE FOOD'S GREAT, BUT THIS GUY, HE'S LIKE AN EATING MACHINE!
MAYBE HE'S A PROFESSIONAL FAT GUY, LIKE A SUMO OR AN OPERA SINGER?
THAT'S THE THING--HE'S NOT EVEN A BIG GUY, COME SEE.
SORRY ABOUT THE DELAY SIR. ENJOY.
NOT A PROBLEM. WE'RE HAVING A WHALE OF A TIME AREN'T WE DEAR?
YES...

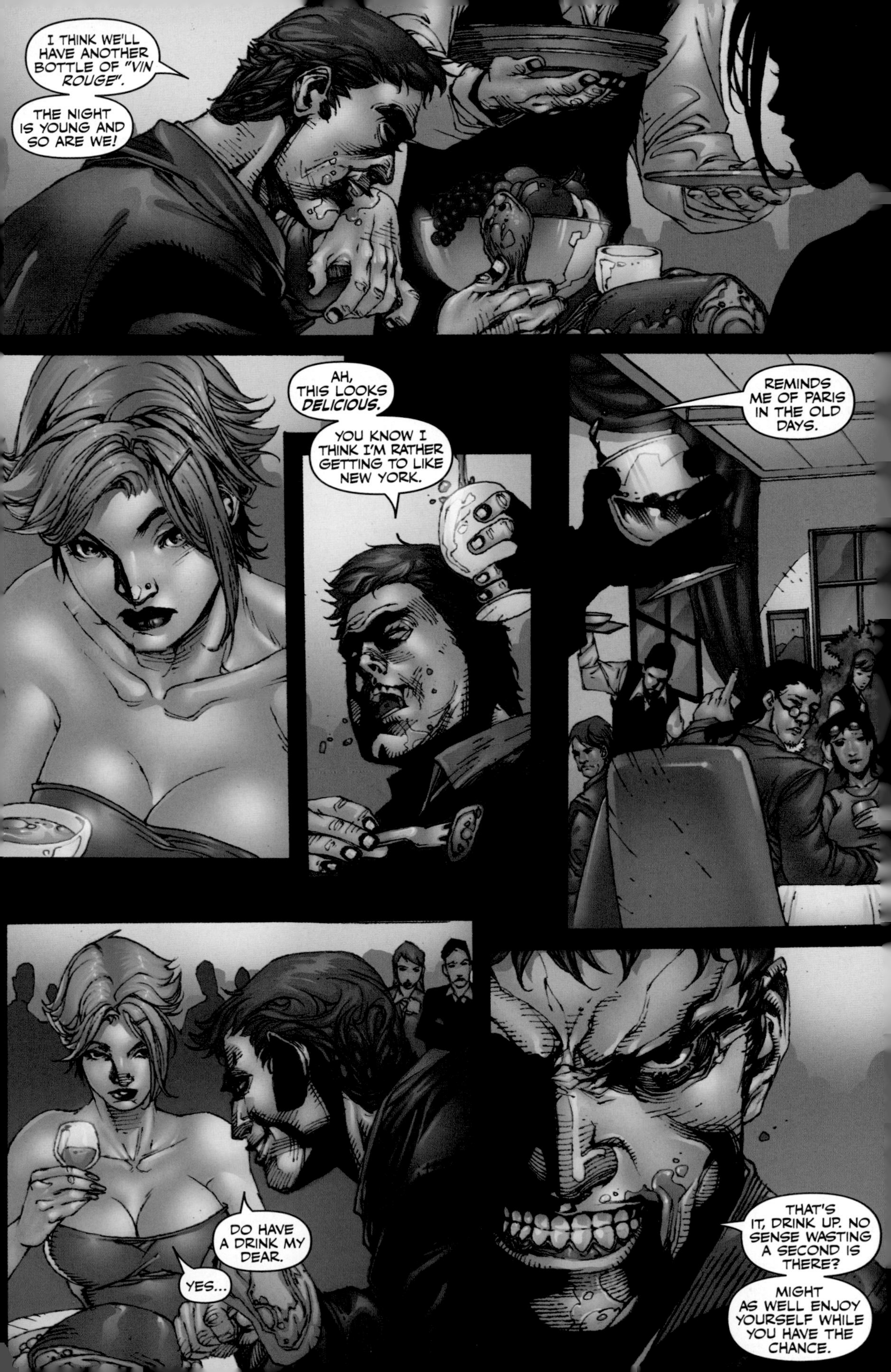

I THINK WE'LL HAVE ANOTHER BOTTLE OF "VIN ROUGE".
THE NIGHT IS YOUNG AND SO ARE WE!
AH, THIS LOOKS DELICIOUS.
YOU KNOW I THINK I'M RATHER GETTING TO LIKE NEW YORK.
REMINDS ME OF PARIS IN THE OLD DAYS.
DO HAVE A DRINK MY DEAR.
YES...
THAT'S IT, DRINK UP. NO SENSE WASTING A SECOND IS THERE?
MIGHT AS WELL ENJOY YOURSELF WHILE YOU HAVE THE CHANCE.

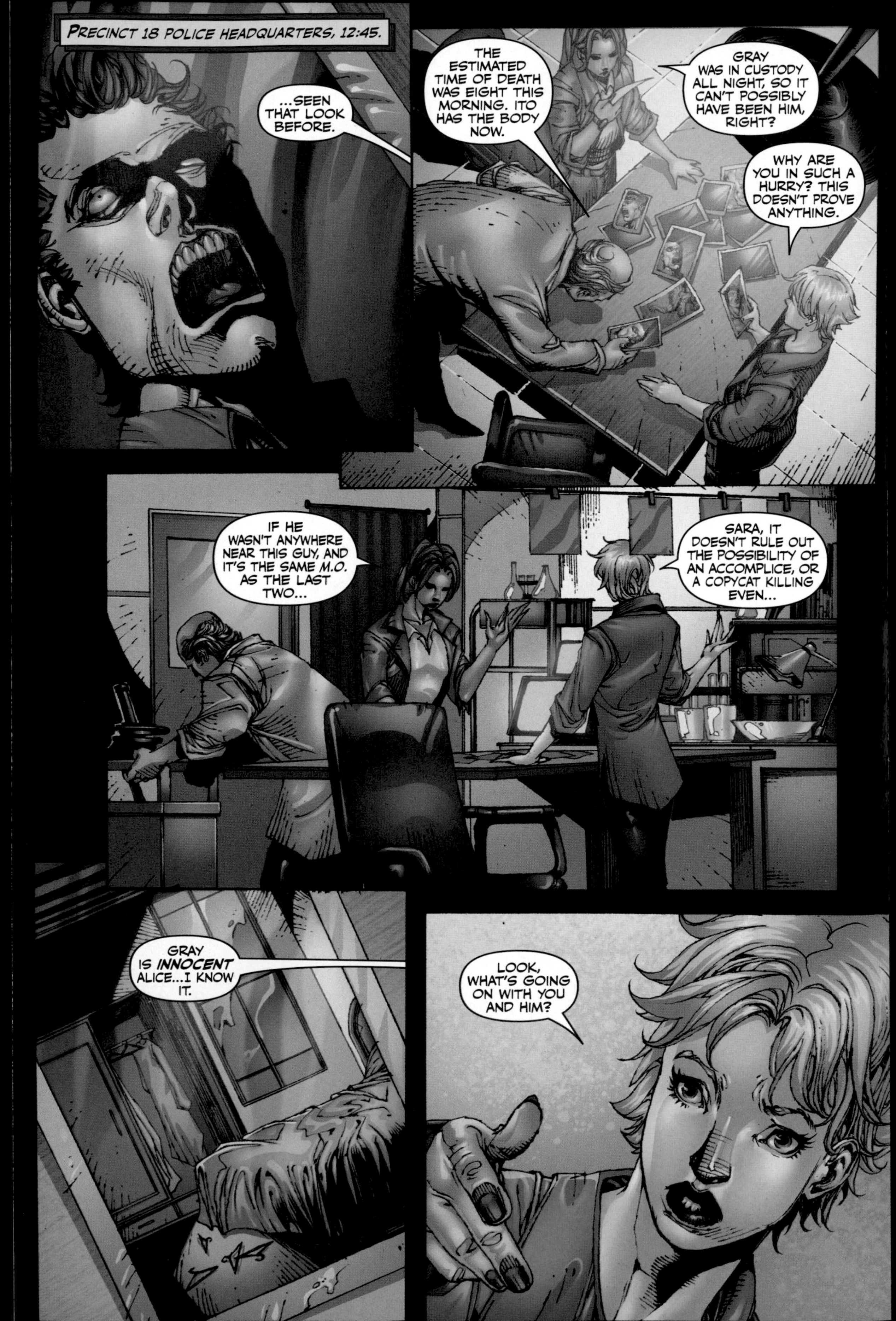
PRECINCT 18 POLICE HEADQUARTERS, 12:45.
...SEEN THAT LOOK BEFORE.
THE ESTIMATED TIME OF DEATH WAS EIGHT THIS MORNING. ITO HAS THE BODY NOW.
GRAY WAS IN CUSTODY ALL NIGHT, SO IT CAN'T POSSIBLY HAVE BEEN HIM, RIGHT?
WHY ARE YOU IN SUCH A HURRY? THIS DOESN'T PROVE ANYTHING.
IF HE WASN'T ANYWHERE NEAR THIS GUY, AND IT'S THE SAME M.O. AS THE LAST TWO...
SARA, IT DOESN'T RULE OUT THE POSSIBILITY OF AN ACCOMPLICE, OR A COPYCAT KILLING EVEN...
GRAY IS INNOCENT ALICE...I KNOW IT.
LOOK, WHAT'S GOING ON WITH YOU AND HIM?

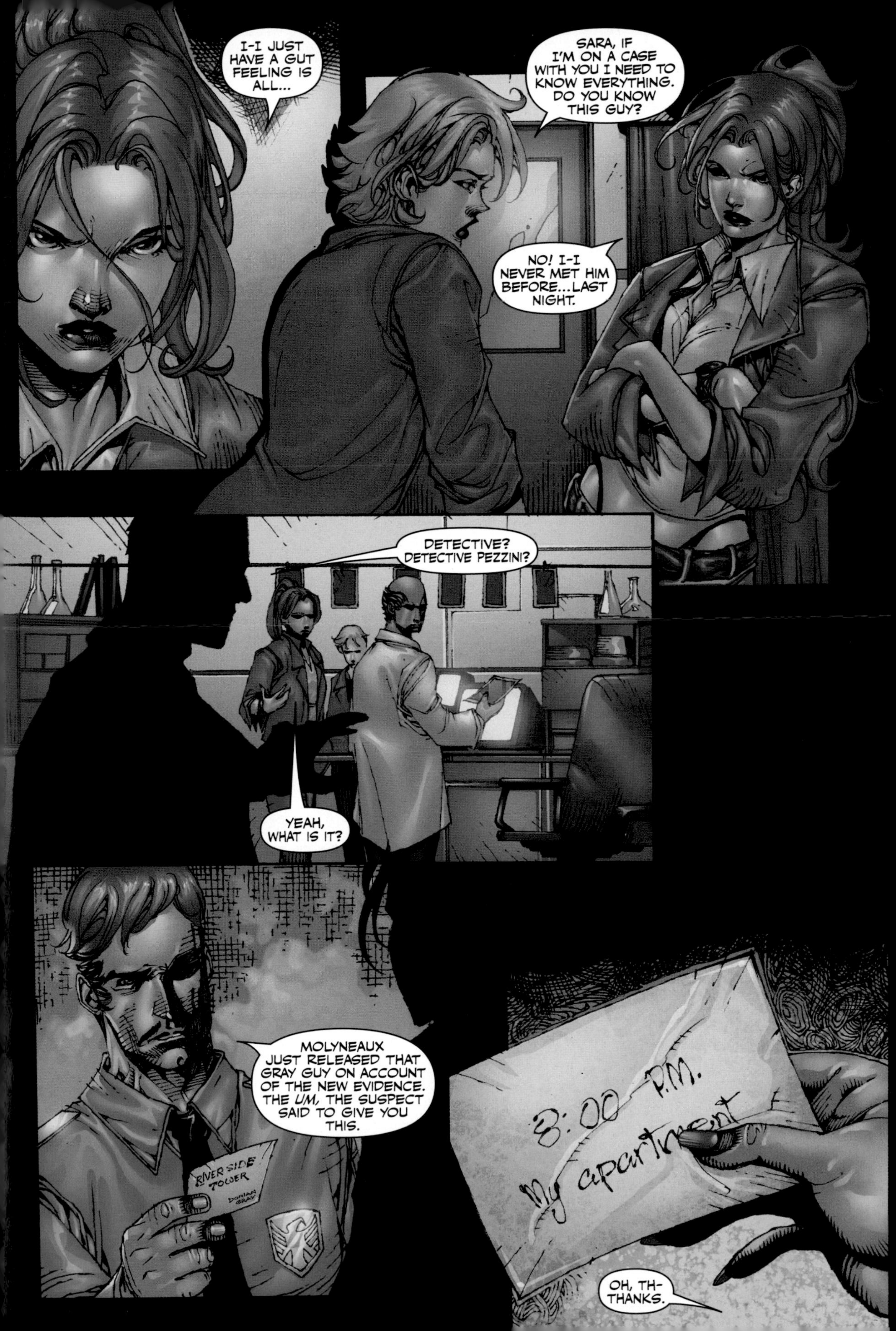
I-I JUST HAVE A GUT FEELING IS ALL...
SARA, IF I'M ON A CASE WITH YOU I NEED TO KNOW EVERYTHING. DO YOU KNOW THIS GUY?
NO! I-I NEVER MET HIM BEFORE...LAST NIGHT.
DETECTIVE? DETECTIVE PEZZINI?
YEAH, WHAT IS IT?
MOLYNEAUX JUST RELEASED THAT GRAY GUY ON ACCOUNT OF THE NEW EVIDENCE. THE UM, THE SUSPECT SAID TO GIVE YOU THIS.
RIVERSIDE TOWER
DORIAN GRAY
8:00 P.M.
My apartment
OH, TH-THANKS.

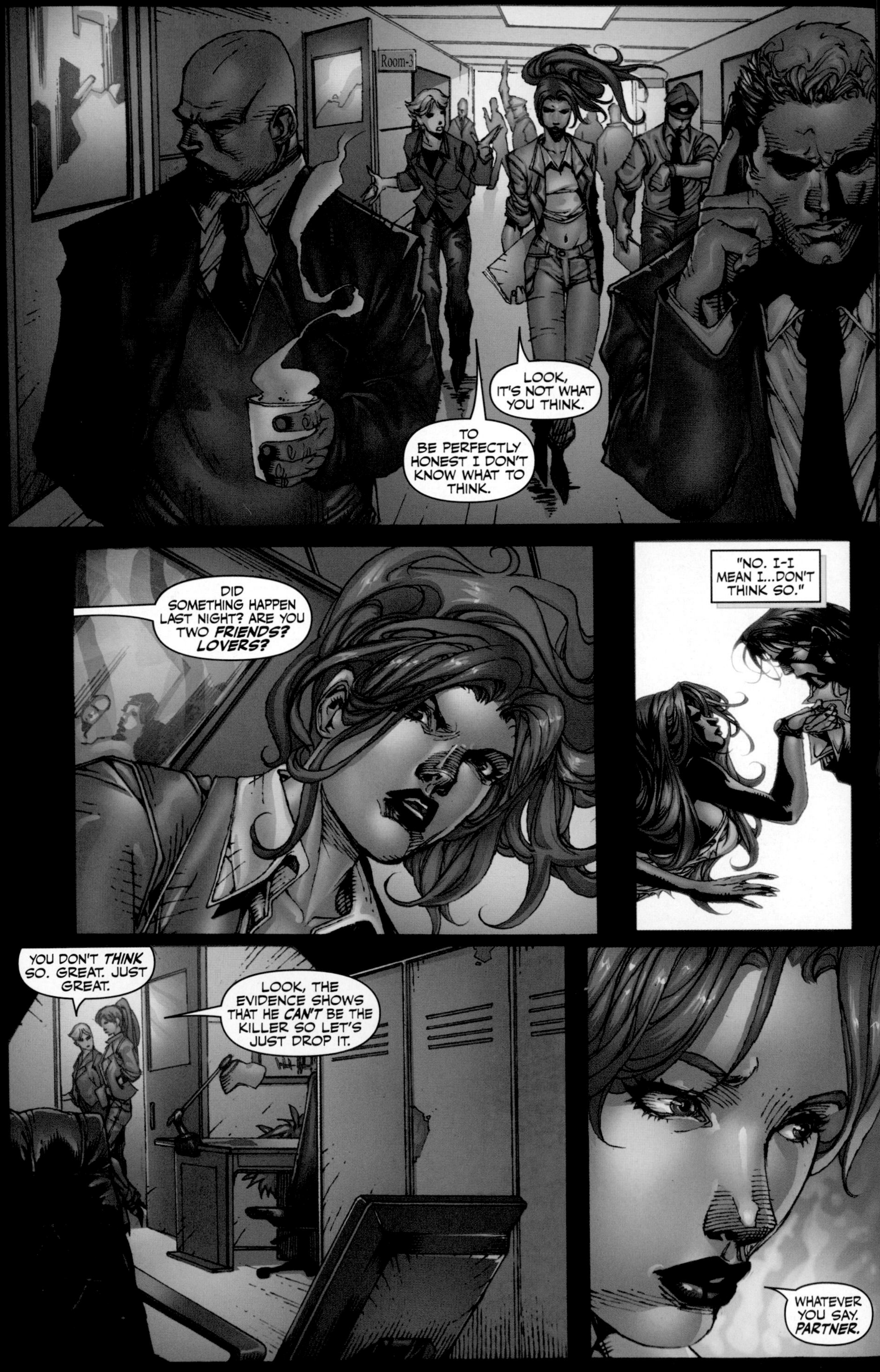
Room-3
LOOK, IT'S NOT WHAT YOU THINK.
TO BE PERFECTLY HONEST I DON'T KNOW WHAT TO THINK.
DID SOMETHING HAPPEN LAST NIGHT? ARE YOU TWO *FRIENDS? LOVERS?*
"NO. I-I MEAN I...DON'T THINK SO."
YOU DON'T *THINK* SO. GREAT. JUST GREAT.
LOOK, THE EVIDENCE SHOWS THAT HE *CAN'T* BE THE KILLER SO LET'S JUST DROP IT.
WHATEVER YOU SAY. *PARTNER.*

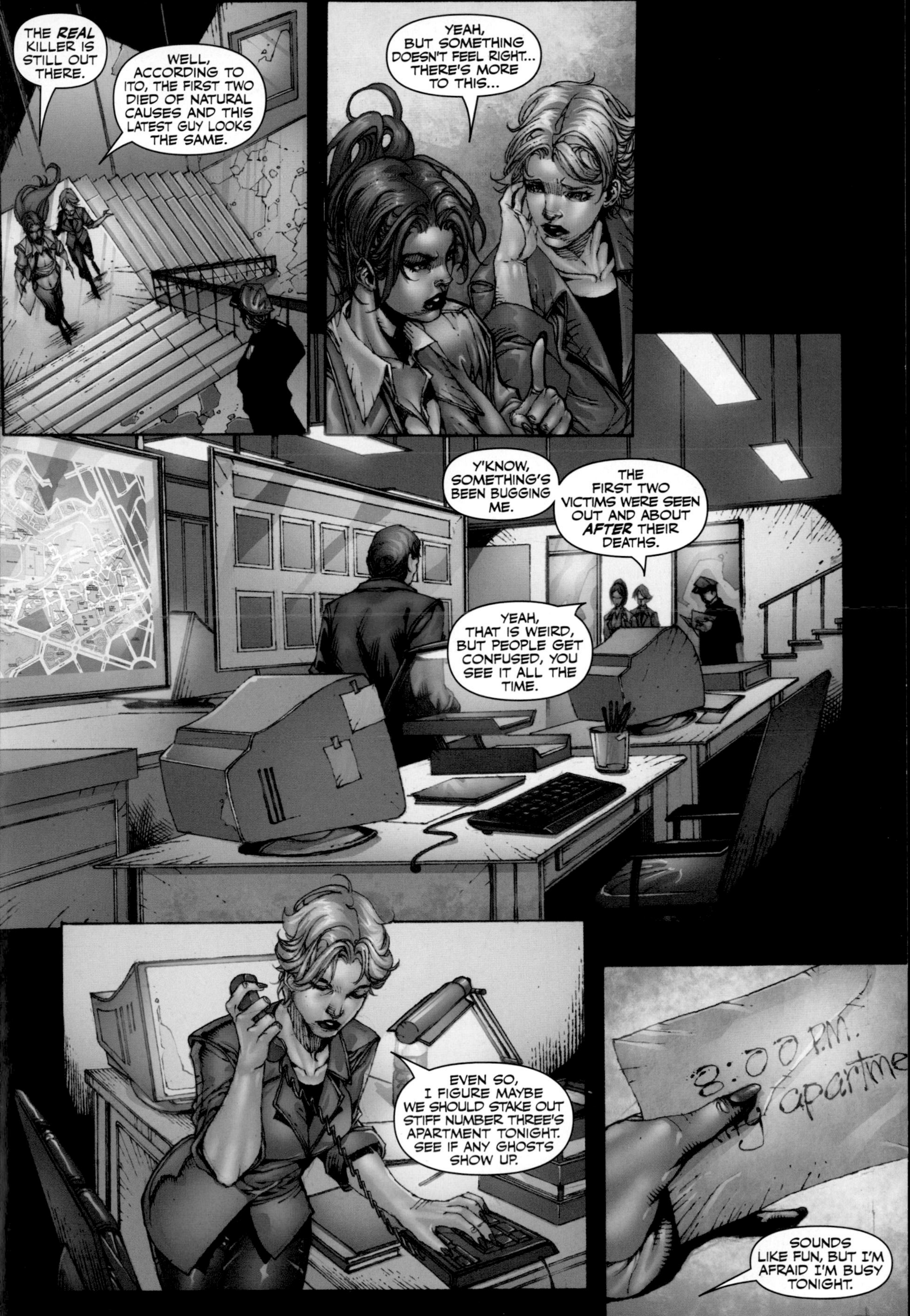
THE REAL KILLER IS STILL OUT THERE.
WELL, ACCORDING TO ITO, THE FIRST TWO DIED OF NATURAL CAUSES AND THIS LATEST GUY LOOKS THE SAME.
YEAH, BUT SOMETHING DOESN'T FEEL RIGHT... THERE'S MORE TO THIS...
Y'KNOW, SOMETHING'S BEEN BUGGING ME.
THE FIRST TWO VICTIMS WERE SEEN OUT AND ABOUT AFTER THEIR DEATHS.
YEAH, THAT IS WEIRD, BUT PEOPLE GET CONFUSED, YOU SEE IT ALL THE TIME.
EVEN SO, I FIGURE MAYBE WE SHOULD STAKE OUT STIFF NUMBER THREE'S APARTMENT TONIGHT. SEE IF ANY GHOSTS SHOW UP.
8:00 P.M.
apartme
SOUNDS LIKE FUN, BUT I'M AFRAID I'M BUSY TONIGHT.

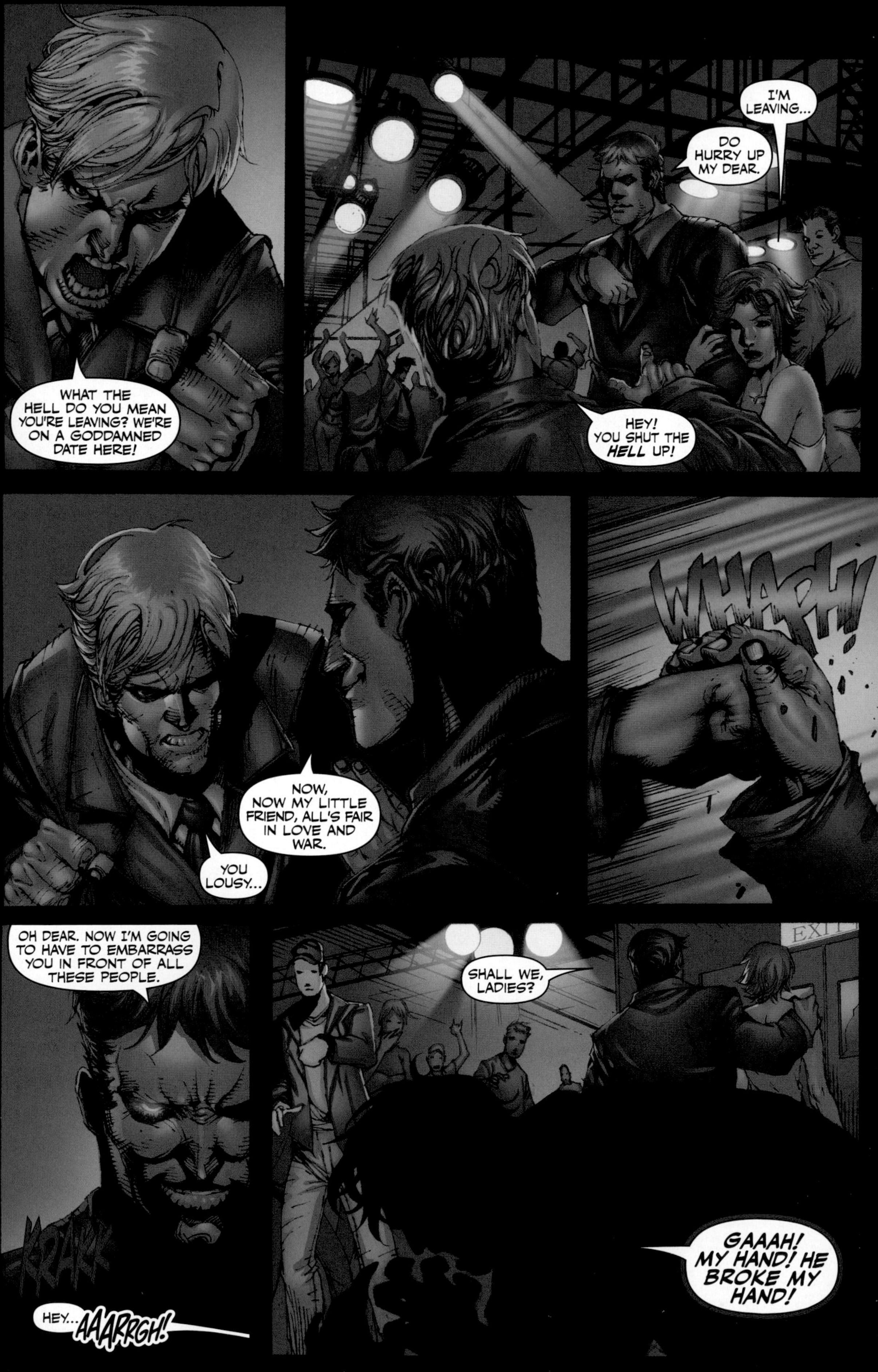
WHAT THE HELL DO YOU MEAN YOU'RE LEAVING? WE'RE ON A GODDAMNED DATE HERE!
I'M LEAVING...
DO HURRY UP MY DEAR.
HEY! YOU SHUT THE HELL UP!
NOW, NOW MY LITTLE FRIEND, ALL'S FAIR IN LOVE AND WAR.
YOU LOUSY...
WHAP!
OH DEAR. NOW I'M GOING TO HAVE TO EMBARRASS YOU IN FRONT OF ALL THESE PEOPLE.
HEY...AAARRGH!
SHALL WE, LADIES?
EXIT
GAAAH! MY HAND! HE BROKE MY HAND!

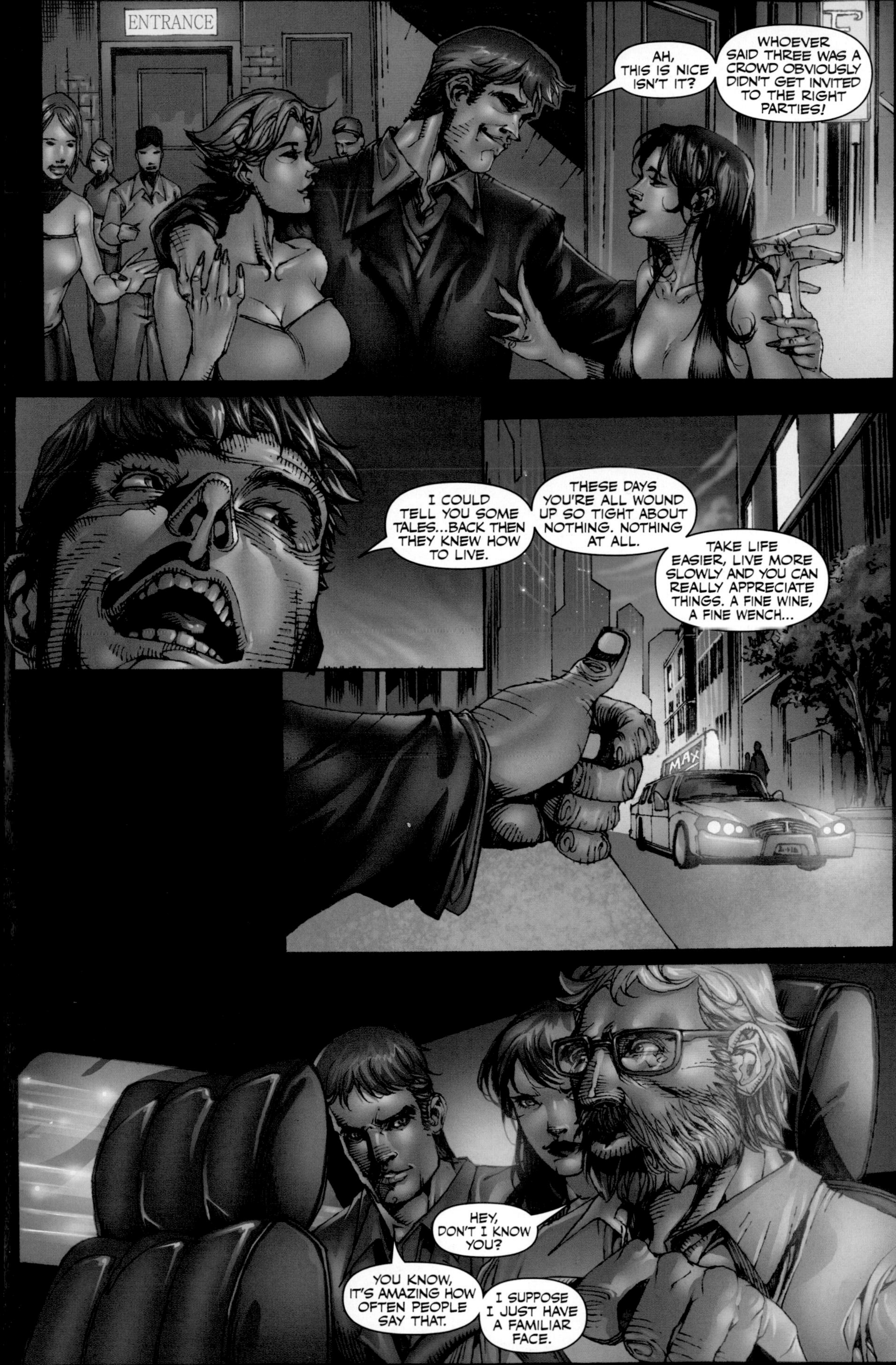
ENTRANCE
AH, THIS IS NICE ISN'T IT?
WHOEVER SAID THREE WAS A CROWD OBVIOUSLY DIDN'T GET INVITED TO THE RIGHT PARTIES!
I COULD TELL YOU SOME TALES...BACK THEN THEY KNEW HOW TO LIVE.
THESE DAYS YOU'RE ALL WOUND UP SO TIGHT ABOUT NOTHING. NOTHING AT ALL.
TAKE LIFE EASIER, LIVE MORE SLOWLY AND YOU CAN REALLY APPRECIATE THINGS. A FINE WINE, A FINE WENCH...
MAX
HEY, DON'T I KNOW YOU?
YOU KNOW, IT'S AMAZING HOW OFTEN PEOPLE SAY THAT.
I SUPPOSE I JUST HAVE A FAMILIAR FACE.

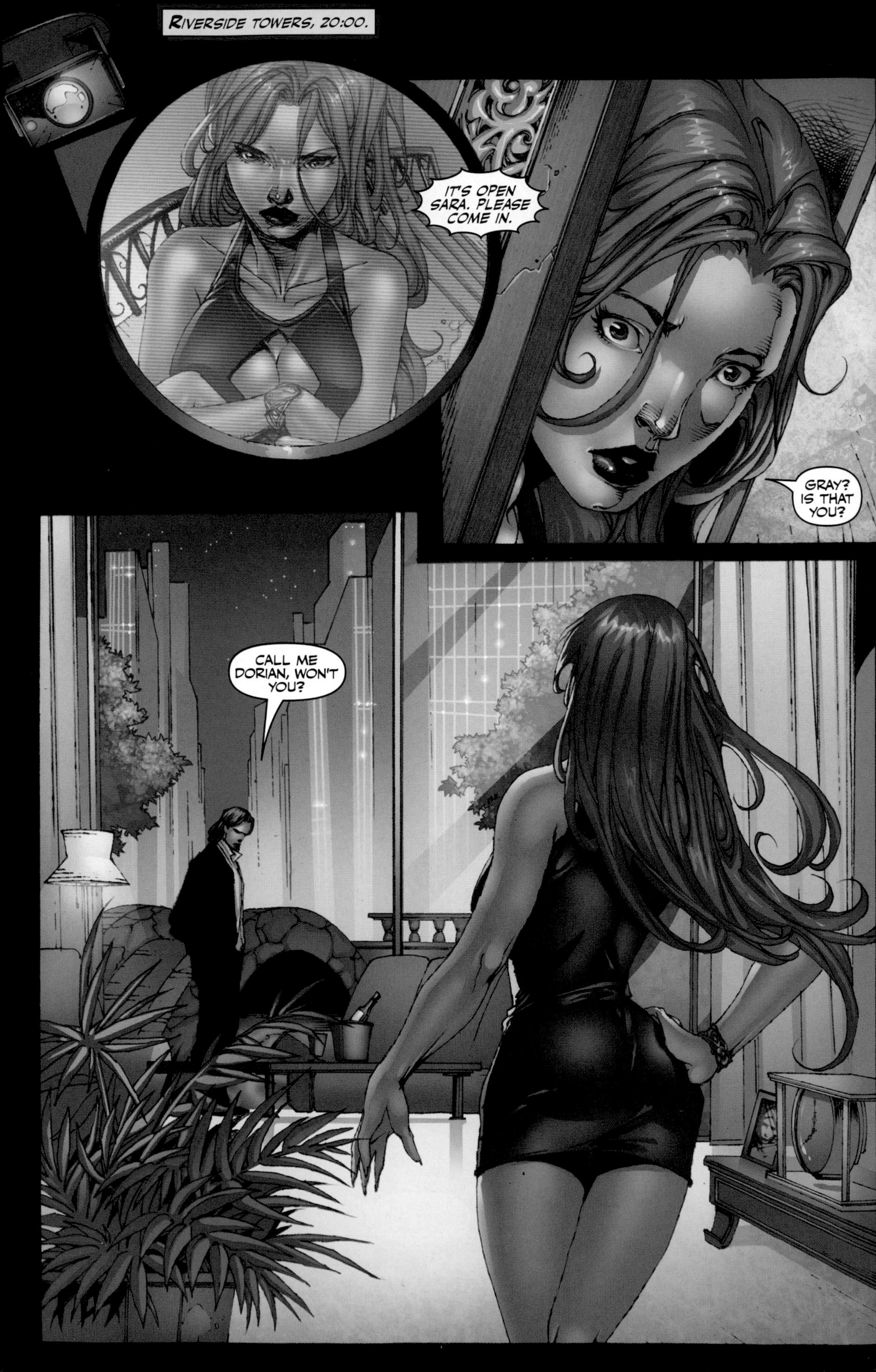
RIVERSIDE TOWERS, 20:00.
IT'S OPEN SARA. PLEASE COME IN.
GRAY? IS THAT YOU?
CALL ME DORIAN, WON'T YOU?

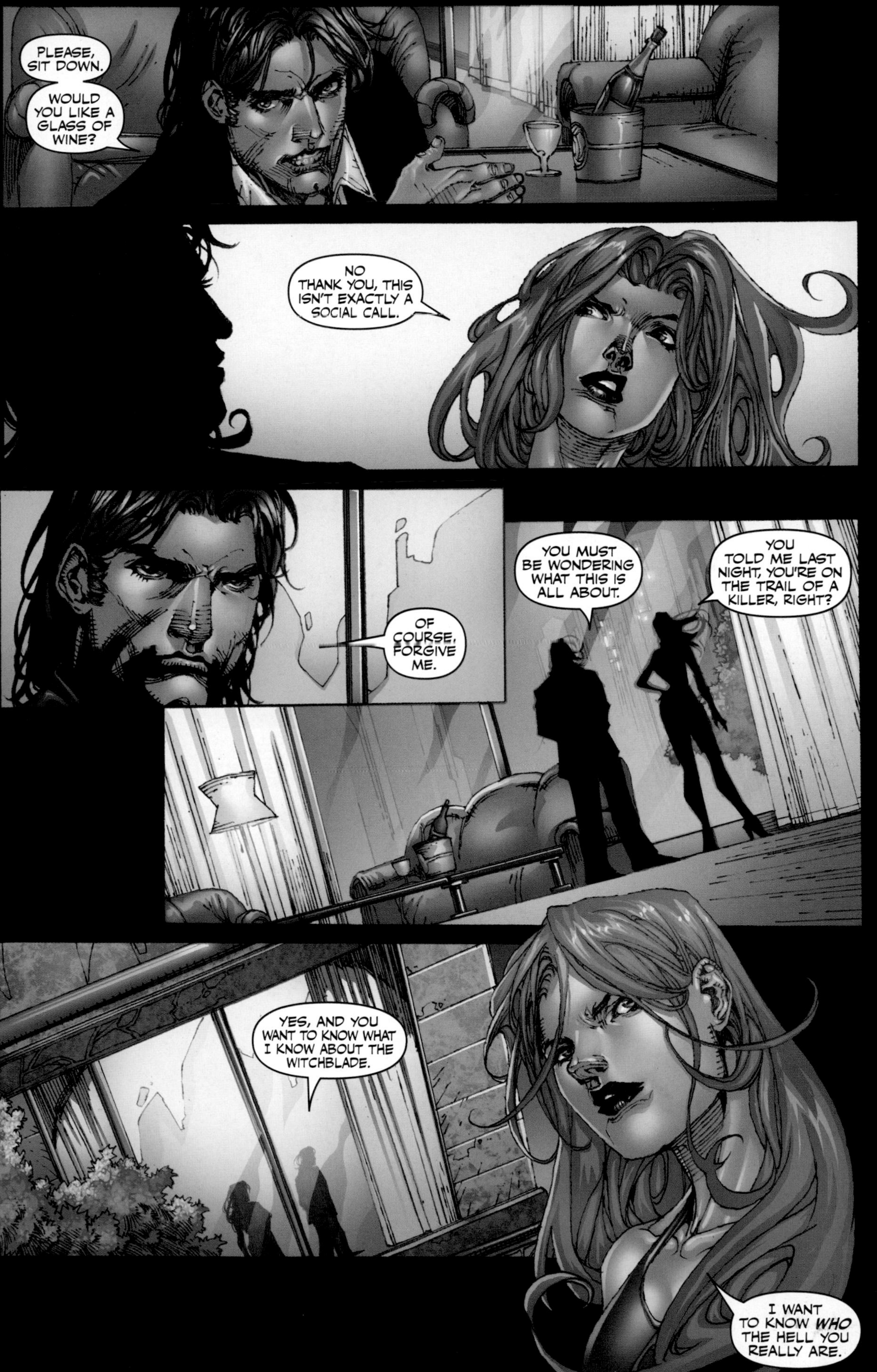
PLEASE, SIT DOWN.
WOULD YOU LIKE A GLASS OF WINE?
NO THANK YOU, THIS ISN'T EXACTLY A SOCIAL CALL.
OF COURSE, FORGIVE ME.
YOU MUST BE WONDERING WHAT THIS IS ALL ABOUT.
YOU TOLD ME LAST NIGHT, YOU'RE ON THE TRAIL OF A KILLER, RIGHT?
YES, AND YOU WANT TO KNOW WHAT I KNOW ABOUT THE WITCHBLADE.
I WANT TO KNOW *WHO* THE HELL YOU REALLY ARE.

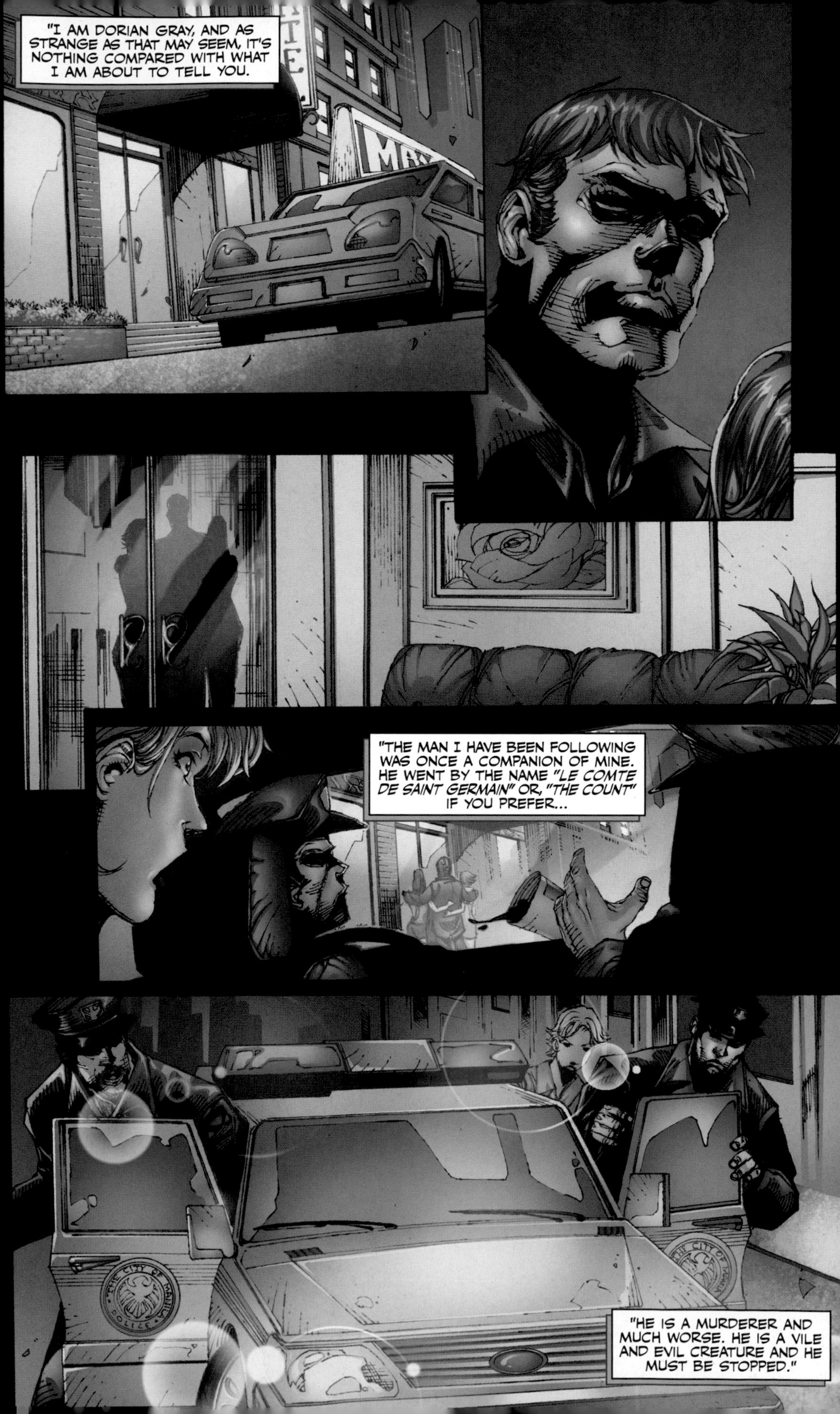
"I AM DORIAN GRAY, AND AS STRANGE AS THAT MAY SEEM, IT'S NOTHING COMPARED WITH WHAT I AM ABOUT TO TELL YOU.
"THE MAN I HAVE BEEN FOLLOWING WAS ONCE A COMPANION OF MINE. HE WENT BY THE NAME "LE COMTE DE SAINT GERMAIN" OR, "THE COUNT" IF YOU PREFER...
"HE IS A MURDERER AND MUCH WORSE. HE IS A VILE AND EVIL CREATURE AND HE MUST BE STOPPED."

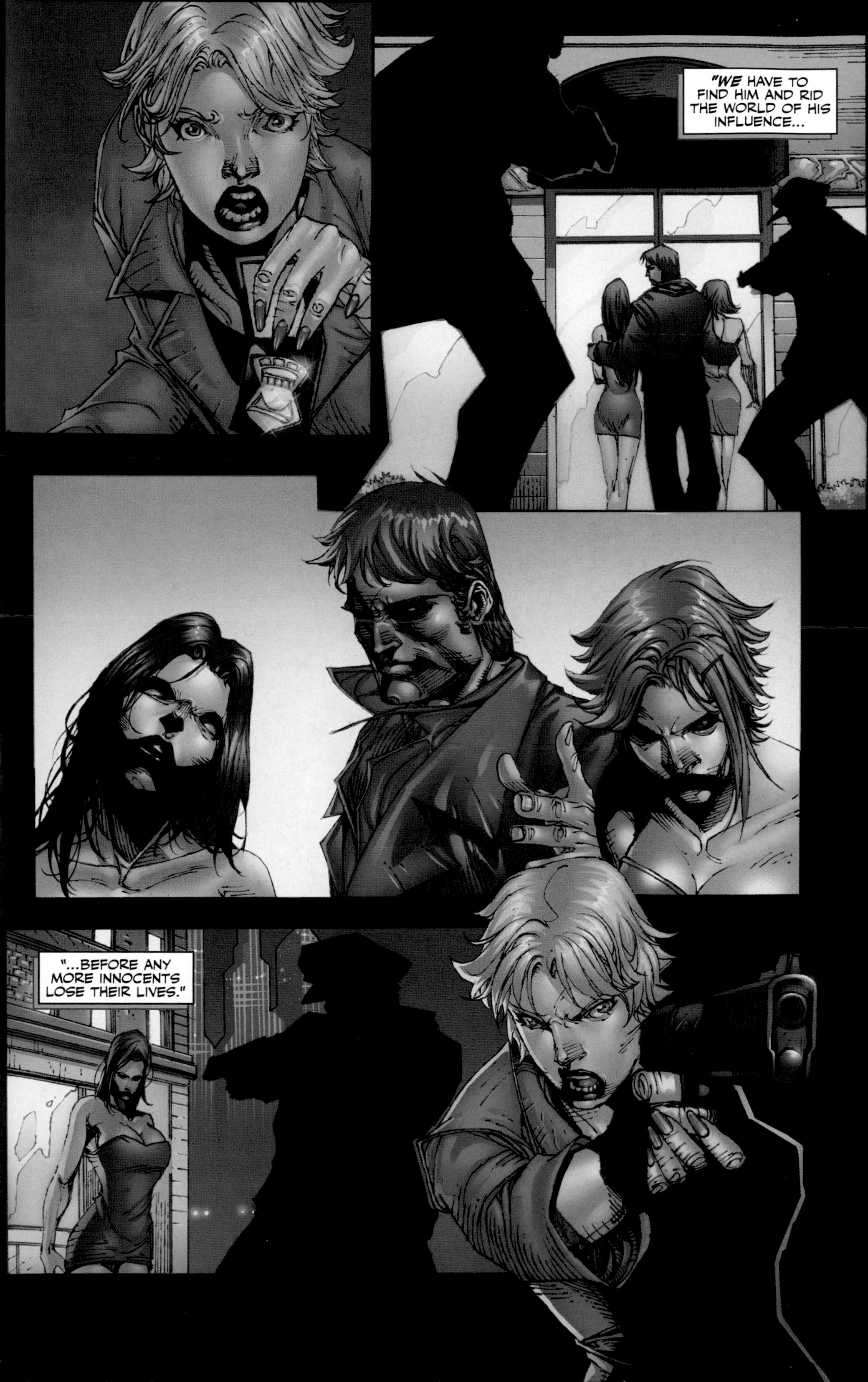
"WE HAVE TO FIND HIM AND RID THE WORLD OF HIS INFLUENCE...
"...BEFORE ANY MORE INNOCENTS LOSE THEIR LIVES."

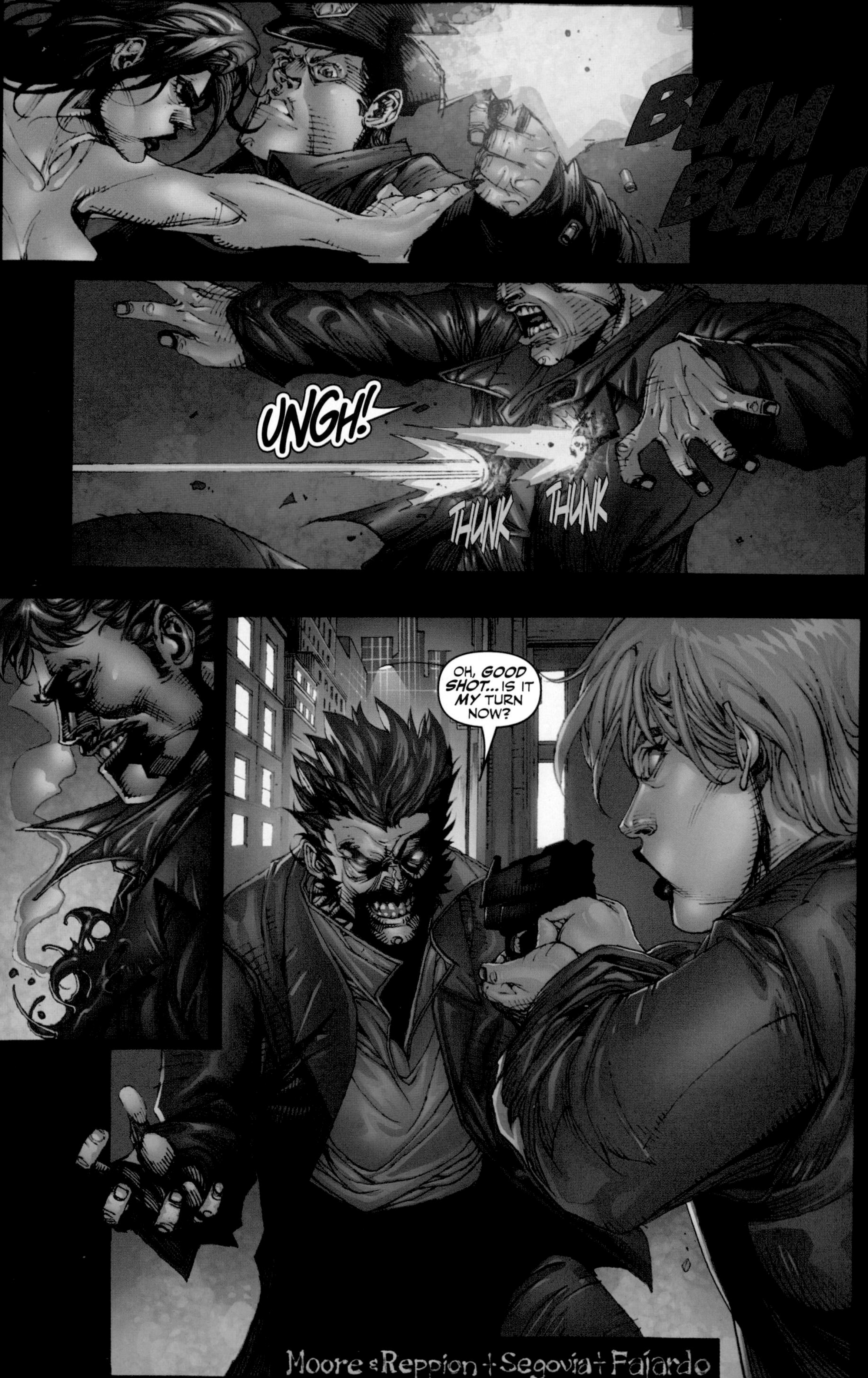
BLAM
BLAM
UNGH!
THUNK
THUNK
OH, GOOD SHOT... IS IT MY TURN NOW?
Moore & Reppion + Segovia + Fajardo

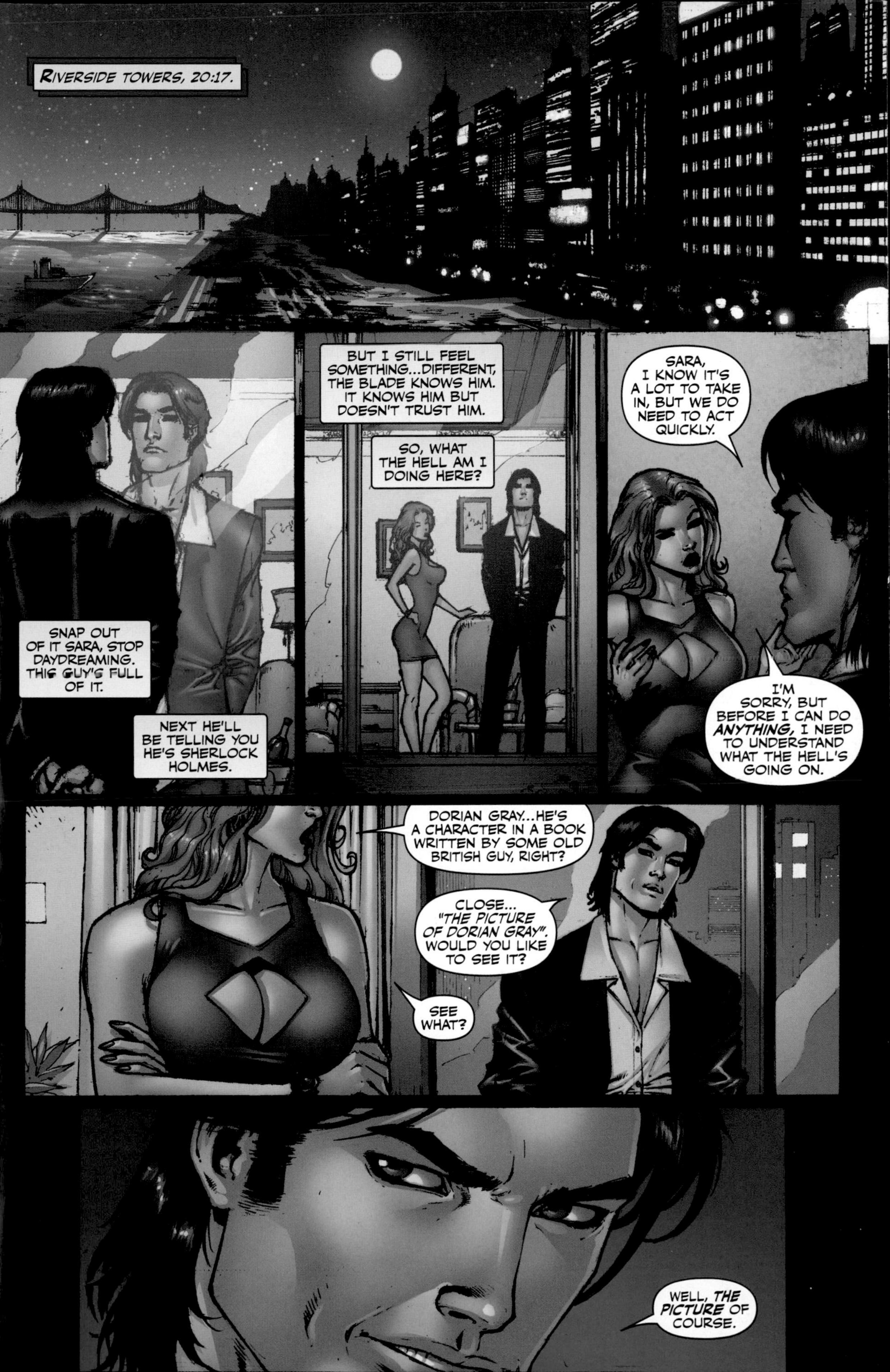
RIVERSIDE TOWERS, 20:17.
SNAP OUT OF IT SARA, STOP DAYDREAMING. THIS GUY'S FULL OF IT.
NEXT HE'LL BE TELLING YOU HE'S SHERLOCK HOLMES.
BUT I STILL FEEL SOMETHING...DIFFERENT, THE BLADE KNOWS HIM. IT KNOWS HIM BUT DOESN'T TRUST HIM.
SO, WHAT THE HELL AM I DOING HERE?
SARA, I KNOW IT'S A LOT TO TAKE IN, BUT WE DO NEED TO ACT QUICKLY.
I'M SORRY, BUT BEFORE I CAN DO *ANYTHING,* I NEED TO UNDERSTAND WHAT THE HELL'S GOING ON.
DORIAN GRAY...HE'S A CHARACTER IN A BOOK WRITTEN BY SOME OLD BRITISH GUY, RIGHT?
CLOSE... *"THE PICTURE OF DORIAN GRAY".* WOULD YOU LIKE TO SEE IT?
SEE WHAT?
WELL, *THE PICTURE* OF COURSE.

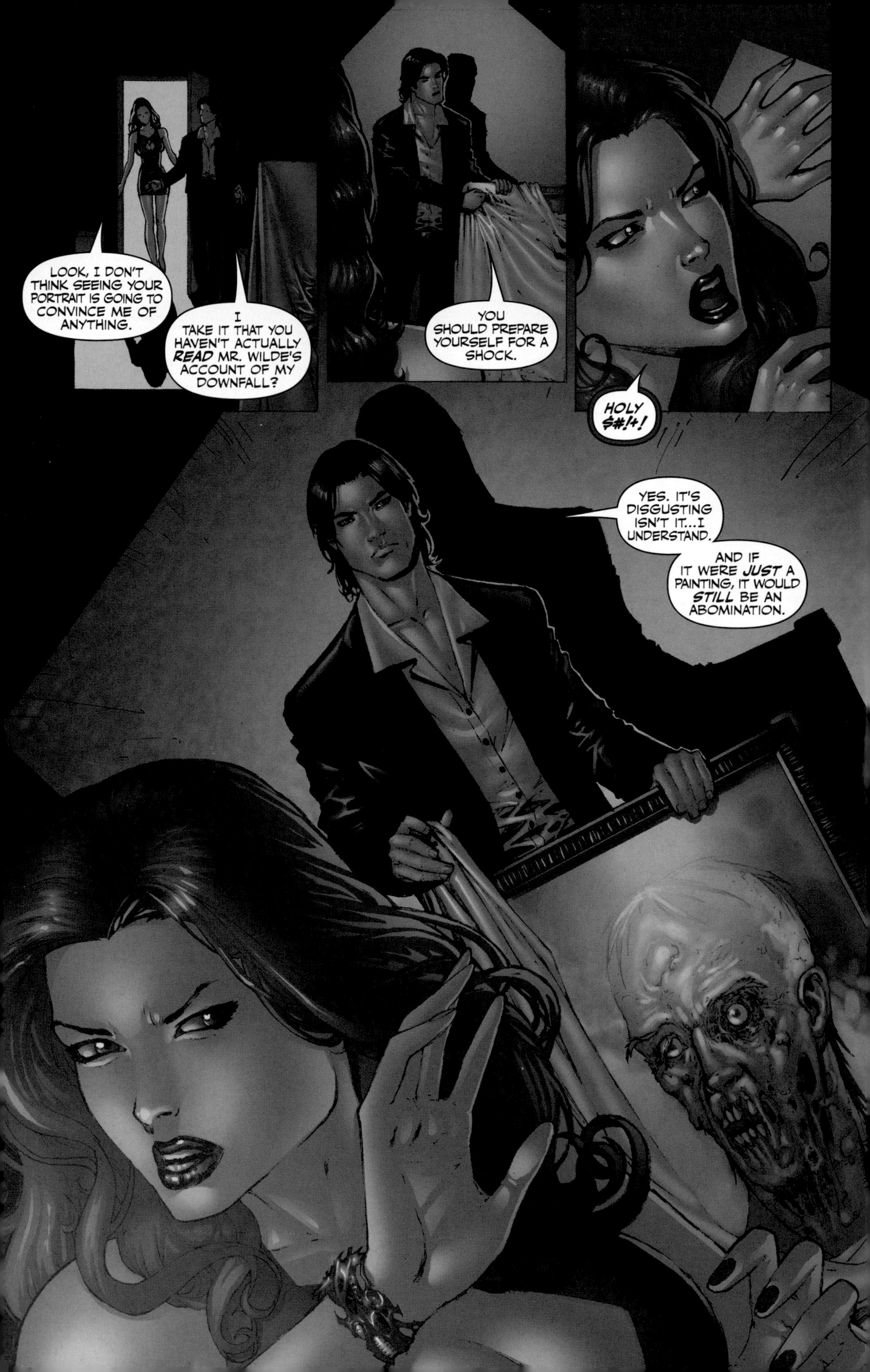
LOOK, I DON'T THINK SEEING YOUR PORTRAIT IS GOING TO CONVINCE ME OF ANYTHING.
I TAKE IT THAT YOU HAVEN'T ACTUALLY READ MR. WILDE'S ACCOUNT OF MY DOWNFALL?
YOU SHOULD PREPARE YOURSELF FOR A SHOCK.
HOLY $#!+!
YES. IT'S DISGUSTING ISN'T IT...I UNDERSTAND.
AND IF IT WERE JUST A PAINTING, IT WOULD STILL BE AN ABOMINATION.

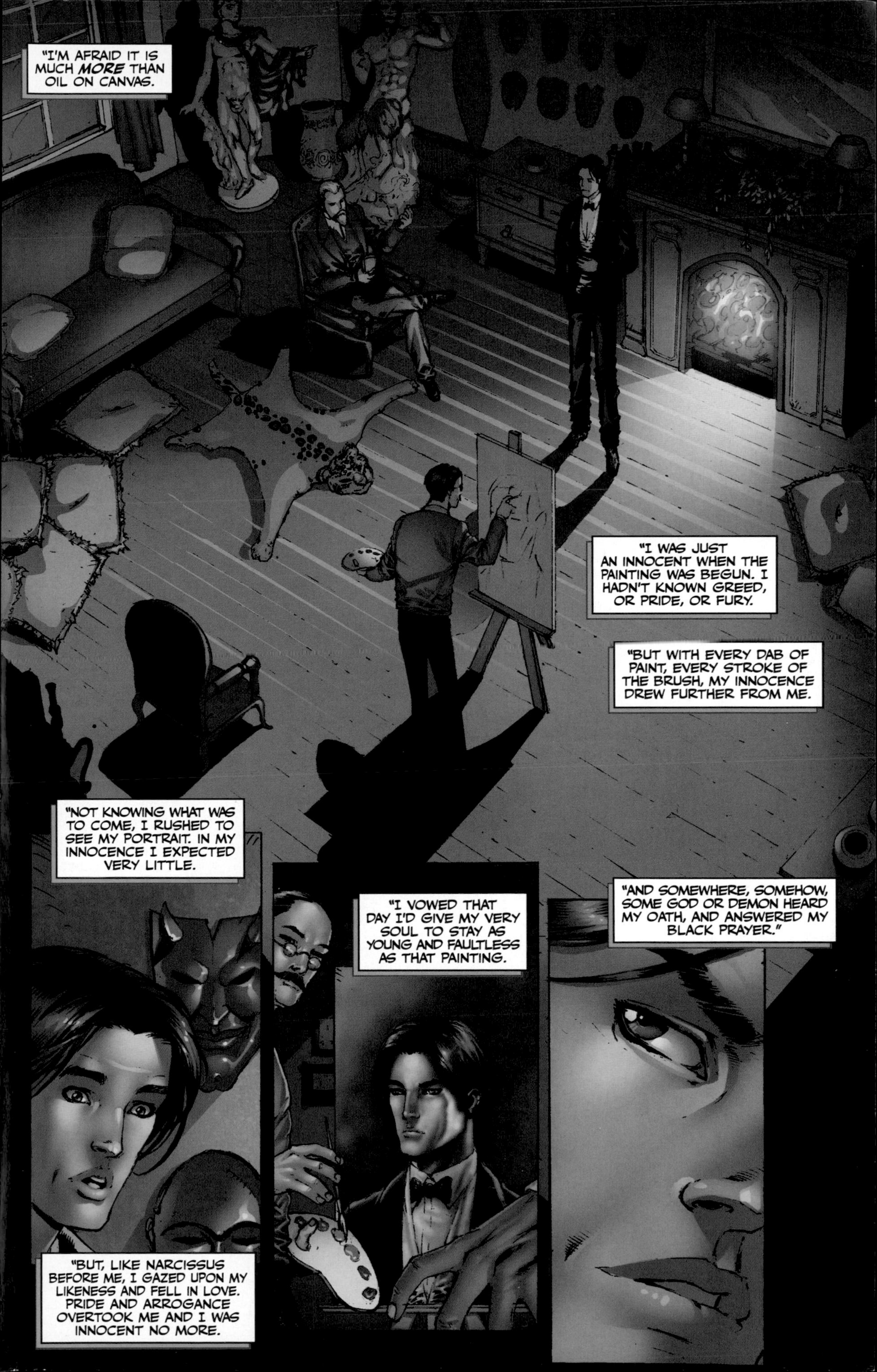
"I'M AFRAID IT IS MUCH MORE THAN OIL ON CANVAS.
"I WAS JUST AN INNOCENT WHEN THE PAINTING WAS BEGUN. I HADN'T KNOWN GREED, OR PRIDE, OR FURY.
"BUT WITH EVERY DAB OF PAINT, EVERY STROKE OF THE BRUSH, MY INNOCENCE DREW FURTHER FROM ME.
"NOT KNOWING WHAT WAS TO COME, I RUSHED TO SEE MY PORTRAIT. IN MY INNOCENCE I EXPECTED VERY LITTLE.
"BUT, LIKE NARCISSUS BEFORE ME, I GAZED UPON MY LIKENESS AND FELL IN LOVE. PRIDE AND ARROGANCE OVERTOOK ME AND I WAS INNOCENT NO MORE.
"I VOWED THAT DAY I'D GIVE MY VERY SOUL TO STAY AS YOUNG AND FAULTLESS AS THAT PAINTING.
"AND SOMEWHERE, SOMEHOW, SOME GOD OR DEMON HEARD MY OATH, AND ANSWERED MY BLACK PRAYER."

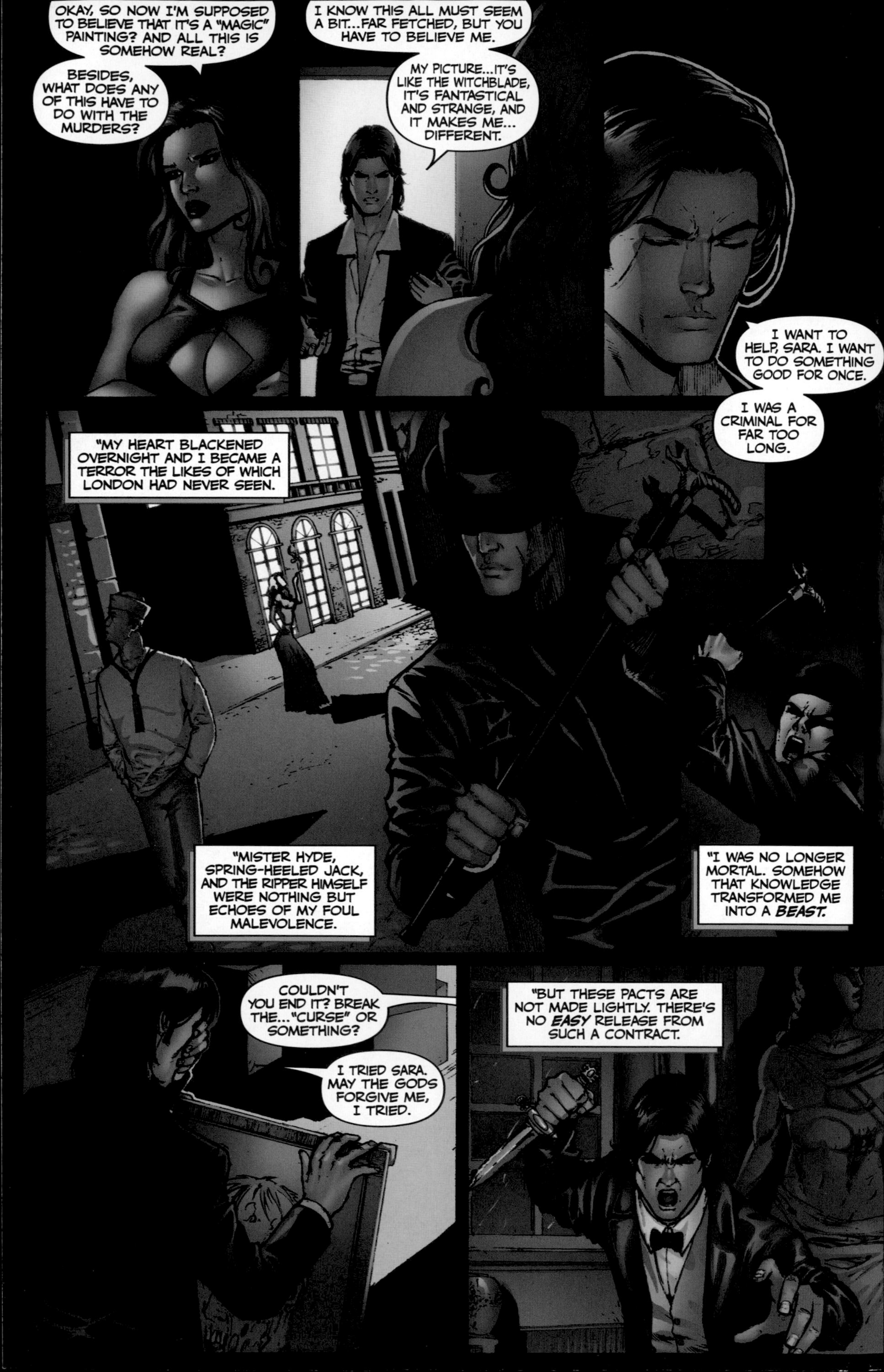
OKAY, SO NOW I'M SUPPOSED TO BELIEVE THAT IT'S A "MAGIC" PAINTING? AND ALL THIS IS SOMEHOW REAL?
BESIDES, WHAT DOES ANY OF THIS HAVE TO DO WITH THE MURDERS?
I KNOW THIS ALL MUST SEEM A BIT...FAR FETCHED, BUT YOU HAVE TO BELIEVE ME.
MY PICTURE...IT'S LIKE THE WITCHBLADE, IT'S FANTASTICAL AND STRANGE, AND IT MAKES ME... DIFFERENT.
I WANT TO HELP, SARA. I WANT TO DO SOMETHING GOOD FOR ONCE.
I WAS A CRIMINAL FOR FAR TOO LONG.
"MY HEART BLACKENED OVERNIGHT AND I BECAME A TERROR THE LIKES OF WHICH LONDON HAD NEVER SEEN.
"MISTER HYDE, SPRING-HEELED JACK, AND THE RIPPER HIMSELF WERE NOTHING BUT ECHOES OF MY FOUL MALEVOLENCE.
"I WAS NO LONGER MORTAL. SOMEHOW THAT KNOWLEDGE TRANSFORMED ME INTO A *BEAST.*
COULDN'T YOU END IT? BREAK THE..."CURSE" OR SOMETHING?
I TRIED SARA. MAY THE GODS FORGIVE ME, I TRIED.
"BUT THESE PACTS ARE NOT MADE LIGHTLY. THERE'S NO *EASY* RELEASE FROM SUCH A CONTRACT.

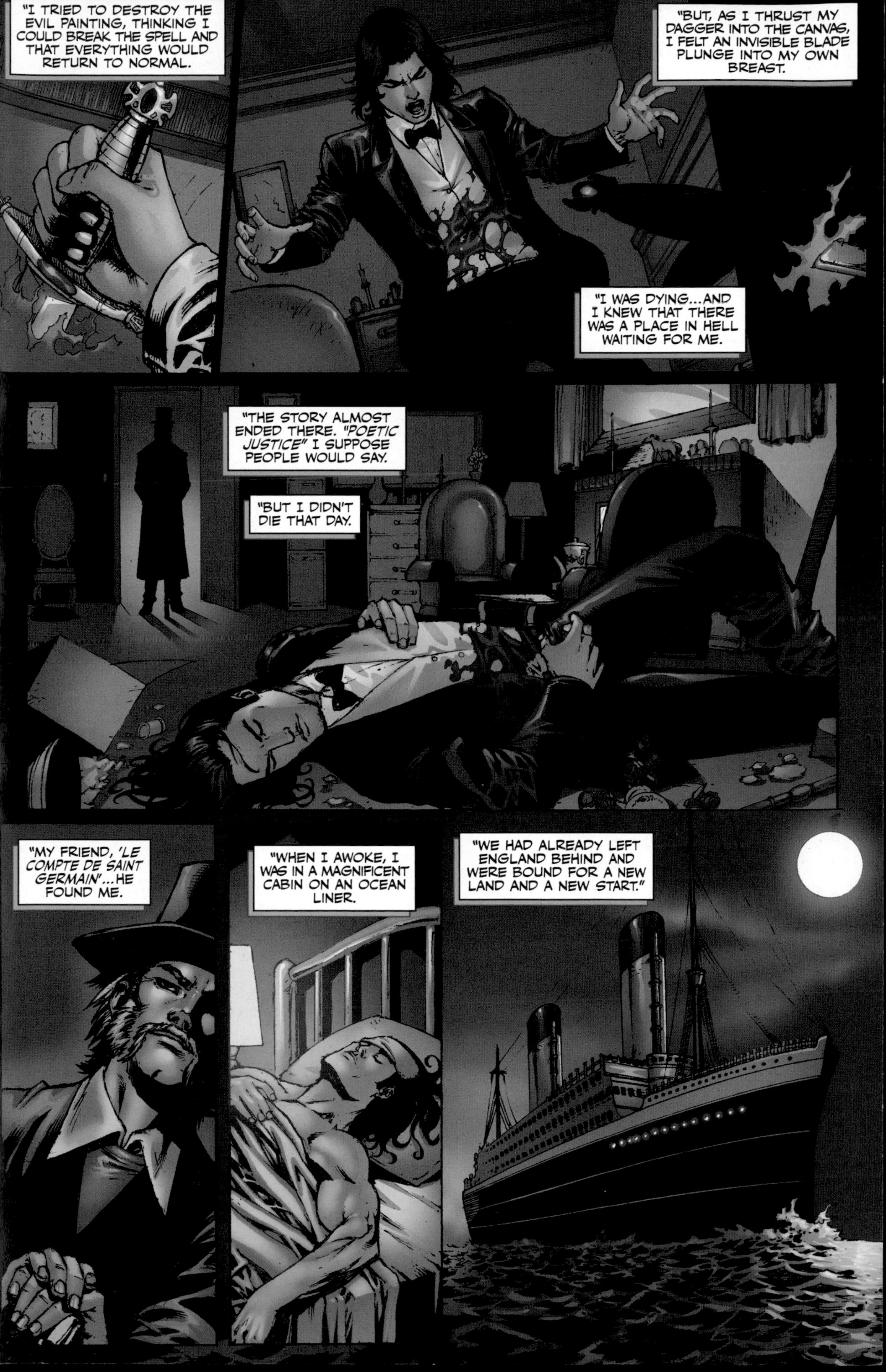
"I TRIED TO DESTROY THE EVIL PAINTING, THINKING I COULD BREAK THE SPELL AND THAT EVERYTHING WOULD RETURN TO NORMAL.
"BUT, AS I THRUST MY DAGGER INTO THE CANVAS, I FELT AN INVISIBLE BLADE PLUNGE INTO MY OWN BREAST.
"I WAS DYING...AND I KNEW THAT THERE WAS A PLACE IN HELL WAITING FOR ME.
"THE STORY ALMOST ENDED THERE. *"POETIC JUSTICE"* I SUPPOSE PEOPLE WOULD SAY.
"BUT I DIDN'T DIE THAT DAY.
"MY FRIEND, *'LE COMPTE DE SAINT GERMAIN'*...HE FOUND ME.
"WHEN I AWOKE, I WAS IN A MAGNIFICENT CABIN ON AN OCEAN LINER.
"WE HAD ALREADY LEFT ENGLAND BEHIND AND WERE BOUND FOR A NEW LAND AND A NEW START."

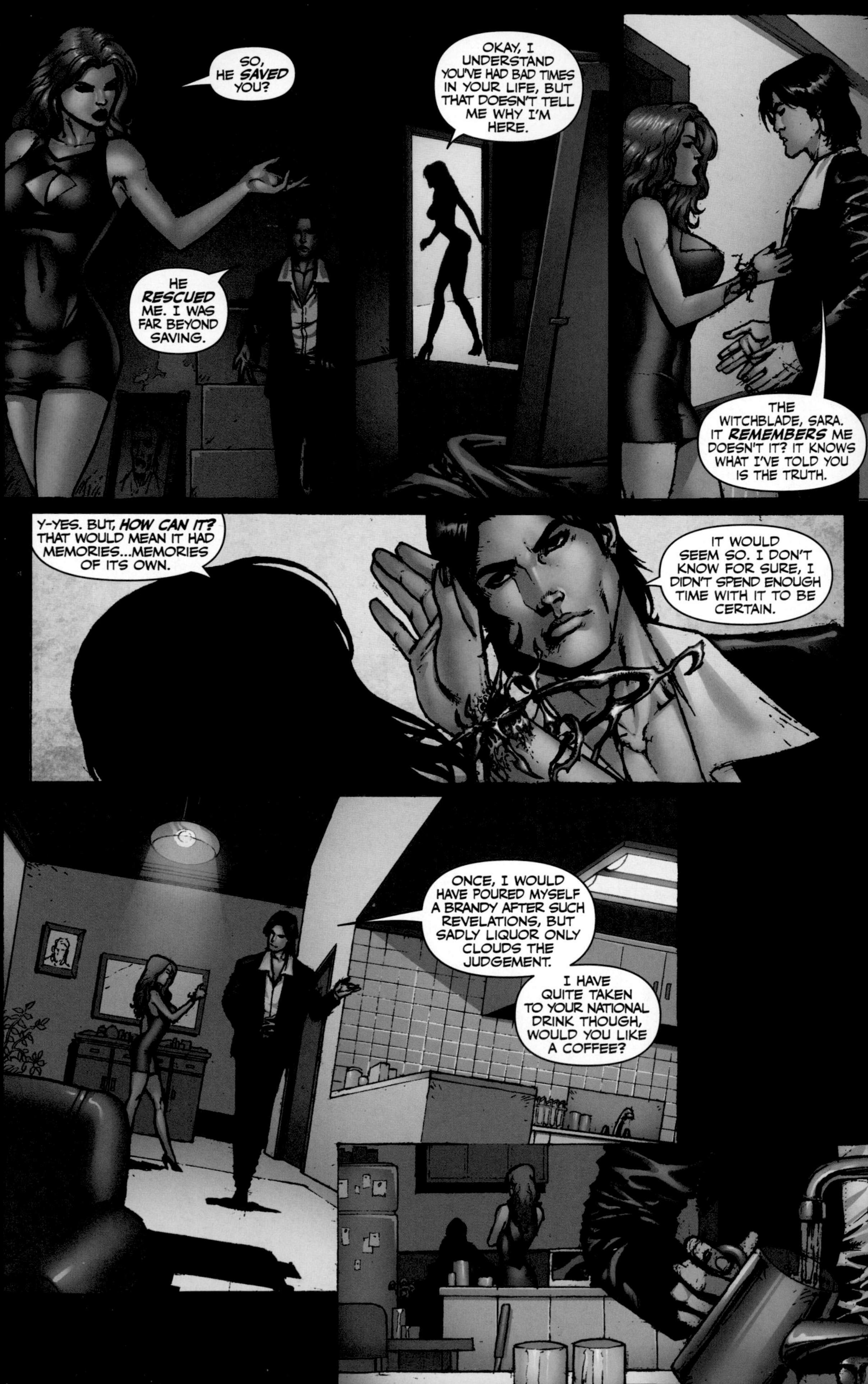
SO, HE *SAVED* YOU?
HE *RESCUED* ME. I WAS FAR BEYOND SAVING.
OKAY, I UNDERSTAND YOU'VE HAD BAD TIMES IN YOUR LIFE, BUT THAT DOESN'T TELL ME WHY I'M HERE.
THE WITCHBLADE, SARA. IT *REMEMBERS* ME DOESN'T IT? IT KNOWS WHAT I'VE TOLD YOU IS THE TRUTH.
Y-YES. BUT, *HOW CAN IT?* THAT WOULD MEAN IT HAD MEMORIES...MEMORIES OF ITS OWN.
IT WOULD SEEM SO. I DON'T KNOW FOR SURE, I DIDN'T SPEND ENOUGH TIME WITH IT TO BE CERTAIN.
ONCE, I WOULD HAVE POURED MYSELF A BRANDY AFTER SUCH REVELATIONS, BUT SADLY LIQUOR ONLY CLOUDS THE JUDGEMENT.
I HAVE QUITE TAKEN TO YOUR NATIONAL DRINK THOUGH, WOULD YOU LIKE A COFFEE?

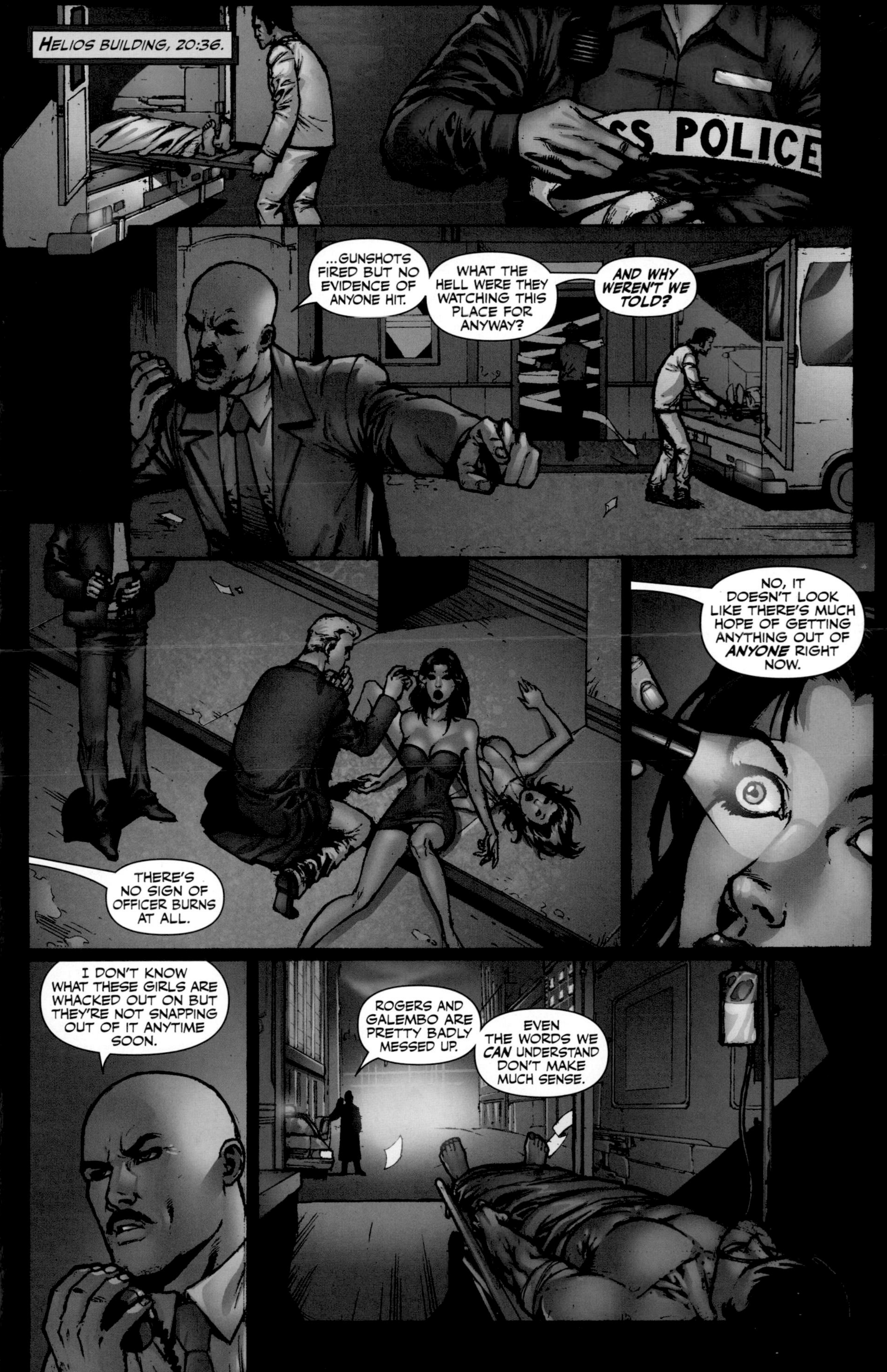
HELIOS BUILDING, 20:36.
...SS POLICE
...GUNSHOTS FIRED BUT NO EVIDENCE OF ANYONE HIT.
WHAT THE HELL WERE THEY WATCHING THIS PLACE FOR ANYWAY?
AND WHY WEREN'T WE TOLD?
THERE'S NO SIGN OF OFFICER BURNS AT ALL.
NO, IT DOESN'T LOOK LIKE THERE'S MUCH HOPE OF GETTING ANYTHING OUT OF ANYONE RIGHT NOW.
I DON'T KNOW WHAT THESE GIRLS ARE WHACKED OUT ON BUT THEY'RE NOT SNAPPING OUT OF IT ANYTIME SOON.
ROGERS AND GALEMBO ARE PRETTY BADLY MESSED UP.
EVEN THE WORDS WE CAN UNDERSTAND DON'T MAKE MUCH SENSE.

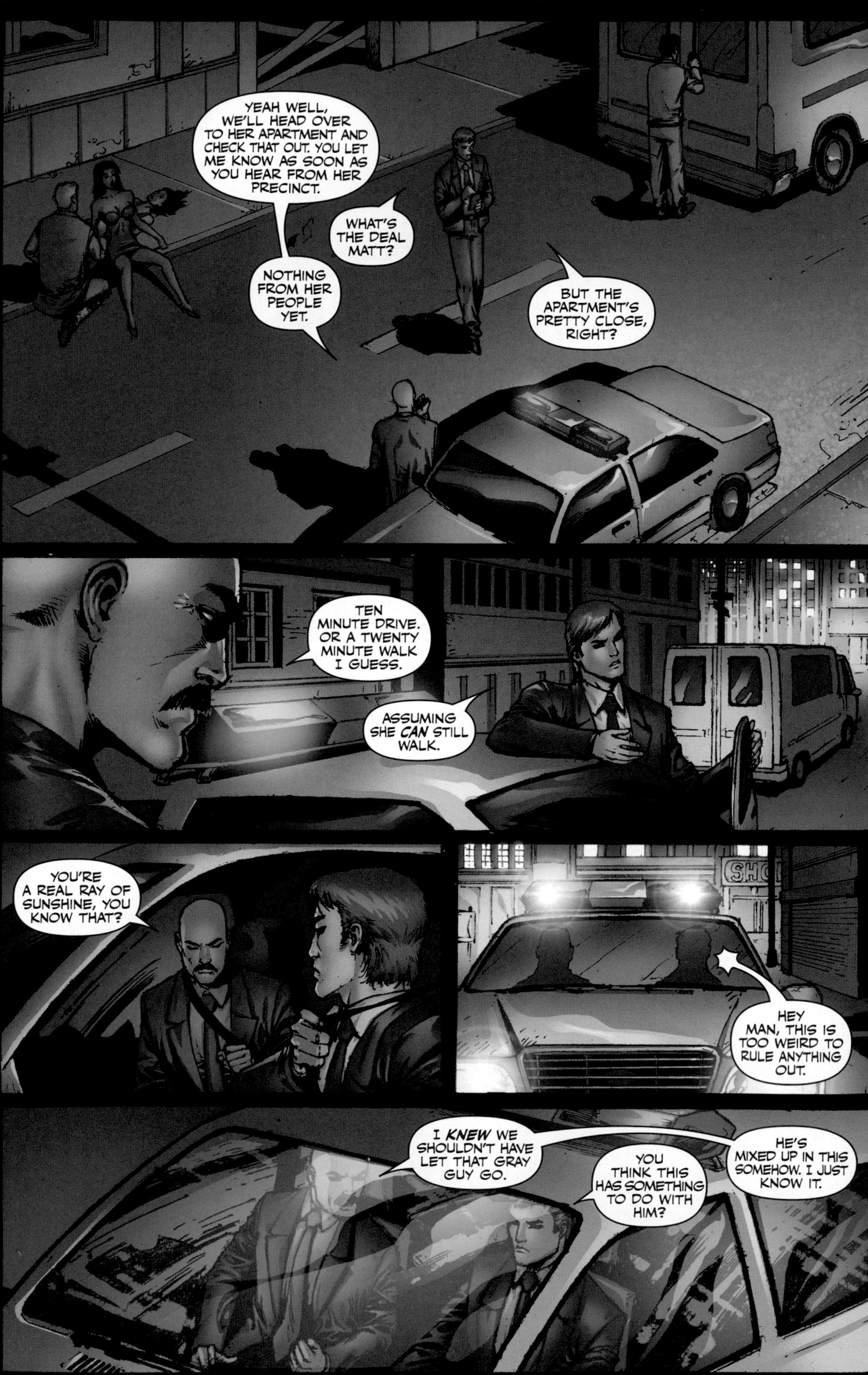

YEAH WELL, WE'LL HEAD OVER TO HER APARTMENT AND CHECK THAT OUT. YOU LET ME KNOW AS SOON AS YOU HEAR FROM HER PRECINCT.
WHAT'S THE DEAL MATT?
NOTHING FROM HER PEOPLE YET.
BUT THE APARTMENT'S PRETTY CLOSE, RIGHT?
TEN MINUTE DRIVE. OR A TWENTY MINUTE WALK I GUESS.
ASSUMING SHE *CAN* STILL WALK.
YOU'RE A REAL RAY OF SUNSHINE, YOU KNOW THAT?
HEY MAN, THIS IS TOO WEIRD TO RULE ANYTHING OUT.
I *KNEW* WE SHOULDN'T HAVE LET THAT GRAY GUY GO.
HE'S MIXED UP IN THIS SOMEHOW. I JUST KNOW IT.
YOU THINK THIS HAS SOMETHING TO DO WITH HIM?

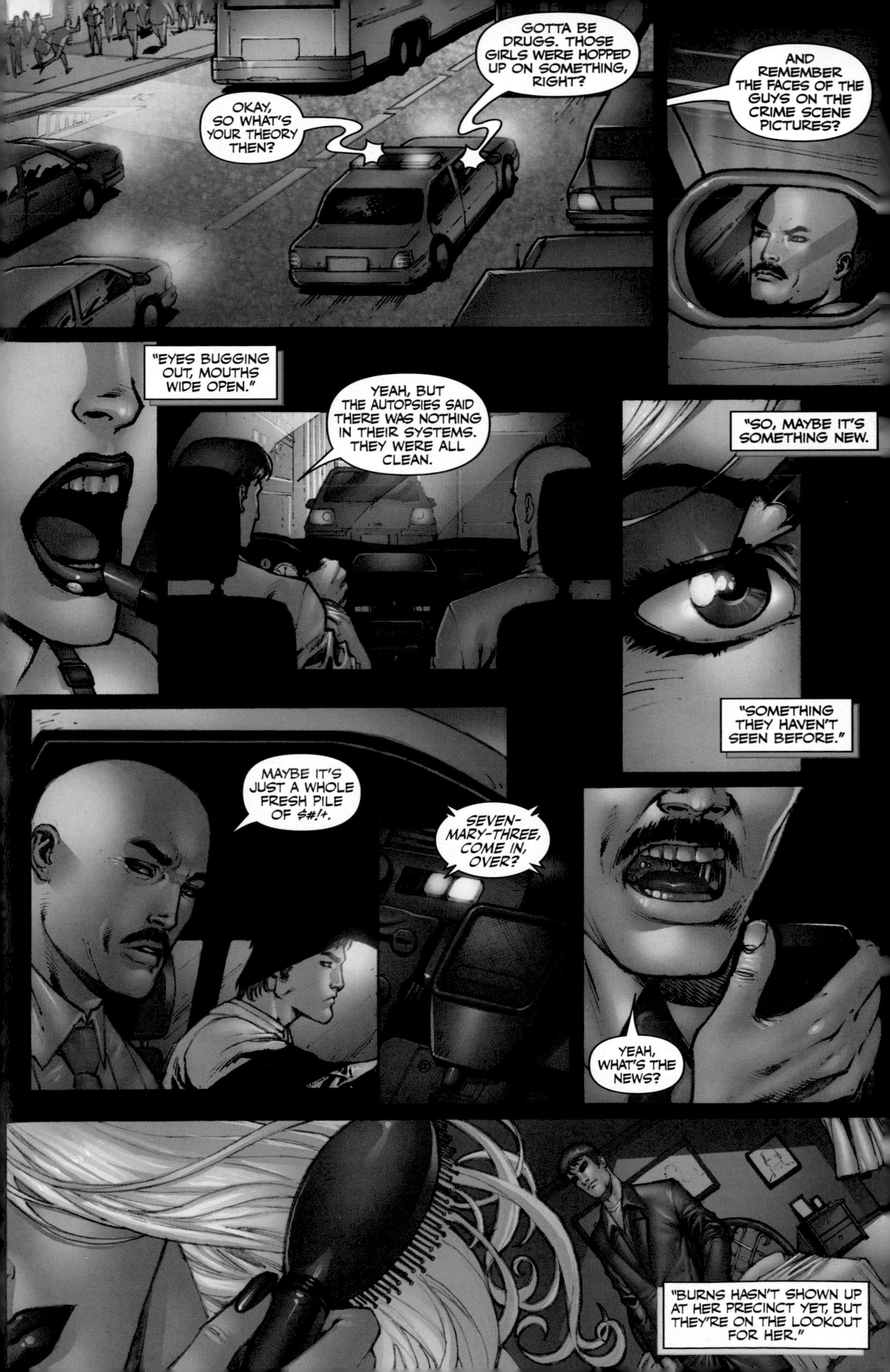
OKAY, SO WHAT'S YOUR THEORY THEN?
GOTTA BE DRUGS. THOSE GIRLS WERE HOPPED UP ON SOMETHING, RIGHT?
AND REMEMBER THE FACES OF THE GUYS ON THE CRIME SCENE PICTURES?
"EYES BUGGING OUT, MOUTHS WIDE OPEN."
YEAH, BUT THE AUTOPSIES SAID THERE WAS NOTHING IN THEIR SYSTEMS. THEY WERE ALL CLEAN.
"SO, MAYBE IT'S SOMETHING NEW.
"SOMETHING THEY HAVEN'T SEEN BEFORE."
MAYBE IT'S JUST A WHOLE FRESH PILE OF $#!+.
SEVEN-MARY-THREE, COME IN, OVER?
YEAH, WHAT'S THE NEWS?
"BURNS HASN'T SHOWN UP AT HER PRECINCT YET, BUT THEY'RE ON THE LOOKOUT FOR HER."

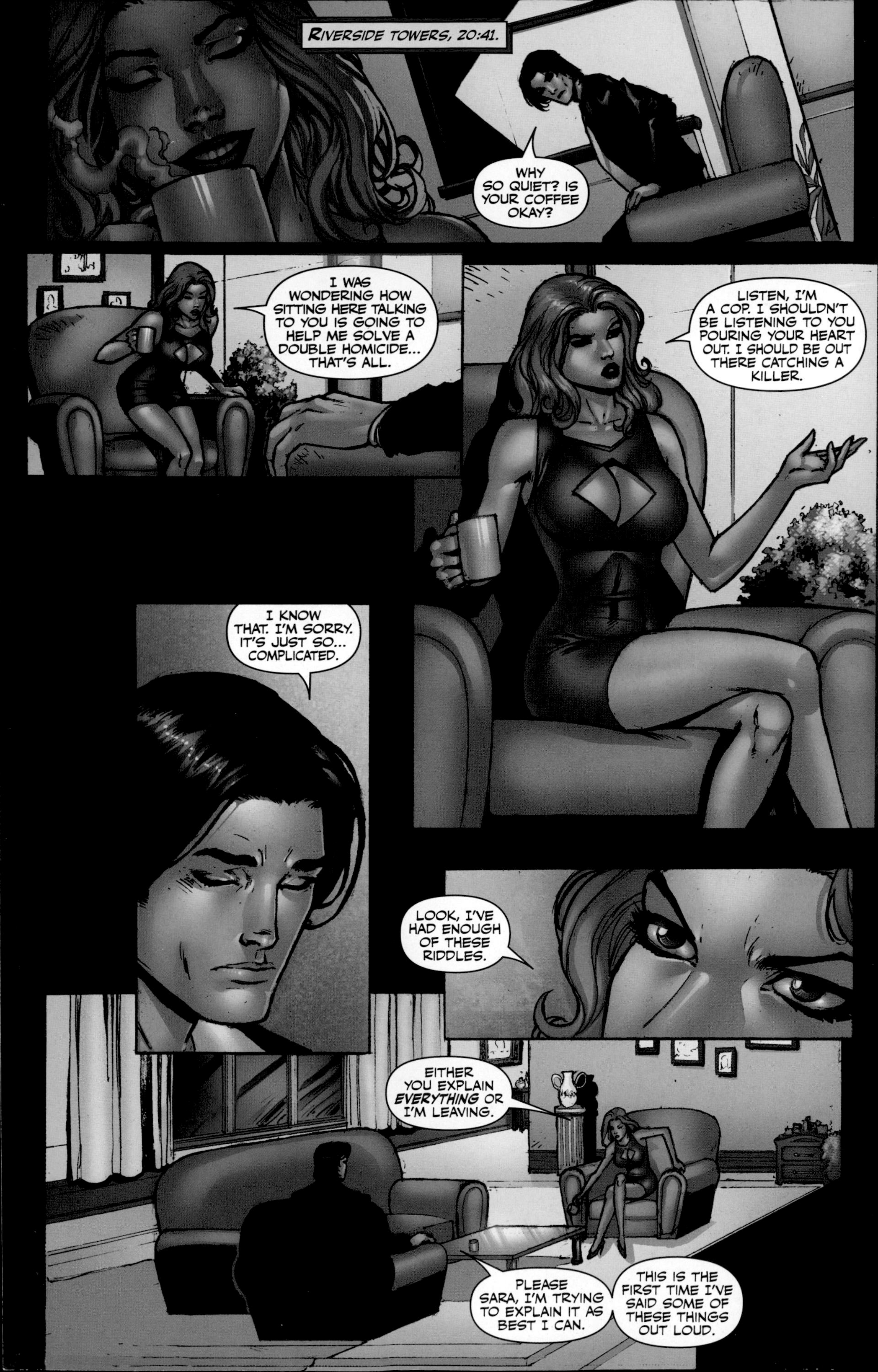
RIVERSIDE TOWERS, 20:41.
WHY SO QUIET? IS YOUR COFFEE OKAY?
I WAS WONDERING HOW SITTING HERE TALKING TO YOU IS GOING TO HELP ME SOLVE A DOUBLE HOMICIDE... THAT'S ALL.
LISTEN, I'M A COP. I SHOULDN'T BE LISTENING TO YOU POURING YOUR HEART OUT. I SHOULD BE OUT THERE CATCHING A KILLER.
I KNOW THAT. I'M SORRY. IT'S JUST SO... COMPLICATED.
LOOK, I'VE HAD ENOUGH OF THESE RIDDLES.
EITHER YOU EXPLAIN *EVERYTHING* OR I'M LEAVING.
PLEASE SARA, I'M TRYING TO EXPLAIN IT AS BEST I CAN.
THIS IS THE FIRST TIME I'VE SAID SOME OF THESE THINGS OUT LOUD.

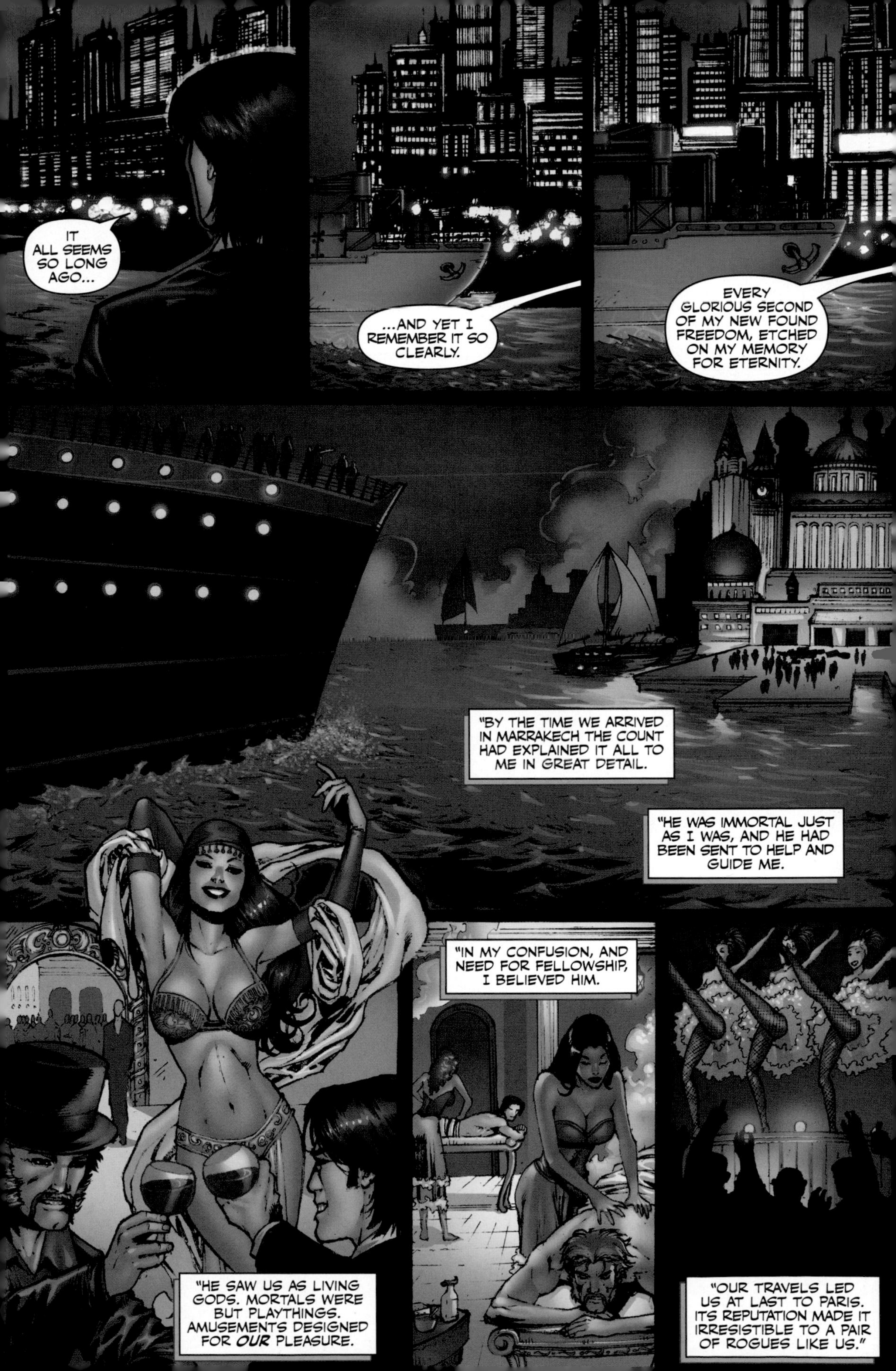
IT ALL SEEMS SO LONG AGO...
...AND YET I REMEMBER IT SO CLEARLY.
EVERY GLORIOUS SECOND OF MY NEW FOUND FREEDOM, ETCHED ON MY MEMORY FOR ETERNITY.
"BY THE TIME WE ARRIVED IN MARRAKECH THE COUNT HAD EXPLAINED IT ALL TO ME IN GREAT DETAIL.
"HE WAS IMMORTAL JUST AS I WAS, AND HE HAD BEEN SENT TO HELP AND GUIDE ME.
"HE SAW US AS LIVING GODS. MORTALS WERE BUT PLAYTHINGS. AMUSEMENTS DESIGNED FOR *OUR* PLEASURE.
"IN MY CONFUSION, AND NEED FOR FELLOWSHIP, I BELIEVED HIM.
"OUR TRAVELS LED US AT LAST TO PARIS. ITS REPUTATION MADE IT IRRESISTIBLE TO A PAIR OF ROGUES LIKE US."

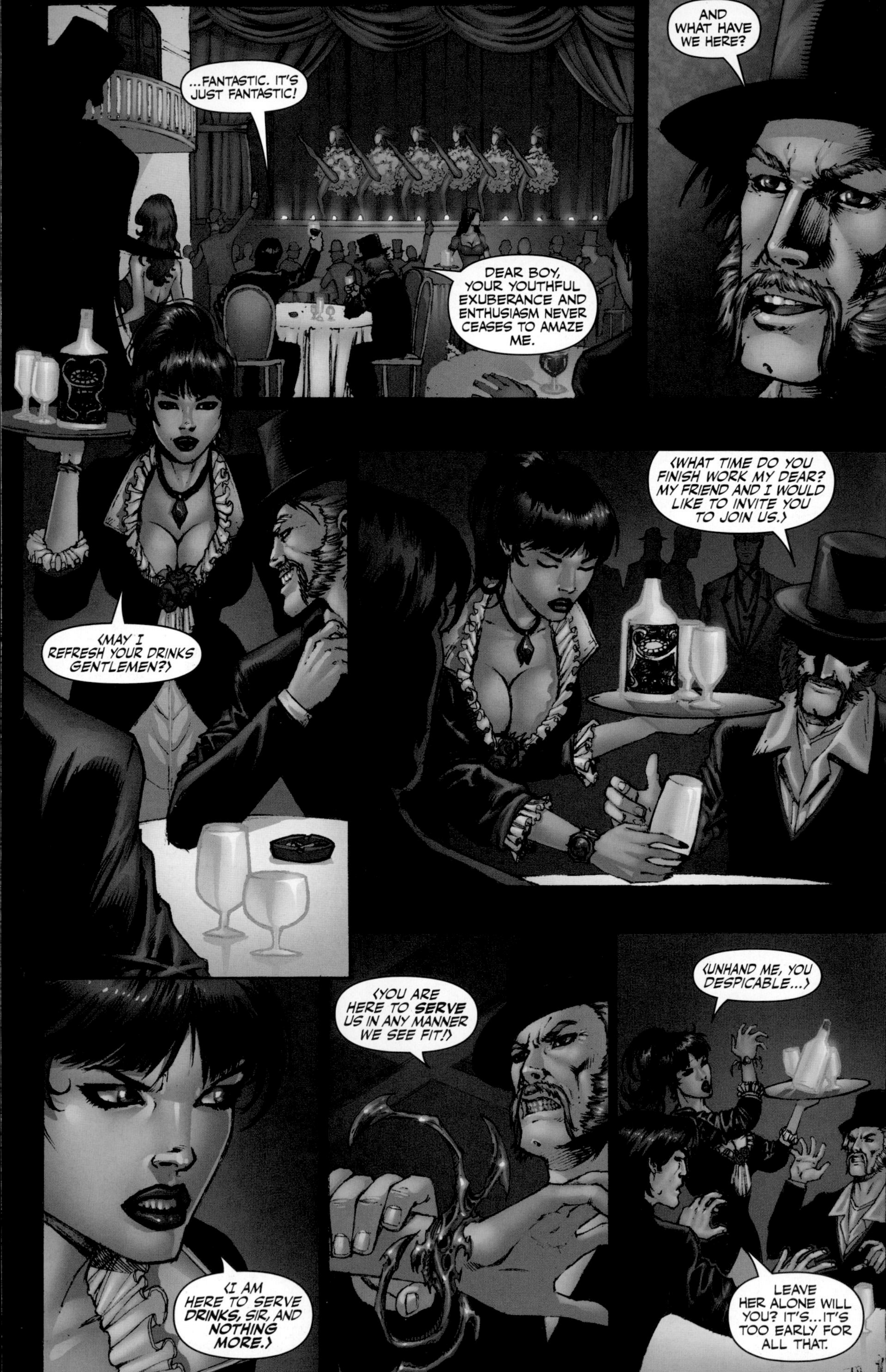
...FANTASTIC. IT'S JUST FANTASTIC!
DEAR BOY, YOUR YOUTHFUL EXUBERANCE AND ENTHUSIASM NEVER CEASES TO AMAZE ME.
AND WHAT HAVE WE HERE?
‹MAY I REFRESH YOUR DRINKS GENTLEMEN?›
‹WHAT TIME DO YOU FINISH WORK MY DEAR? MY FRIEND AND I WOULD LIKE TO INVITE YOU TO JOIN US.›
‹I AM HERE TO SERVE DRINKS, SIR, AND NOTHING MORE.›
‹YOU ARE HERE TO SERVE US IN ANY MANNER WE SEE FIT!›
‹UNHAND ME, YOU DESPICABLE...›
LEAVE HER ALONE WILL YOU? IT'S...IT'S TOO EARLY FOR ALL THAT.

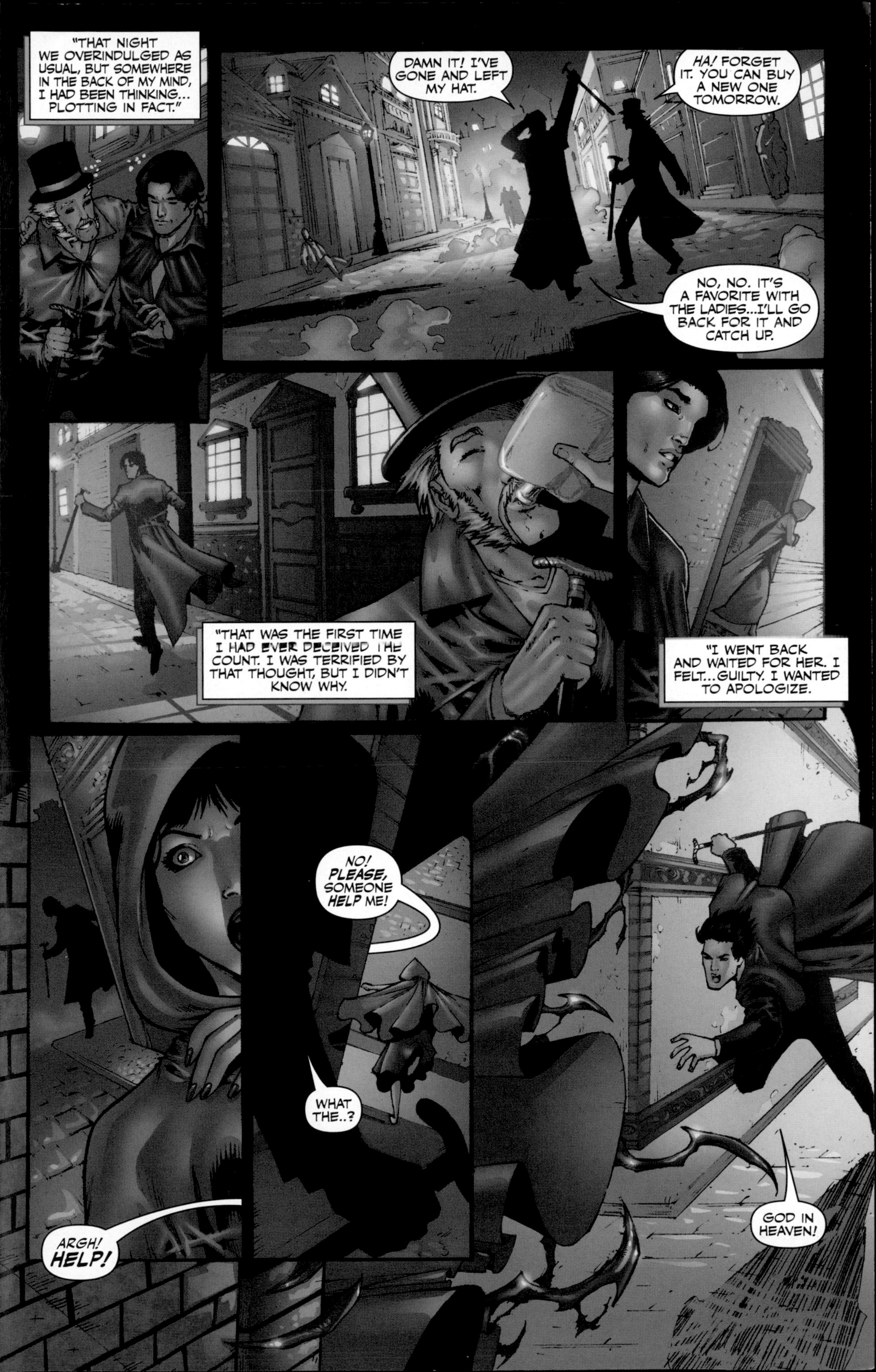
"THAT NIGHT WE OVERINDULGED AS USUAL, BUT SOMEWHERE IN THE BACK OF MY MIND, I HAD BEEN THINKING... PLOTTING IN FACT."
DAMN IT! I'VE GONE AND LEFT MY HAT.
HA! FORGET IT. YOU CAN BUY A NEW ONE TOMORROW.
NO, NO. IT'S A FAVORITE WITH THE LADIES...I'LL GO BACK FOR IT AND CATCH UP.
"THAT WAS THE FIRST TIME I HAD EVER DECEIVED THE COUNT. I WAS TERRIFIED BY THAT THOUGHT, BUT I DIDN'T KNOW WHY.
"I WENT BACK AND WAITED FOR HER. I FELT...GUILTY. I WANTED TO APOLOGIZE.
ARGH! HELP!
NO! PLEASE, SOMEONE HELP ME!
WHAT THE..?
GOD IN HEAVEN!

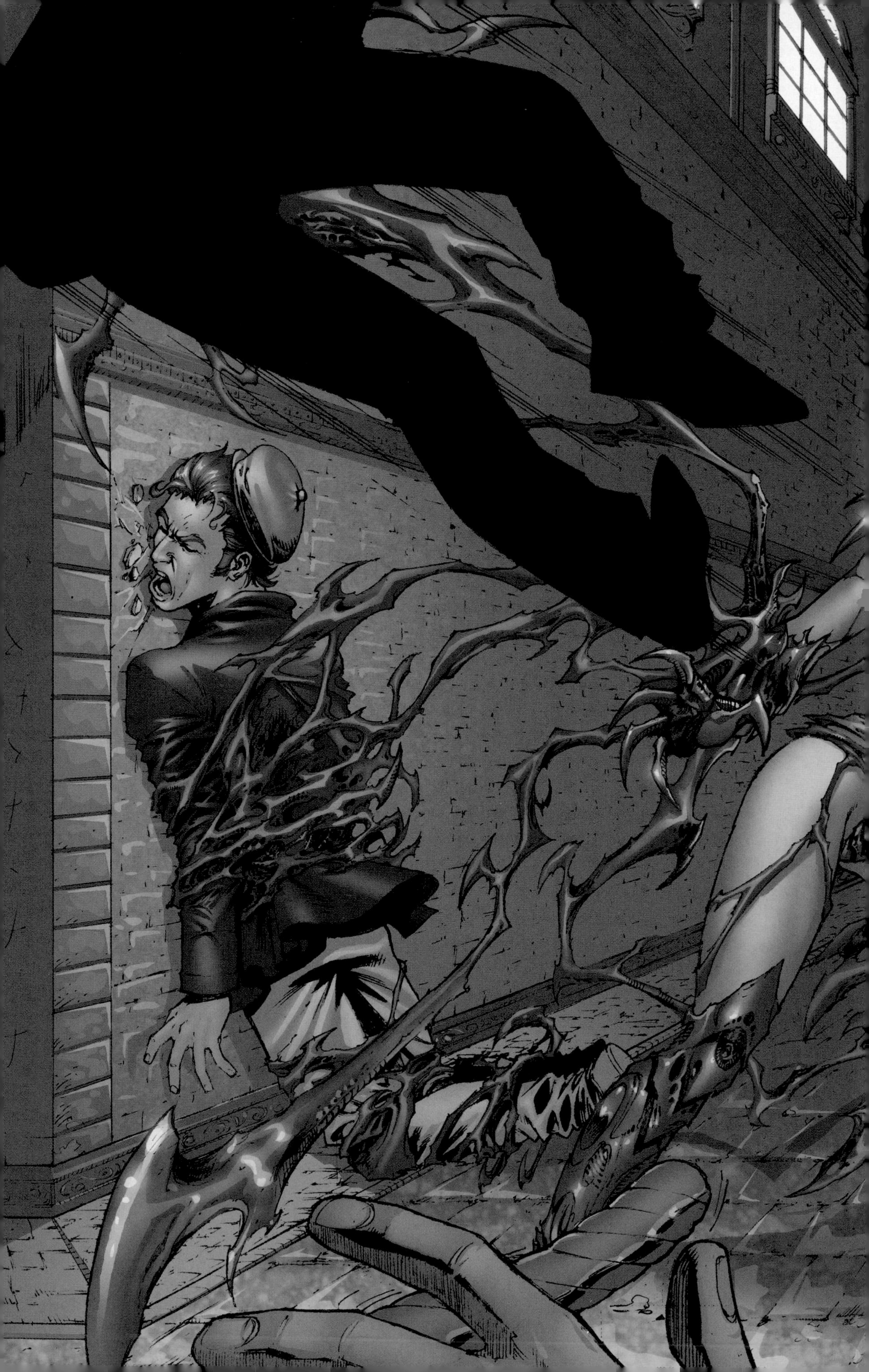

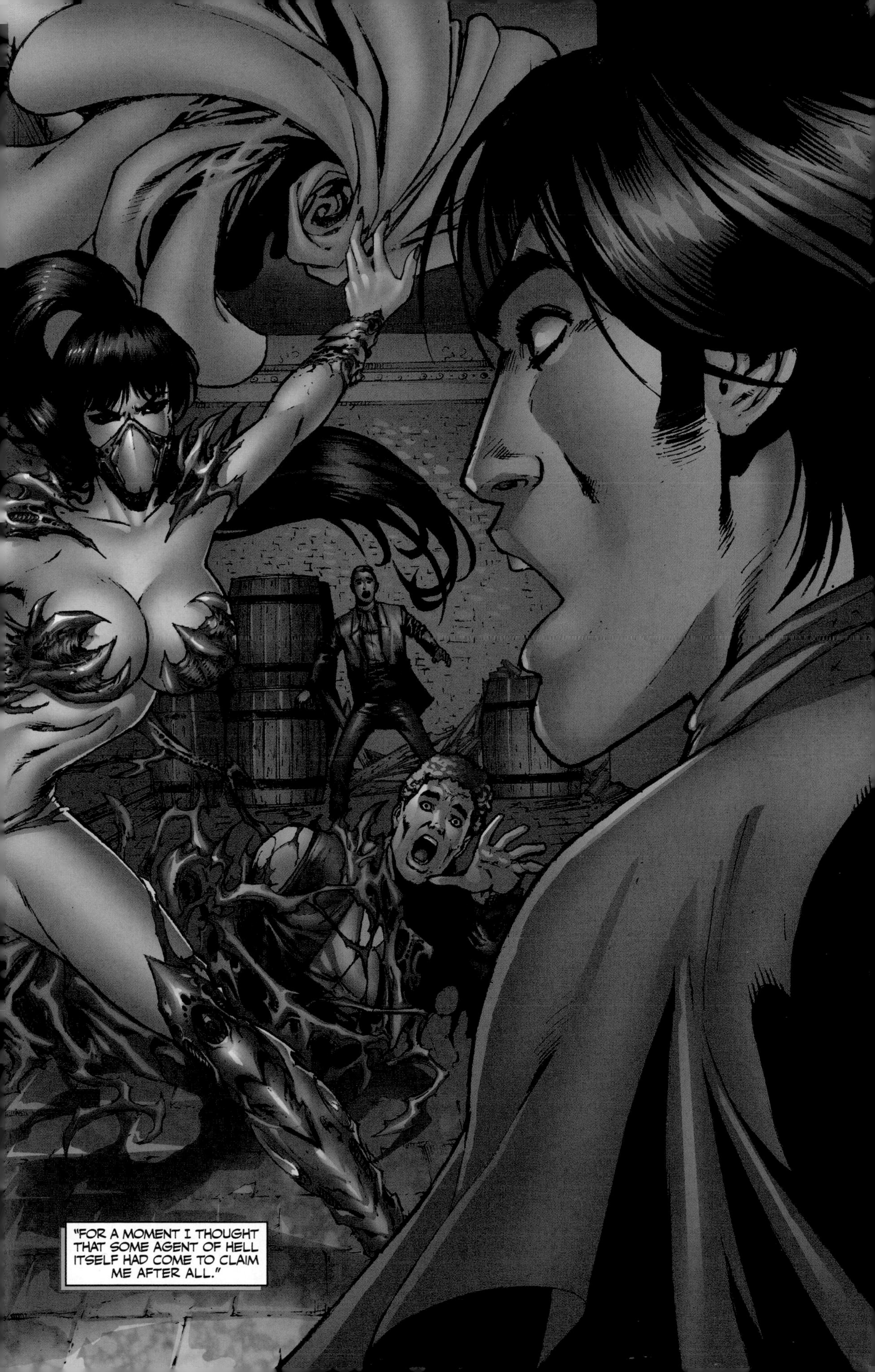
"FOR A MOMENT I THOUGHT THAT SOME AGENT OF HELL ITSELF HAD COME TO CLAIM ME AFTER ALL."

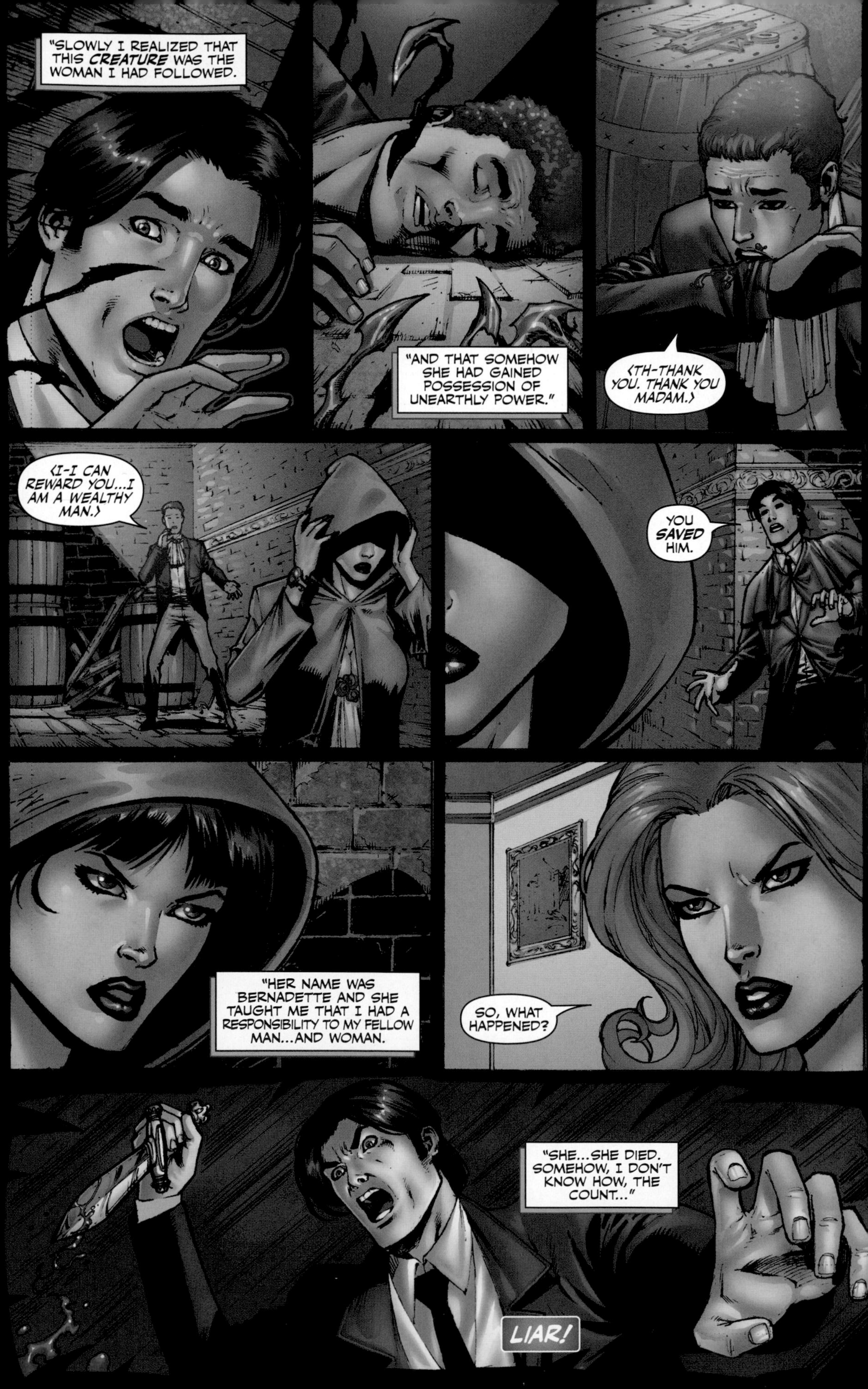
"SLOWLY I REALIZED THAT THIS CREATURE WAS THE WOMAN I HAD FOLLOWED.
"AND THAT SOMEHOW SHE HAD GAINED POSSESSION OF UNEARTHLY POWER."
<TH-THANK YOU. THANK YOU MADAM.>
<I-I CAN REWARD YOU...I AM A WEALTHY MAN.>
YOU SAVED HIM.
"HER NAME WAS BERNADETTE AND SHE TAUGHT ME THAT I HAD A RESPONSIBILITY TO MY FELLOW MAN...AND WOMAN.
SO, WHAT HAPPENED?
"SHE...SHE DIED. SOMEHOW, I DON'T KNOW HOW, THE COUNT..."
LIAR!

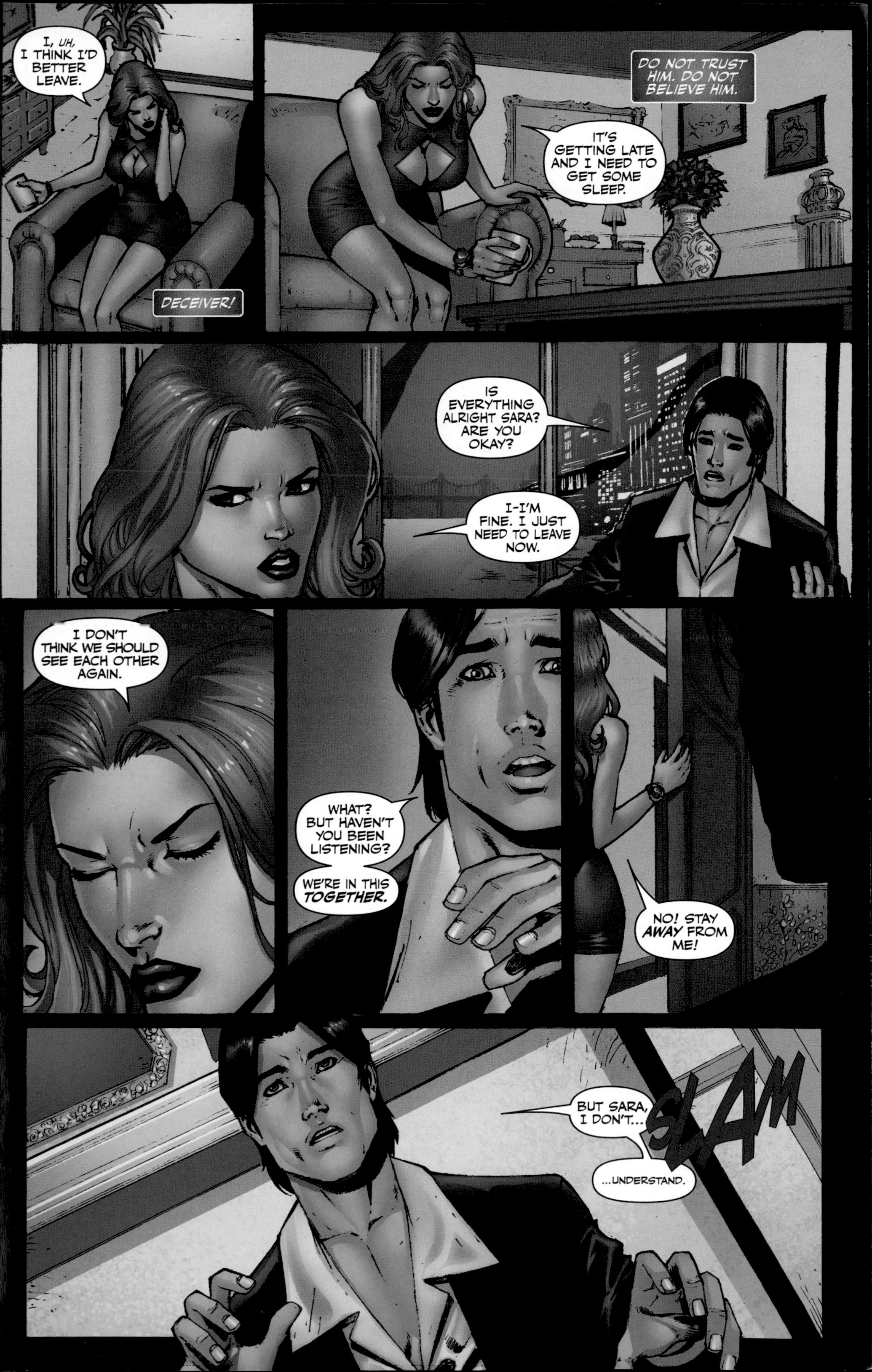
I, *UH*, I THINK I'D BETTER LEAVE.
DECEIVER!
DO NOT TRUST HIM. DO NOT BELIEVE HIM.
IT'S GETTING LATE AND I NEED TO GET SOME SLEEP.
IS EVERYTHING ALRIGHT SARA? ARE YOU OKAY?
I-I'M FINE. I JUST NEED TO LEAVE NOW.
I DON'T THINK WE SHOULD SEE EACH OTHER AGAIN.
WHAT? BUT HAVEN'T YOU BEEN LISTENING?
WE'RE IN THIS ***TOGETHER.***
NO! STAY ***AWAY*** FROM ME!
BUT SARA, I DON'T...
SLAM
...UNDERSTAND.

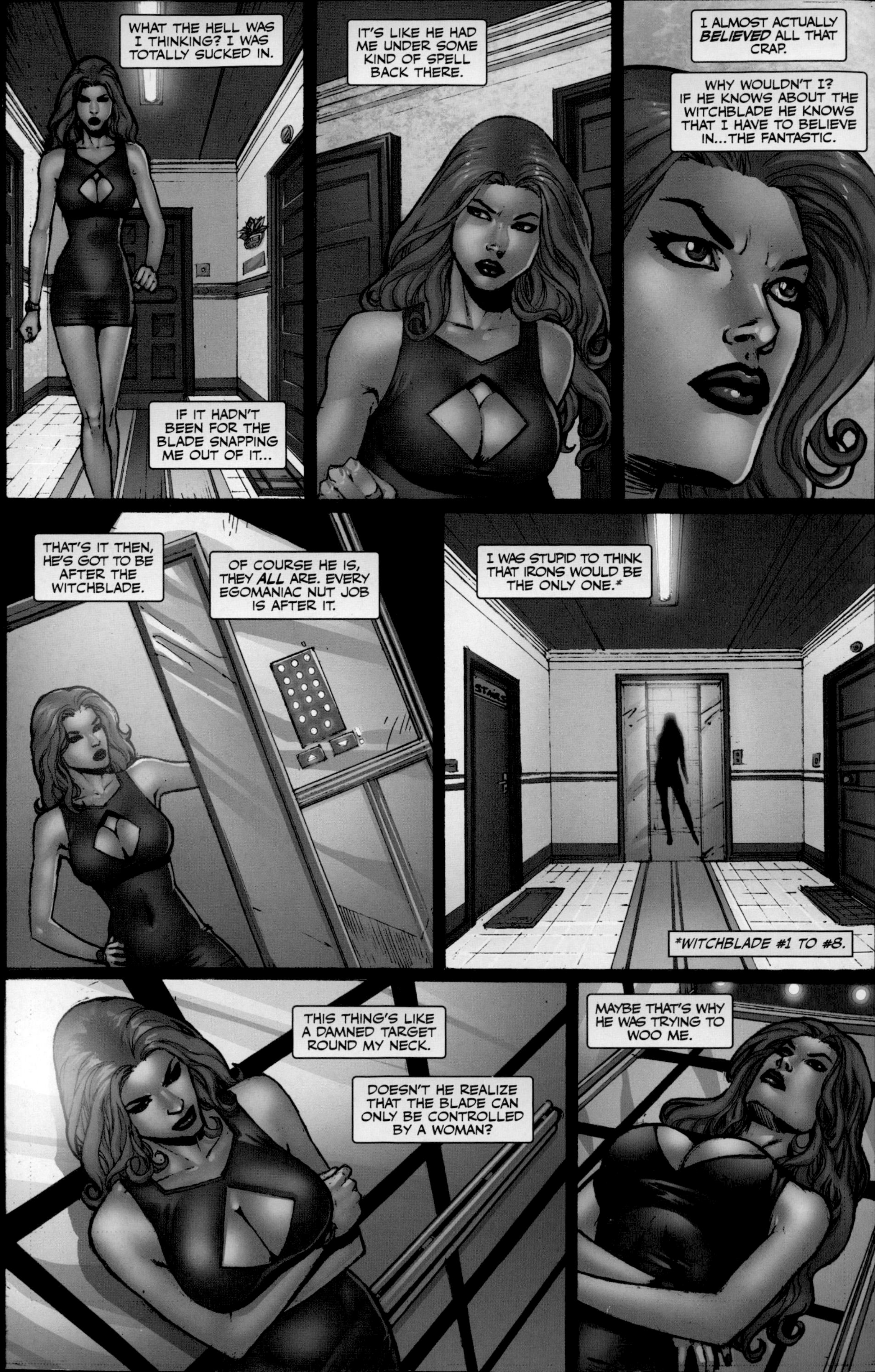
WHAT THE HELL WAS I THINKING? I WAS TOTALLY SUCKED IN.
IF IT HADN'T BEEN FOR THE BLADE SNAPPING ME OUT OF IT...
IT'S LIKE HE HAD ME UNDER SOME KIND OF SPELL BACK THERE.
I ALMOST ACTUALLY BELIEVED ALL THAT CRAP.
WHY WOULDN'T I? IF HE KNOWS ABOUT THE WITCHBLADE HE KNOWS THAT I HAVE TO BELIEVE IN...THE FANTASTIC.
THAT'S IT THEN, HE'S GOT TO BE AFTER THE WITCHBLADE.
OF COURSE HE IS, THEY ALL ARE. EVERY EGOMANIAC NUT JOB IS AFTER IT.
I WAS STUPID TO THINK THAT IRONS WOULD BE THE ONLY ONE.*
STAIRS
*WITCHBLADE #1 TO #8.
THIS THING'S LIKE A DAMNED TARGET ROUND MY NECK.
DOESN'T HE REALIZE THAT THE BLADE CAN ONLY BE CONTROLLED BY A WOMAN?
MAYBE THAT'S WHY HE WAS TRYING TO WOO ME.

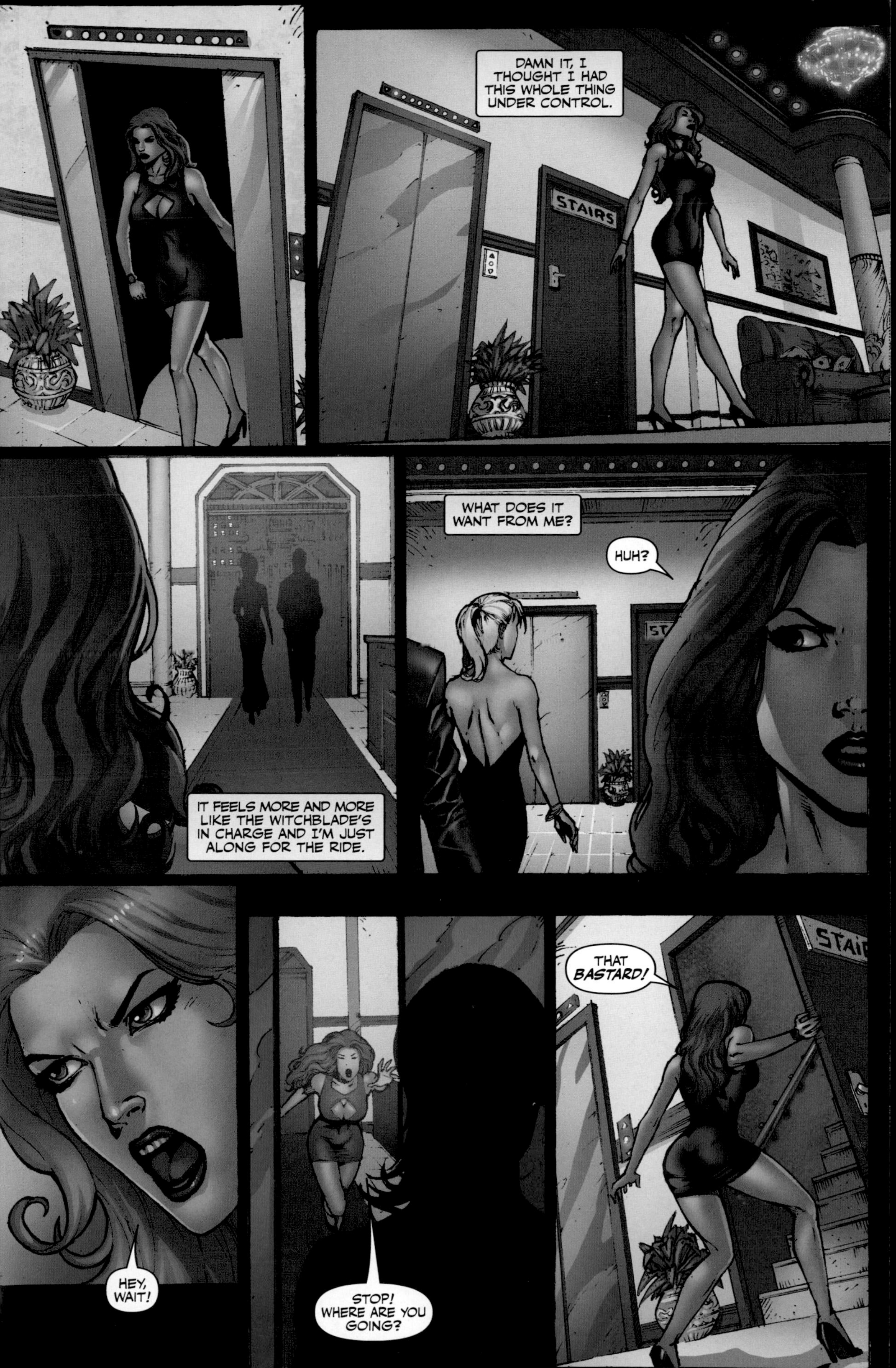
DAMN IT, I THOUGHT I HAD THIS WHOLE THING UNDER CONTROL.
STAIRS
IT FEELS MORE AND MORE LIKE THE WITCHBLADE'S IN CHARGE AND I'M JUST ALONG FOR THE RIDE.
WHAT DOES IT WANT FROM ME?
HUH?
HEY, WAIT!
STOP! WHERE ARE YOU GOING?
THAT *BASTARD!*

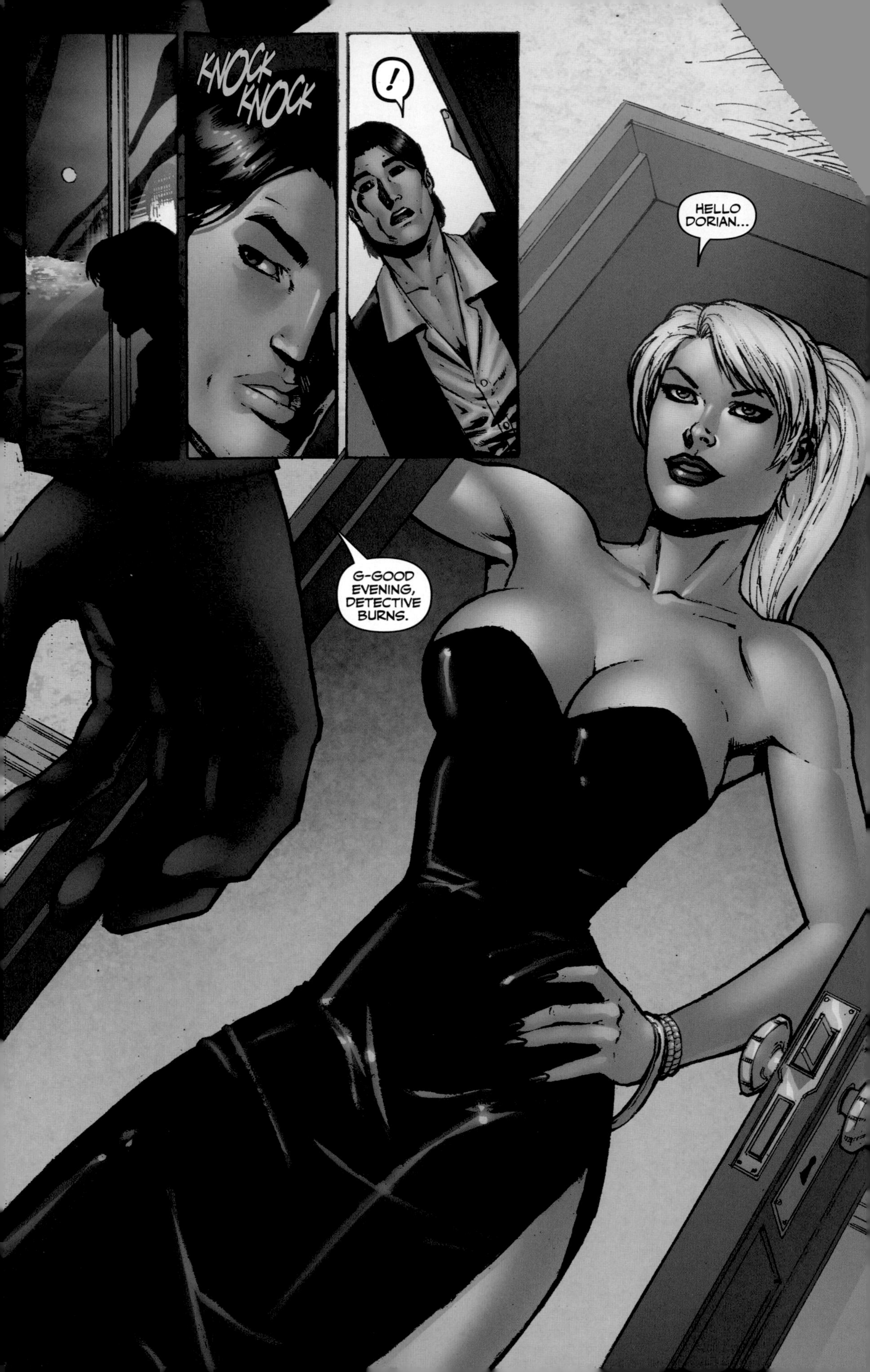
KNOCK KNOCK
!
HELLO DORIAN...
G-GOOD EVENING, DETECTIVE BURNS.

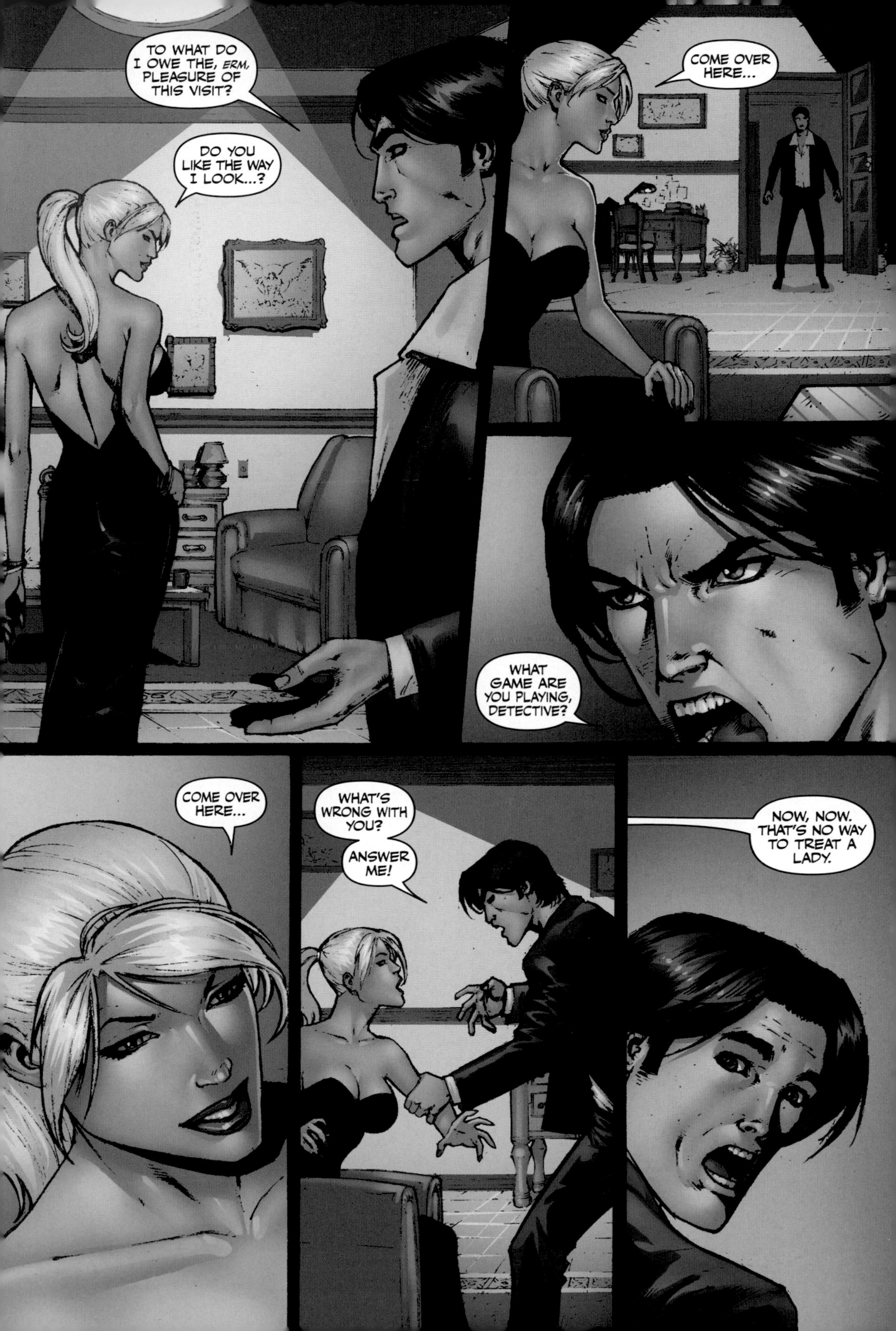
TO WHAT DO I OWE THE, *ERM*, PLEASURE OF THIS VISIT?
DO YOU LIKE THE WAY I LOOK...?
COME OVER HERE...
WHAT GAME ARE YOU PLAYING, DETECTIVE?
COME OVER HERE...
WHAT'S WRONG WITH YOU?
ANSWER ME!
NOW, NOW. THAT'S NO WAY TO TREAT A LADY.

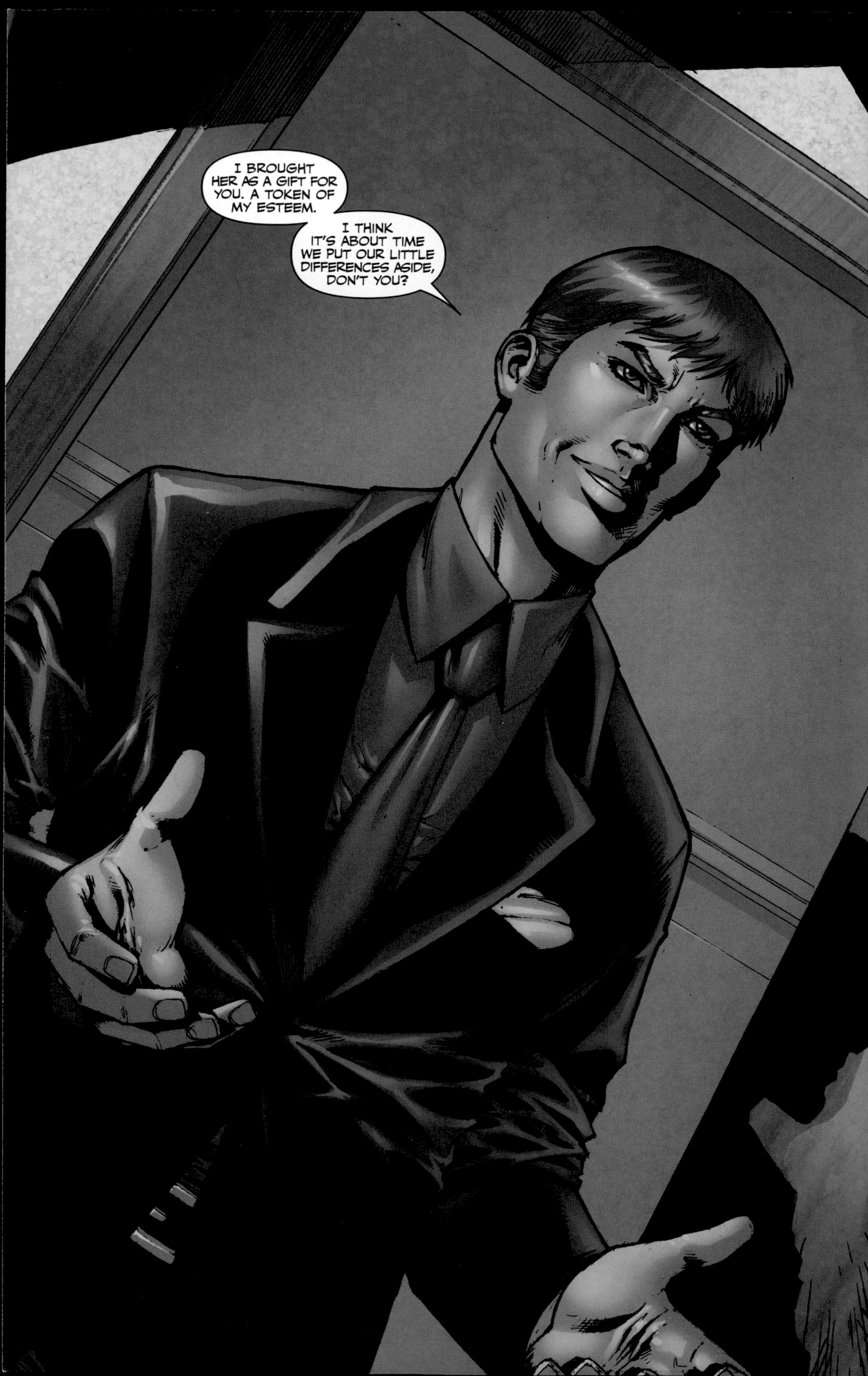
I BROUGHT HER AS A GIFT FOR YOU. A TOKEN OF MY ESTEEM.
I THINK IT'S ABOUT TIME WE PUT OUR LITTLE DIFFERENCES ASIDE, DON'T YOU?

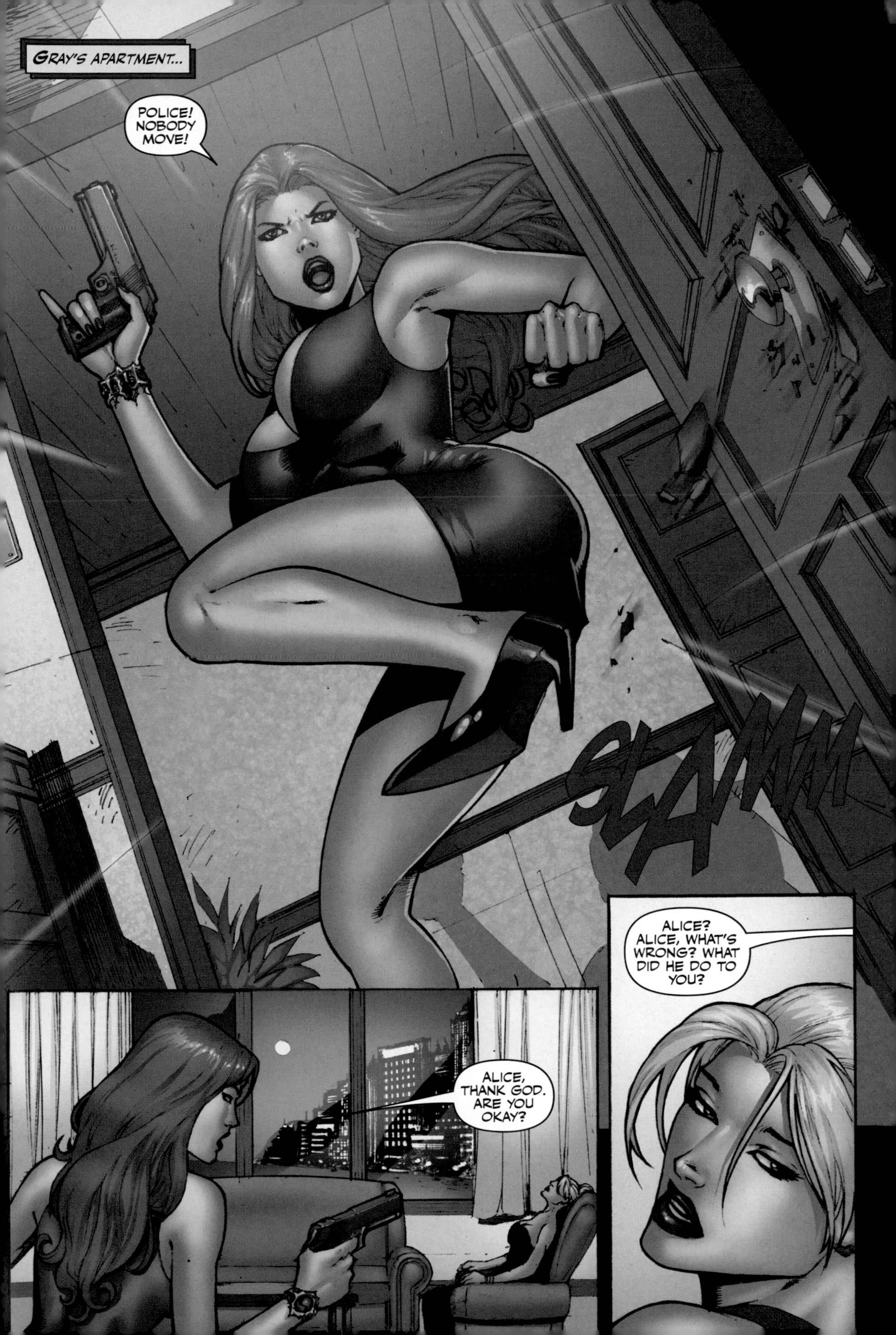
GRAY'S APARTMENT...
POLICE! NOBODY MOVE!
SLAMM
ALICE, THANK GOD. ARE YOU OKAY?
ALICE? ALICE, WHAT'S WRONG? WHAT DID HE DO TO YOU?

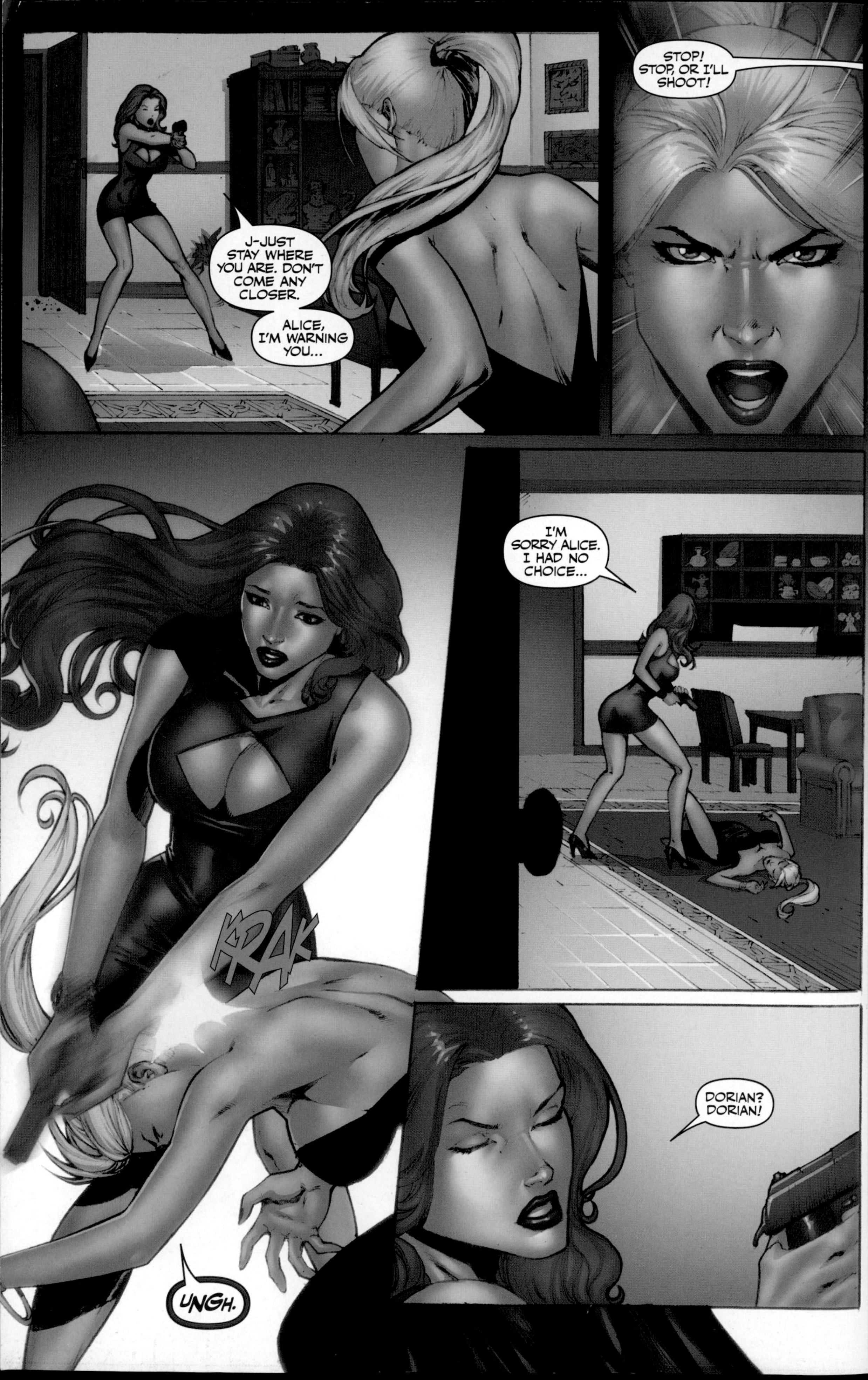
J-JUST STAY WHERE YOU ARE. DON'T COME ANY CLOSER.
ALICE, I'M WARNING YOU...
STOP! STOP, OR I'LL SHOOT!
KRAK
UNGH.
I'M SORRY ALICE. I HAD NO CHOICE...
DORIAN? DORIAN!

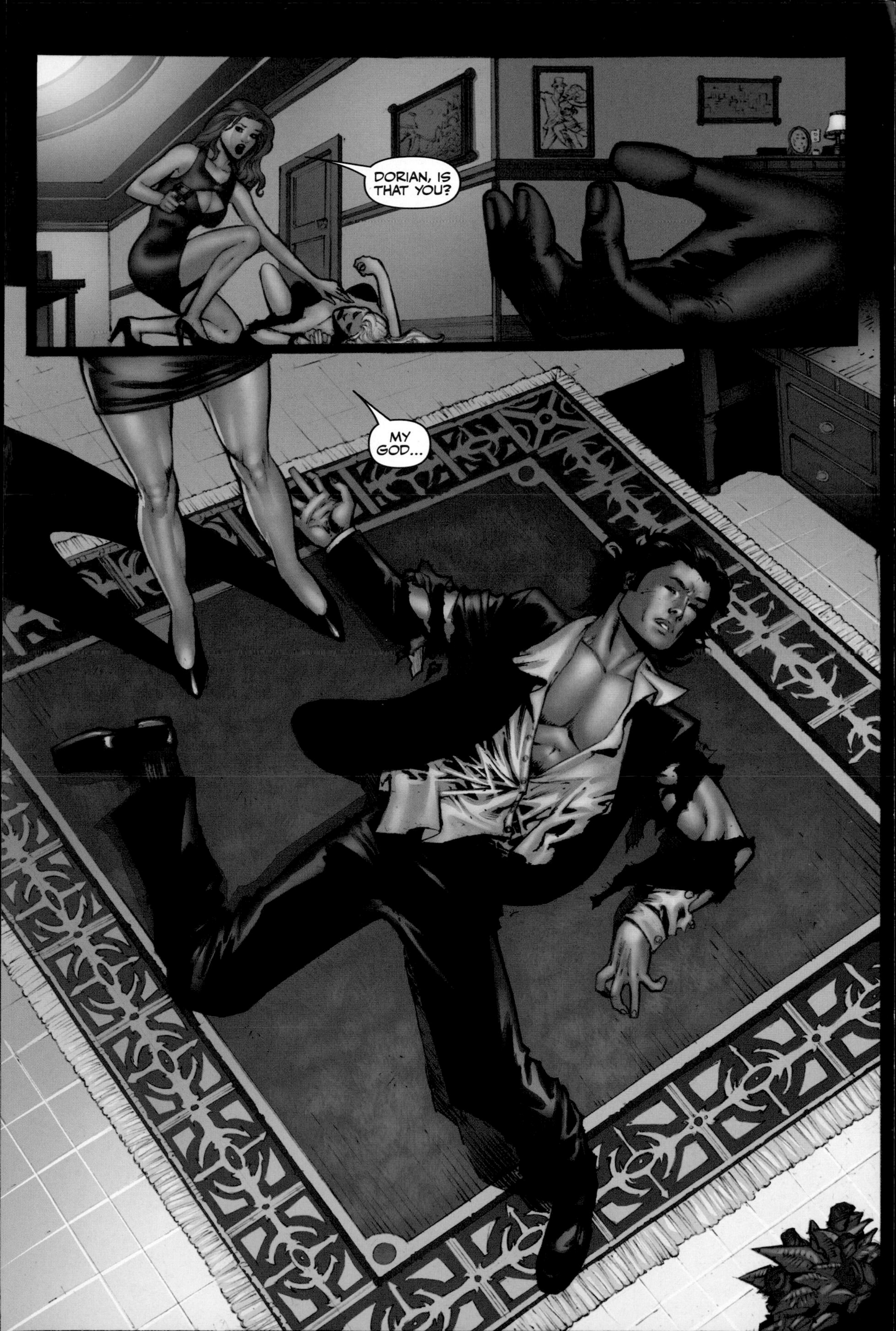
DORIAN, IS THAT YOU?
MY GOD...

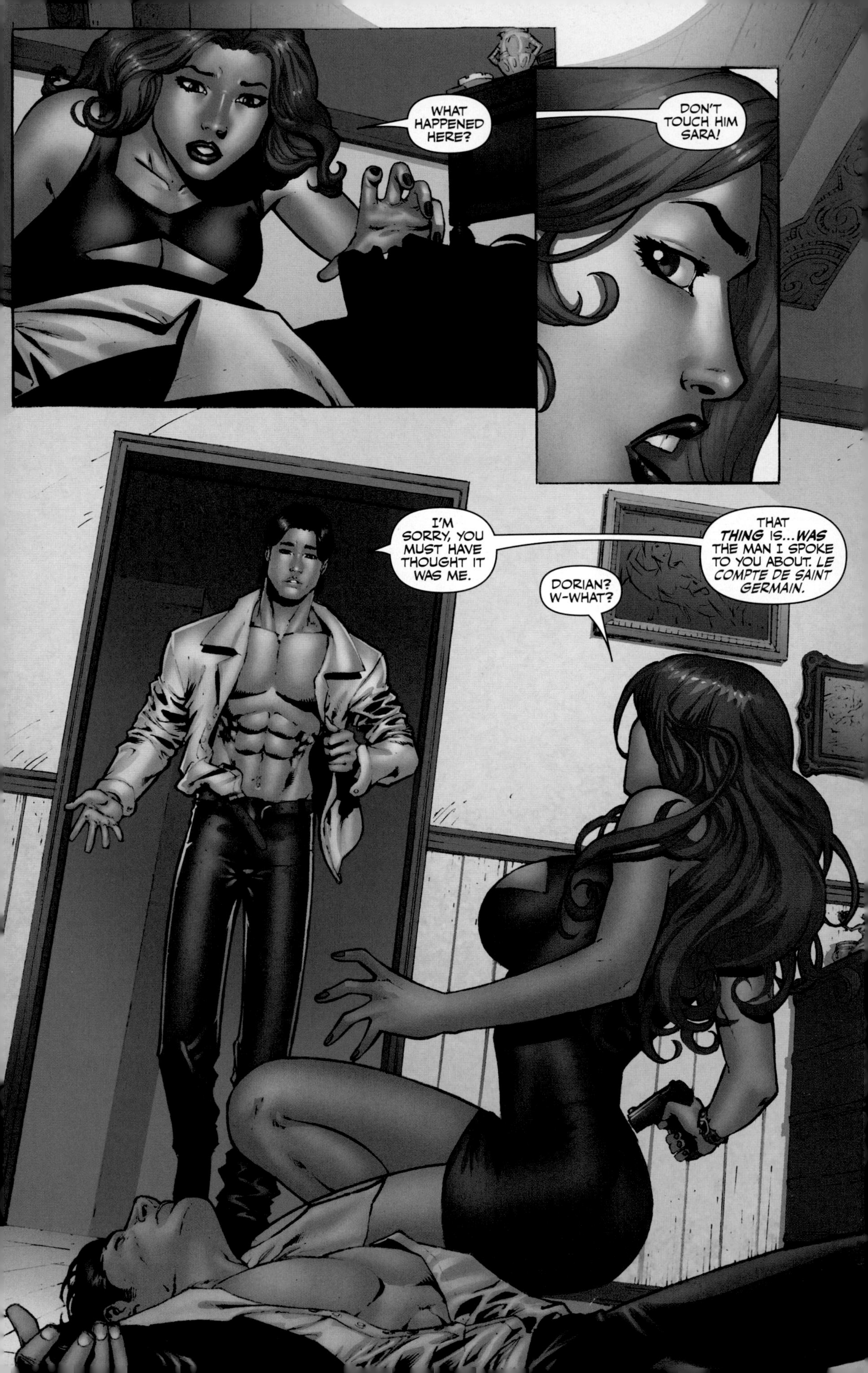
WHAT HAPPENED HERE?
DON'T TOUCH HIM SARA!
I'M SORRY, YOU MUST HAVE THOUGHT IT WAS ME.
THAT *THING* IS...*WAS* THE MAN I SPOKE TO YOU ABOUT. *LE COMPTE DE SAINT GERMAIN.*
DORIAN? W-WHAT?

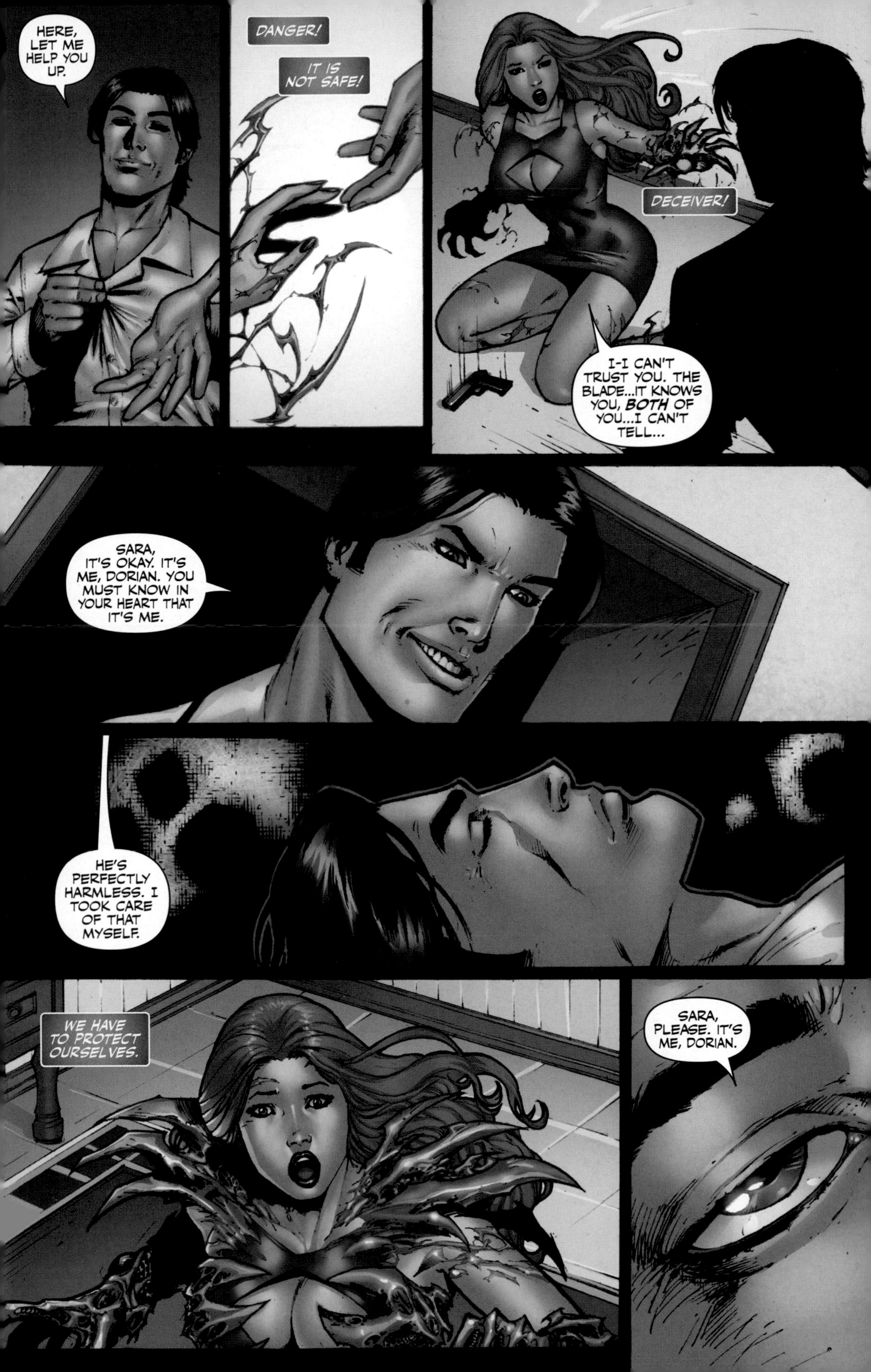
HERE, LET ME HELP YOU UP.
DANGER!
IT IS NOT SAFE!
DECEIVER!
I-I CAN'T TRUST YOU. THE BLADE...IT KNOWS YOU, BOTH OF YOU...I CAN'T TELL...
SARA, IT'S OKAY. IT'S ME, DORIAN. YOU MUST KNOW IN YOUR HEART THAT IT'S ME.
HE'S PERFECTLY HARMLESS. I TOOK CARE OF THAT MYSELF.
WE HAVE TO PROTECT OURSELVES.
SARA, PLEASE. IT'S ME, DORIAN.

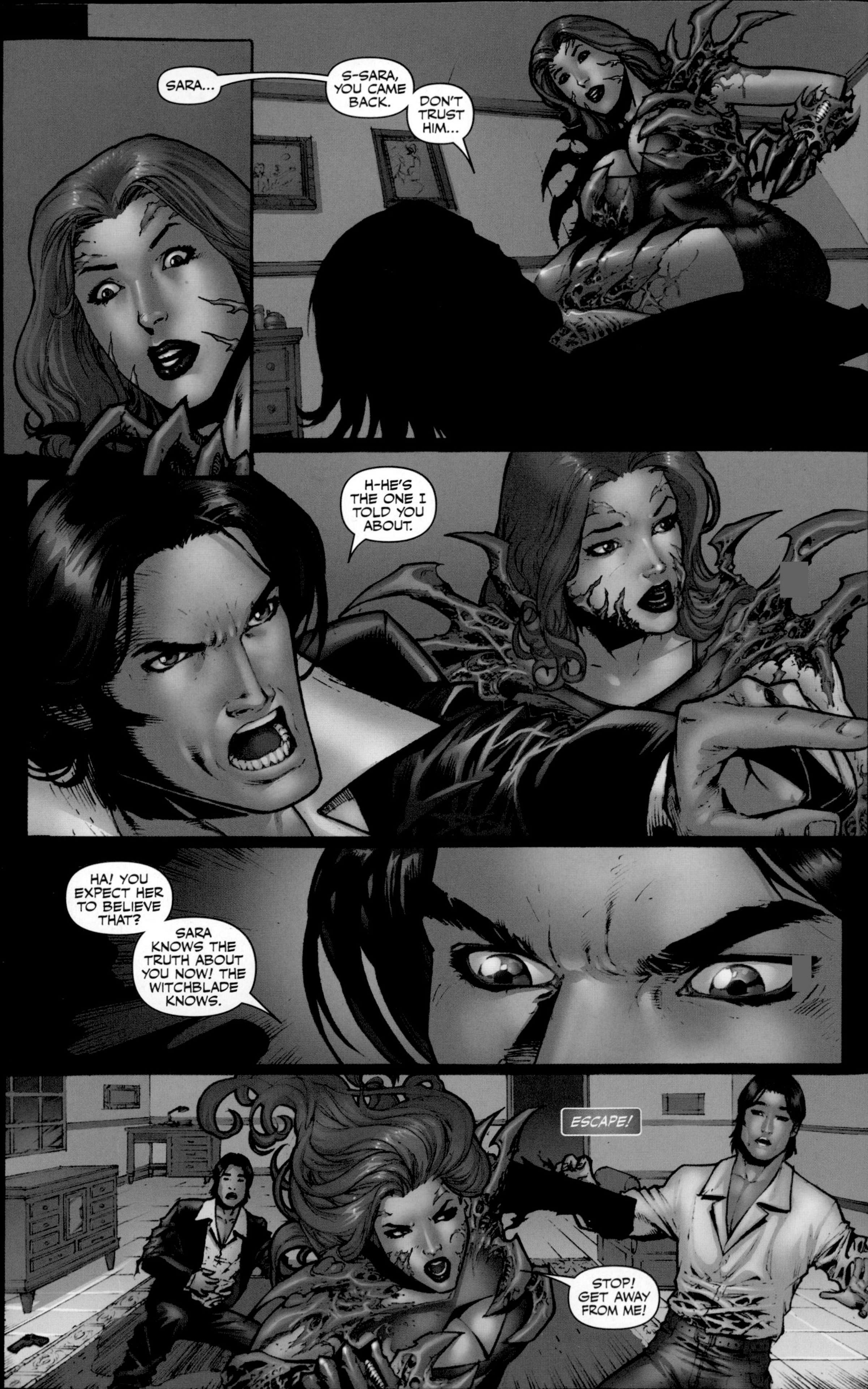
SARA...
S-SARA, YOU CAME BACK.
DON'T TRUST HIM...
H-HE'S THE ONE I TOLD YOU ABOUT.
HA! YOU EXPECT HER TO BELIEVE THAT?
SARA KNOWS THE TRUTH ABOUT YOU NOW! THE WITCHBLADE KNOWS.
ESCAPE!
STOP! GET AWAY FROM ME!

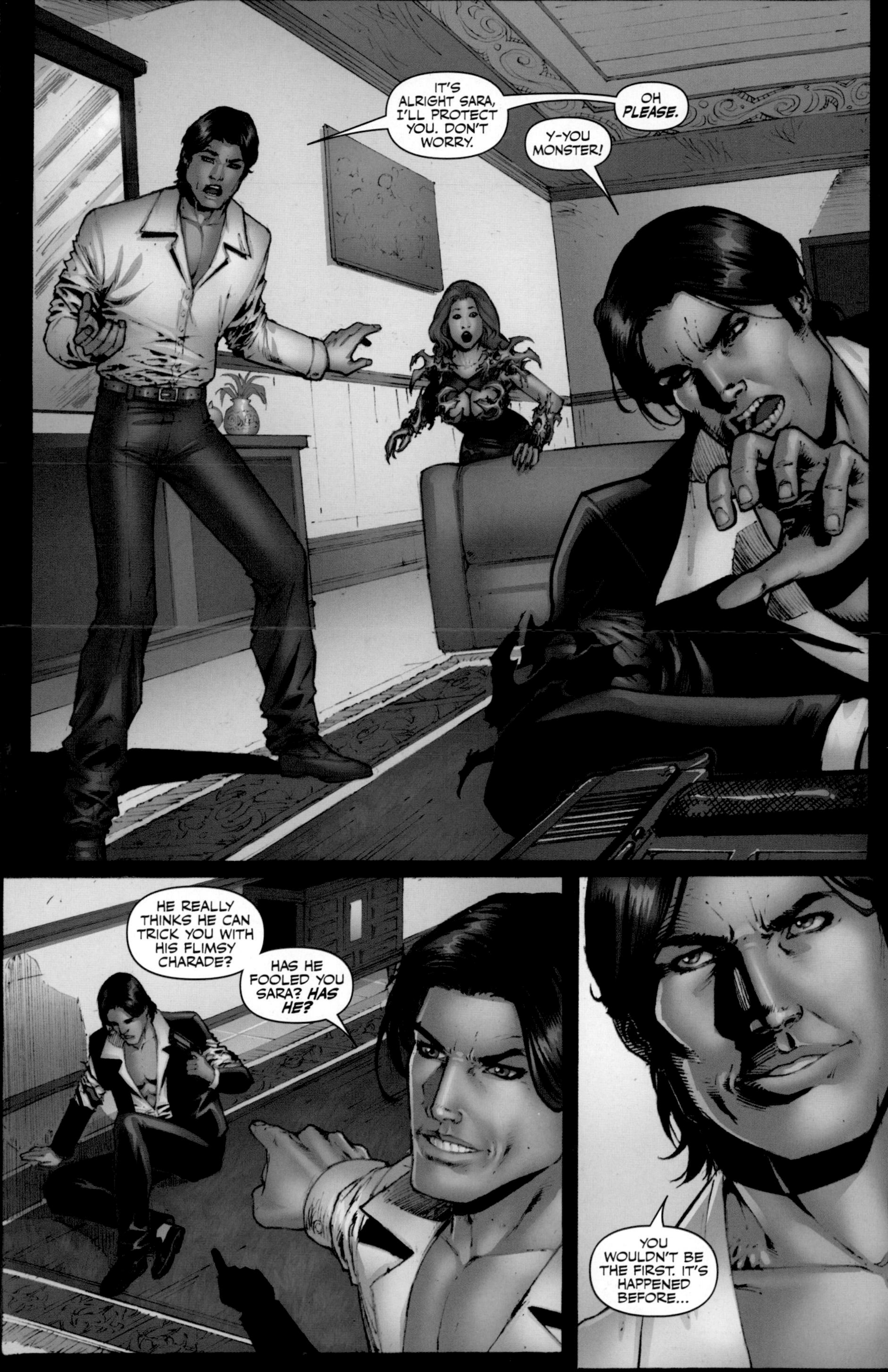
IT'S ALRIGHT SARA, I'LL PROTECT YOU. DON'T WORRY.
OH *PLEASE.*
Y-YOU MONSTER!
HE REALLY THINKS HE CAN TRICK YOU WITH HIS FLIMSY CHARADE?
HAS HE FOOLED YOU SARA? *HAS HE?*
YOU WOULDN'T BE THE FIRST. IT'S HAPPENED BEFORE...

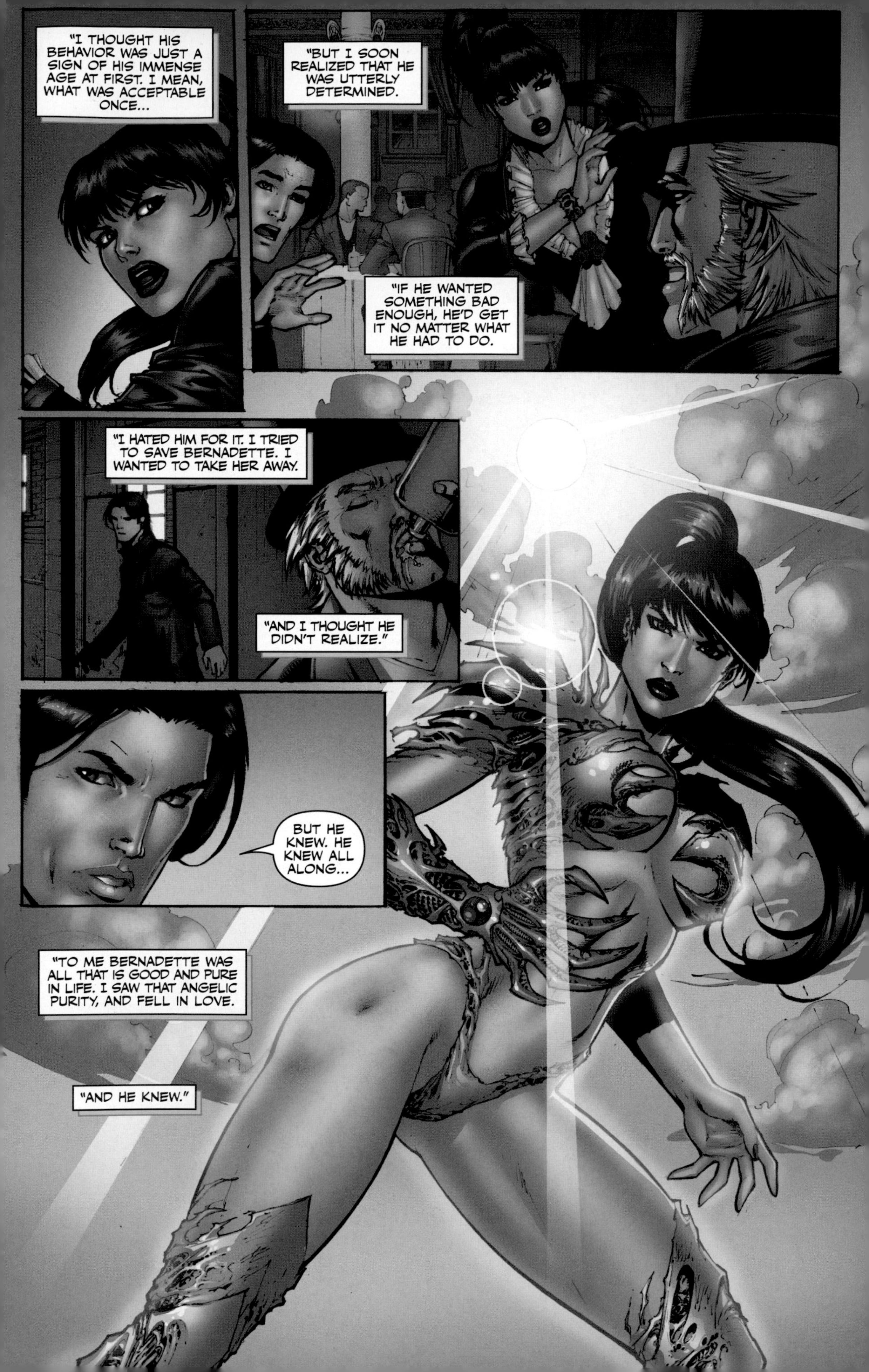
"I THOUGHT HIS BEHAVIOR WAS JUST A SIGN OF HIS IMMENSE AGE AT FIRST. I MEAN, WHAT WAS ACCEPTABLE ONCE...
"BUT I SOON REALIZED THAT HE WAS UTTERLY DETERMINED.
"IF HE WANTED SOMETHING BAD ENOUGH, HE'D GET IT NO MATTER WHAT HE HAD TO DO.
"I HATED HIM FOR IT. I TRIED TO SAVE BERNADETTE. I WANTED TO TAKE HER AWAY.
"AND I THOUGHT HE DIDN'T REALIZE."
BUT HE KNEW. HE KNEW ALL ALONG...
"TO ME BERNADETTE WAS ALL THAT IS GOOD AND PURE IN LIFE. I SAW THAT ANGELIC PURITY, AND FELL IN LOVE.
"AND HE KNEW."

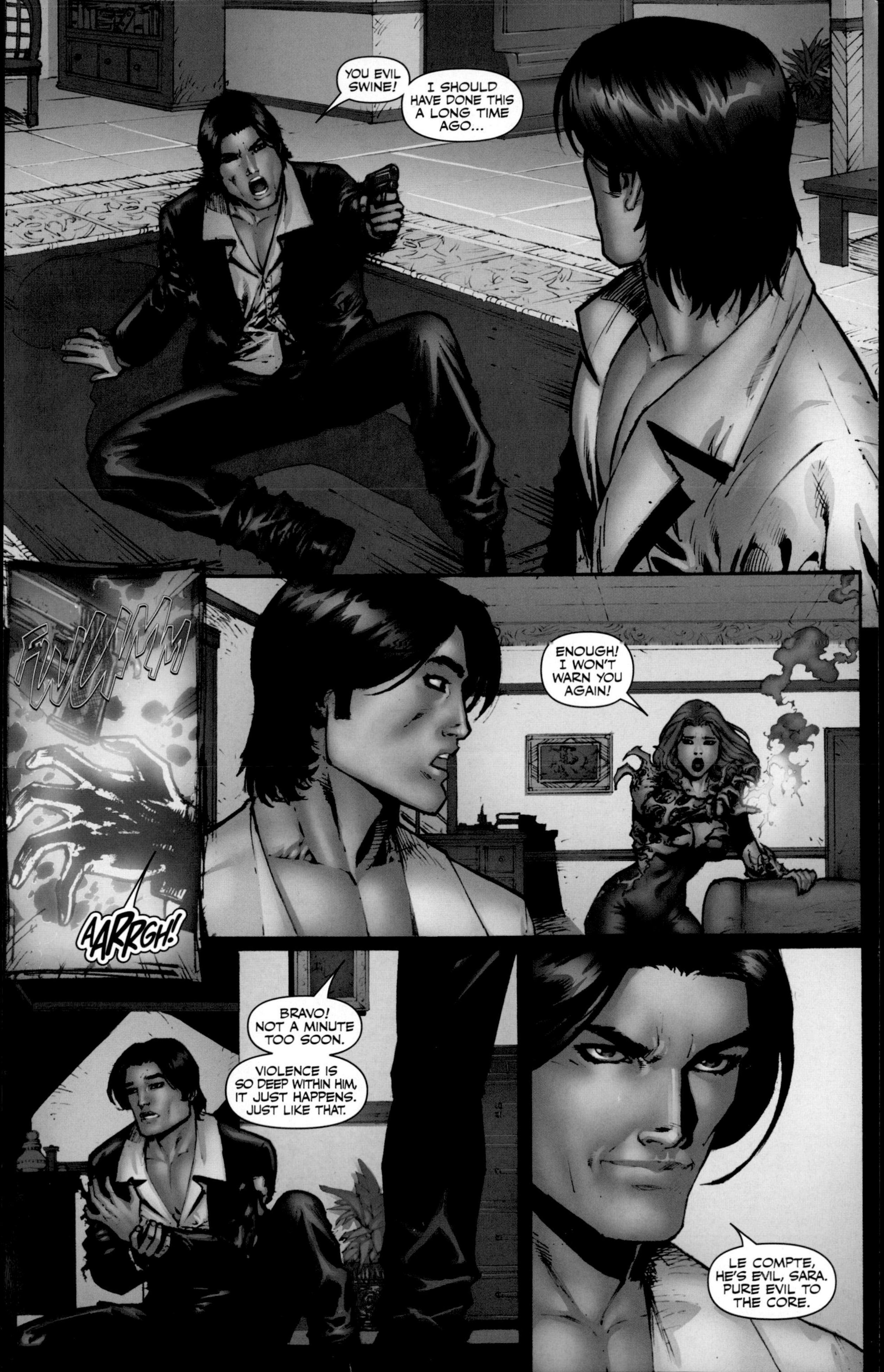
YOU EVIL SWINE!
I SHOULD HAVE DONE THIS A LONG TIME AGO...
FWUMMM
AARRGH!
ENOUGH! I WON'T WARN YOU AGAIN!
BRAVO! NOT A MINUTE TOO SOON.
VIOLENCE IS SO DEEP WITHIN HIM, IT JUST HAPPENS. JUST LIKE THAT.
LE COMPTE, HE'S EVIL, SARA. PURE EVIL TO THE CORE.

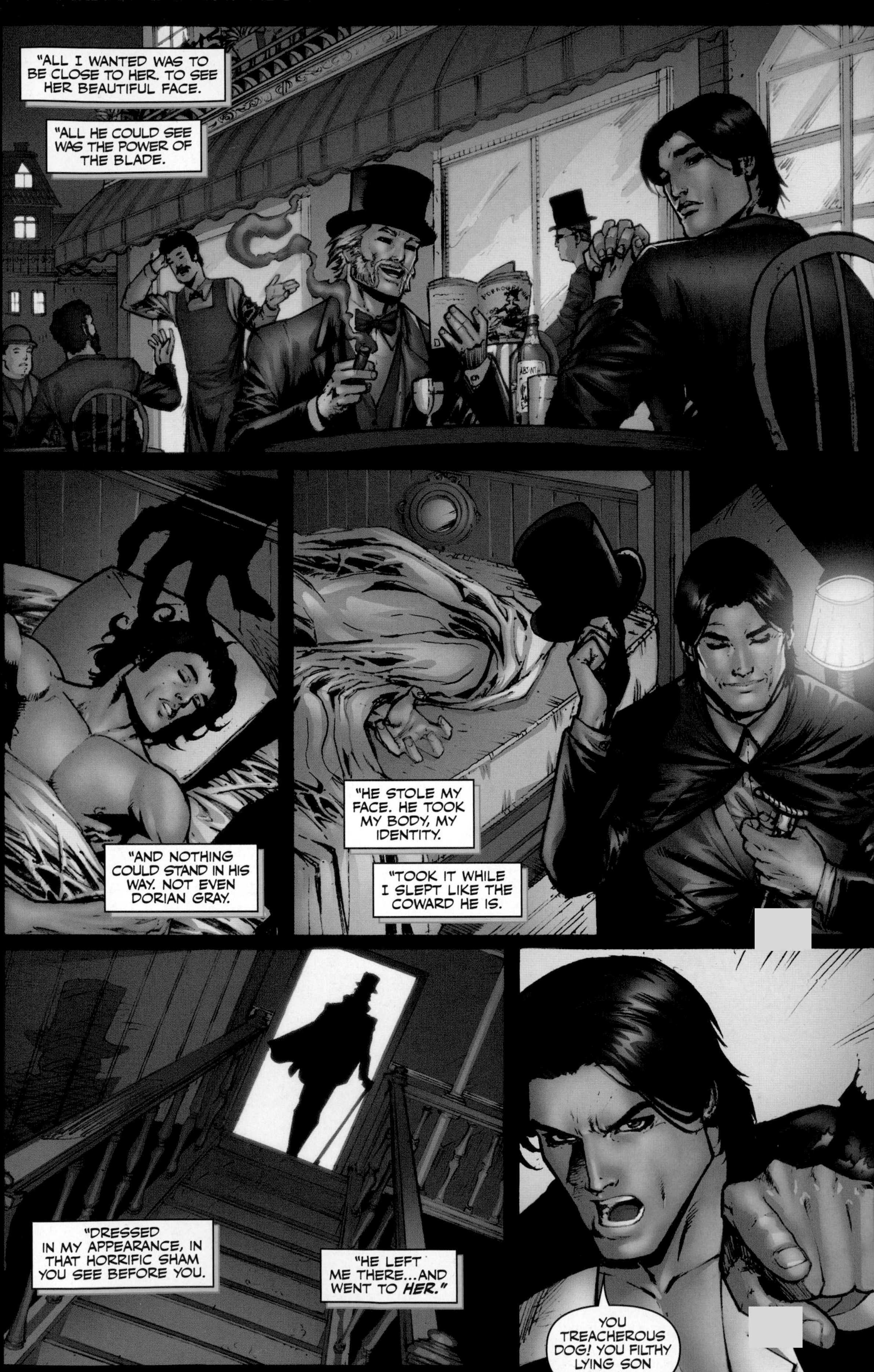
"ALL I WANTED WAS TO BE CLOSE TO HER. TO SEE HER BEAUTIFUL FACE.
"ALL HE COULD SEE WAS THE POWER OF THE BLADE.
"AND NOTHING COULD STAND IN HIS WAY. NOT EVEN DORIAN GRAY.
"HE STOLE MY FACE. HE TOOK MY BODY, MY IDENTITY.
"TOOK IT WHILE I SLEPT LIKE THE COWARD HE IS.
"DRESSED IN MY APPEARANCE, IN THAT HORRIFIC SHAM YOU SEE BEFORE YOU.
"HE LEFT ME THERE...AND WENT TO *HER.*"
YOU TREACHEROUS DOG! YOU FILTHY LYING SON OF A--

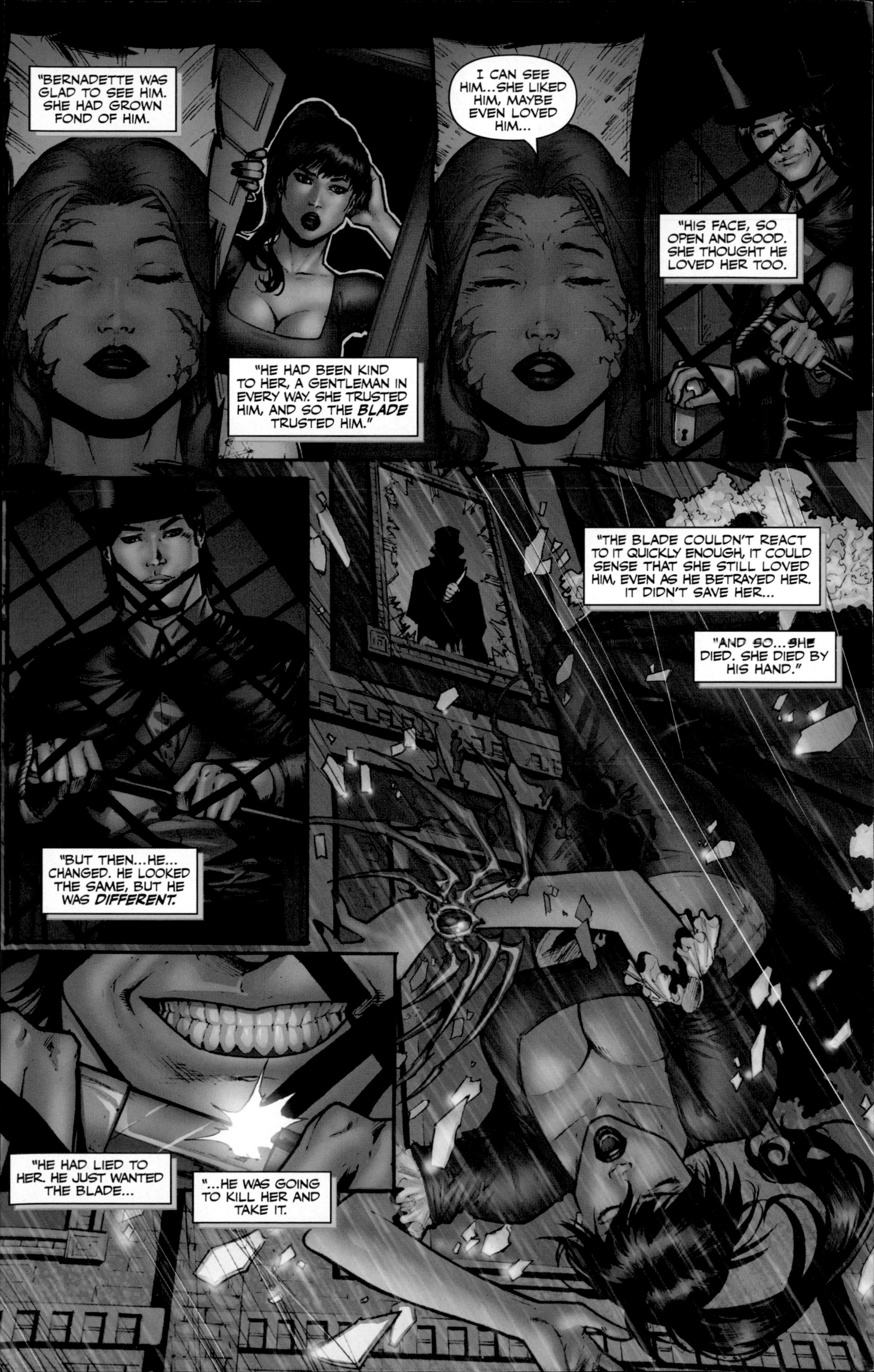
"BERNADETTE WAS GLAD TO SEE HIM. SHE HAD GROWN FOND OF HIM.
"HE HAD BEEN KIND TO HER, A GENTLEMAN IN EVERY WAY. SHE TRUSTED HIM, AND SO THE BLADE TRUSTED HIM."
I CAN SEE HIM...SHE LIKED HIM, MAYBE EVEN LOVED HIM...
"HIS FACE, SO OPEN AND GOOD. SHE THOUGHT HE LOVED HER TOO.
"BUT THEN...HE... CHANGED. HE LOOKED THE SAME, BUT HE WAS DIFFERENT.
"HE HAD LIED TO HER. HE JUST WANTED THE BLADE...
"...HE WAS GOING TO KILL HER AND TAKE IT.
"THE BLADE COULDN'T REACT TO IT QUICKLY ENOUGH, IT COULD SENSE THAT SHE STILL LOVED HIM, EVEN AS HE BETRAYED HER. IT DIDN'T SAVE HER...
"AND SO...SHE DIED. SHE DIED BY HIS HAND."

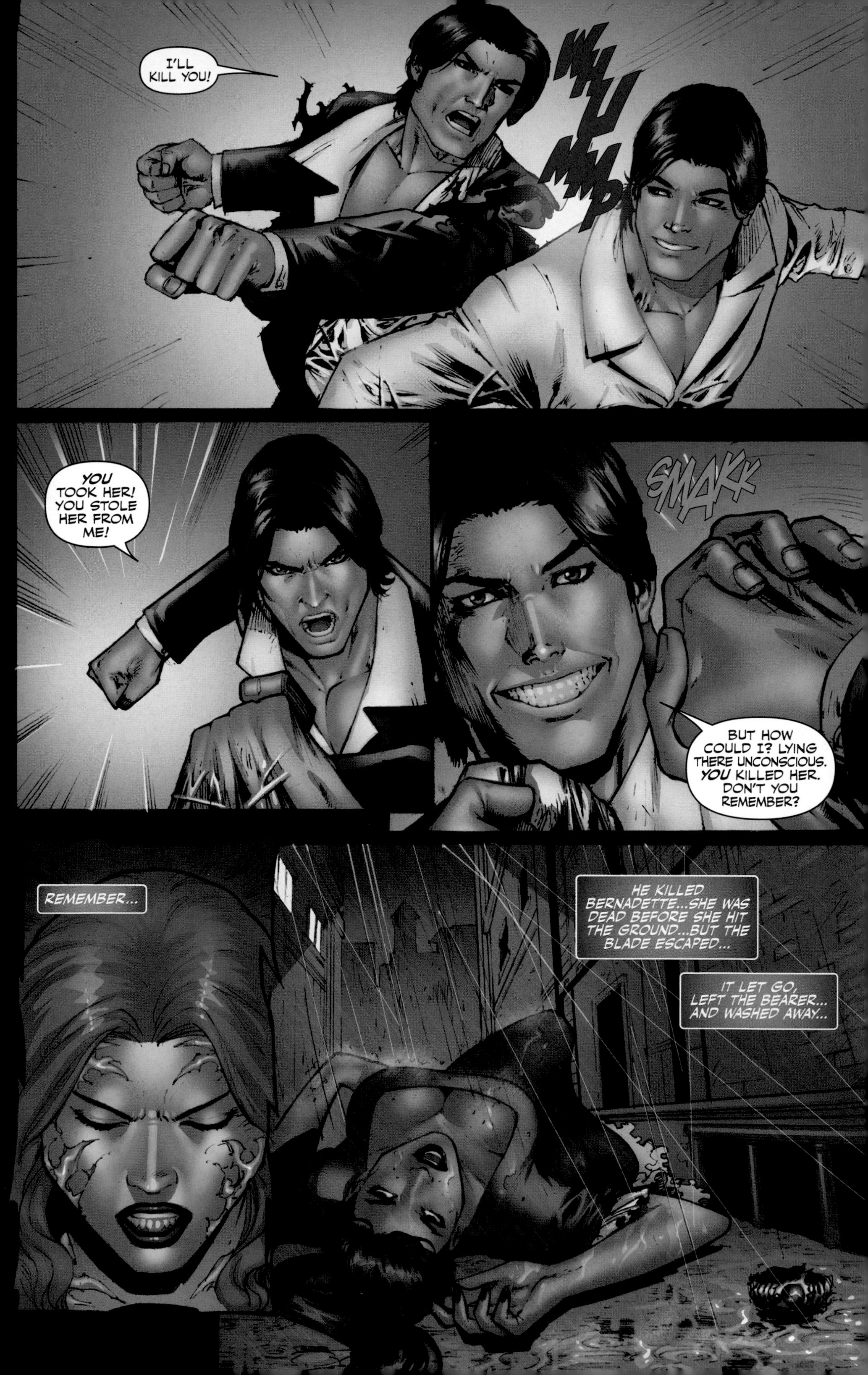
I'LL KILL YOU!
WHUMMP
YOU TOOK HER! YOU STOLE HER FROM ME!
SMAKK
BUT HOW COULD I? LYING THERE UNCONSCIOUS. YOU KILLED HER. DON'T YOU REMEMBER?
REMEMBER...
HE KILLED BERNADETTE...SHE WAS DEAD BEFORE SHE HIT THE GROUND...BUT THE BLADE ESCAPED...
IT LET GO, LEFT THE BEARER... AND WASHED AWAY...

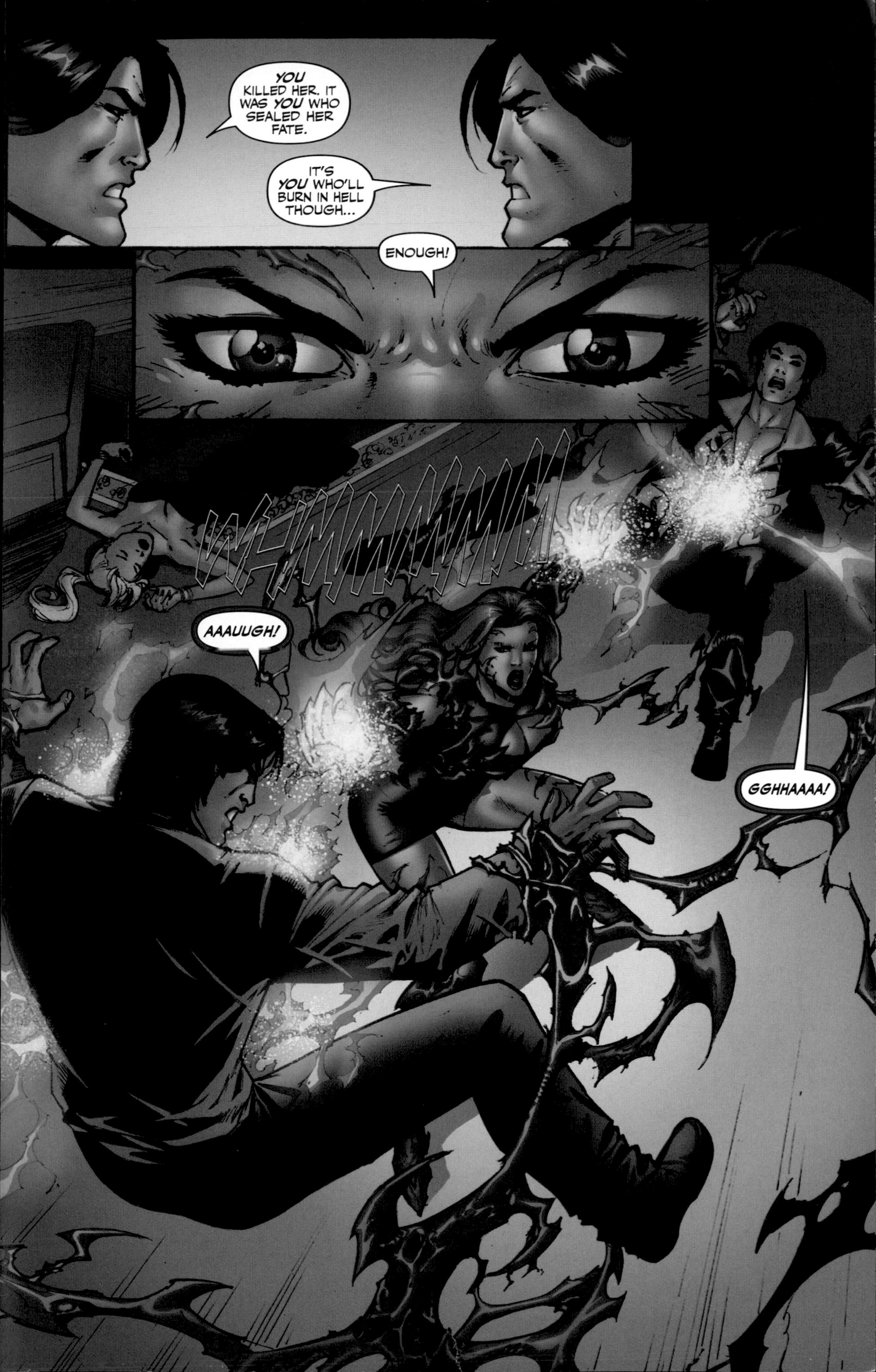
YOU KILLED HER. IT WAS YOU WHO SEALED HER FATE.
IT'S YOU WHO'LL BURN IN HELL THOUGH...
ENOUGH!
WHMMMMMM
AAAUUGH!
GGHHAAAA!

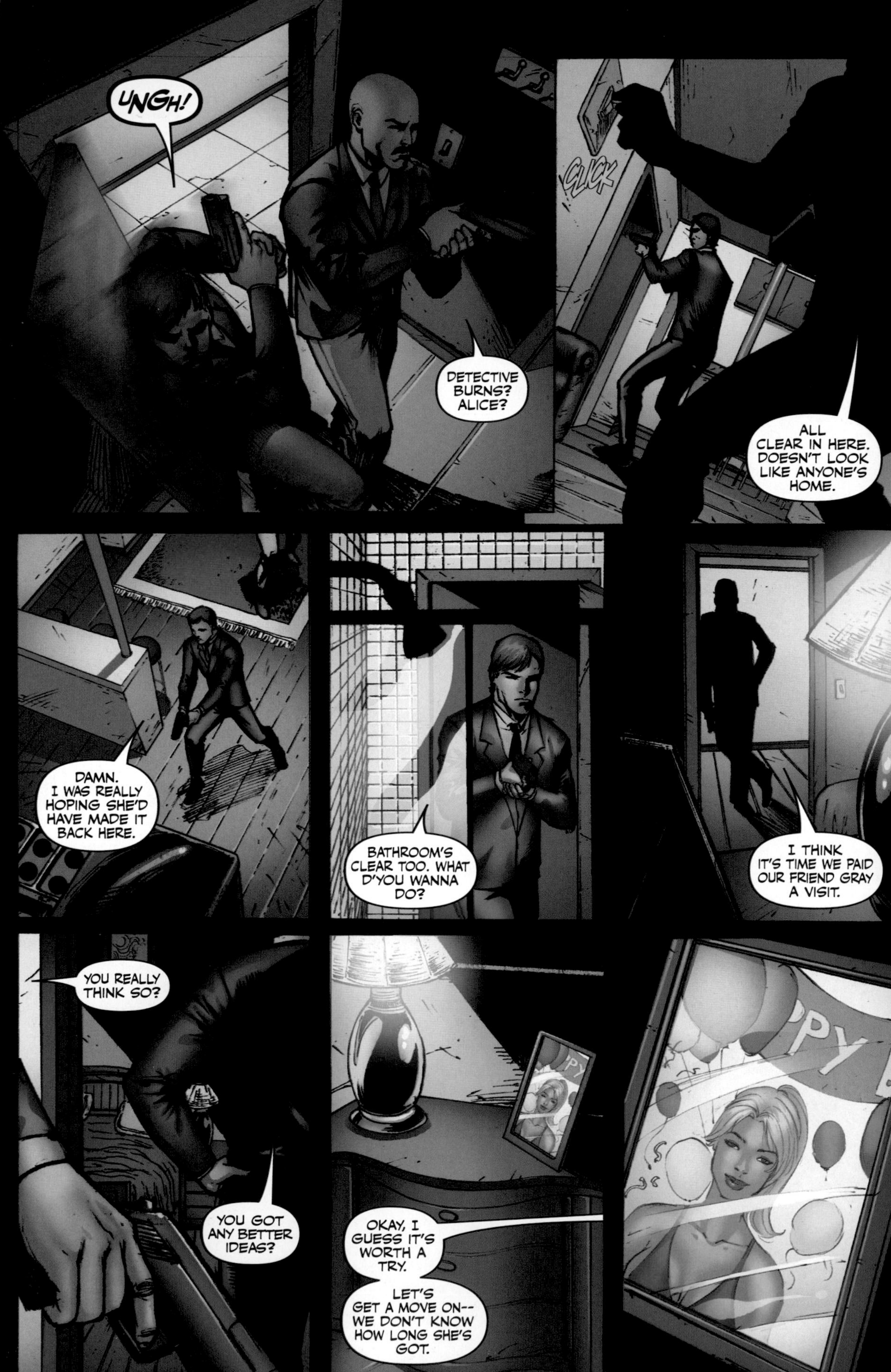
UNGH!
DETECTIVE BURNS? ALICE?
CLICK
ALL CLEAR IN HERE. DOESN'T LOOK LIKE ANYONE'S HOME.
DAMN. I WAS REALLY HOPING SHE'D HAVE MADE IT BACK HERE.
BATHROOM'S CLEAR TOO. WHAT D'YOU WANNA DO?
I THINK IT'S TIME WE PAID OUR FRIEND GRAY A VISIT.
YOU REALLY THINK SO?
YOU GOT ANY BETTER IDEAS?
OKAY, I GUESS IT'S WORTH A TRY.
LET'S GET A MOVE ON-- WE DON'T KNOW HOW LONG SHE'S GOT.

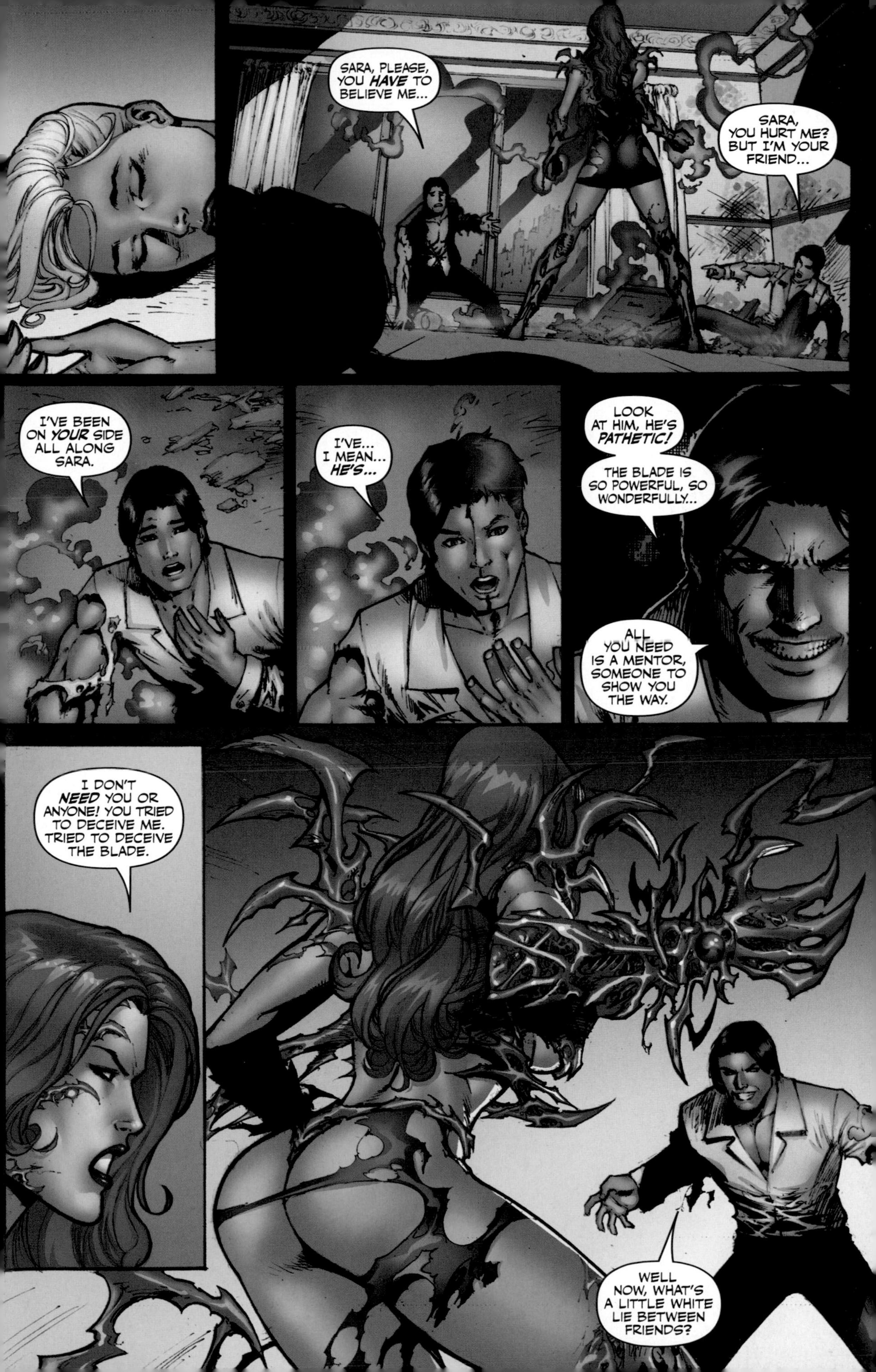
SARA, PLEASE, YOU HAVE TO BELIEVE ME...
SARA, YOU HURT ME? BUT I'M YOUR FRIEND...
I'VE BEEN ON YOUR SIDE ALL ALONG SARA.
I'VE... I MEAN... HE'S...
LOOK AT HIM, HE'S PATHETIC!
THE BLADE IS SO POWERFUL, SO WONDERFULLY...
ALL YOU NEED IS A MENTOR, SOMEONE TO SHOW YOU THE WAY.
I DON'T NEED YOU OR ANYONE! YOU TRIED TO DECEIVE ME. TRIED TO DECEIVE THE BLADE.
WELL NOW, WHAT'S A LITTLE WHITE LIE BETWEEN FRIENDS?

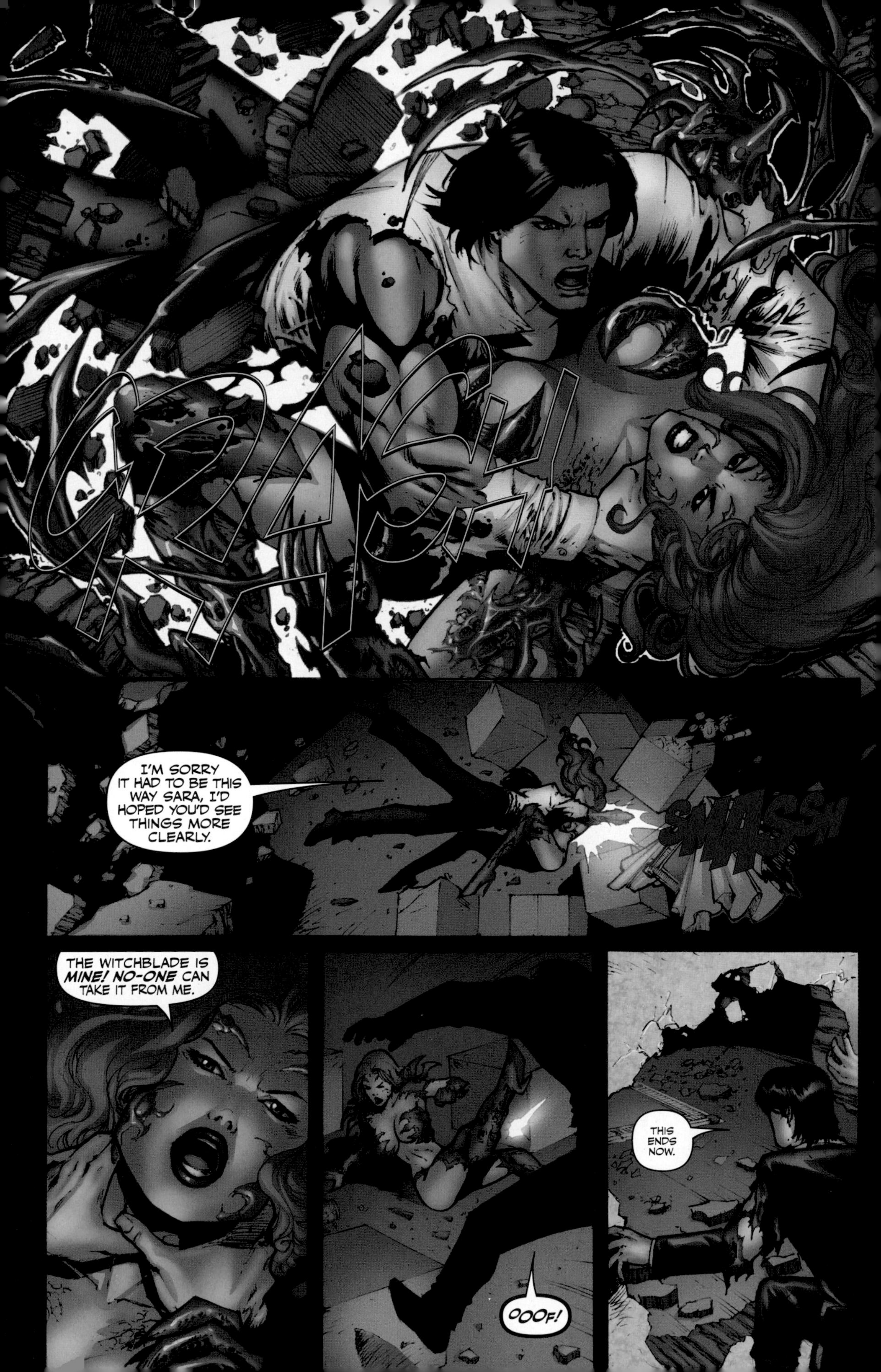

CRASH
I'M SORRY IT HAD TO BE THIS WAY SARA, I'D HOPED YOU'D SEE THINGS MORE CLEARLY.
SMASH
THE WITCHBLADE IS *MINE! NO-ONE* CAN TAKE IT FROM ME.
OOOF!
THIS ENDS NOW.

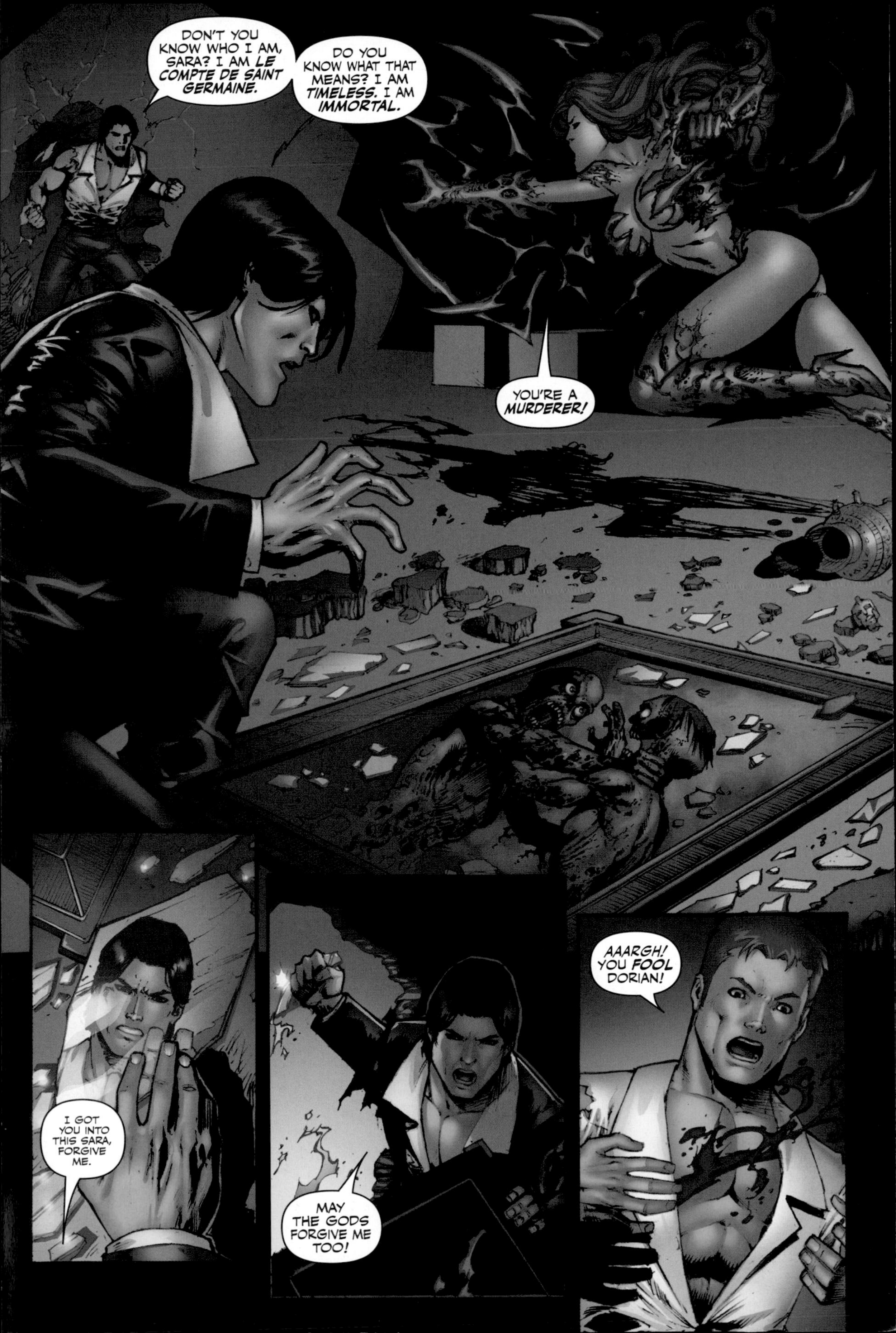
DON'T YOU KNOW WHO I AM, SARA? I AM LE COMPTE DE SAINT GERMAINE.
DO YOU KNOW WHAT THAT MEANS? I AM TIMELESS. I AM IMMORTAL.
YOU'RE A MURDERER!
I GOT YOU INTO THIS SARA, FORGIVE ME.
MAY THE GODS FORGIVE ME TOO!
AAARGH! YOU FOOL DORIAN!

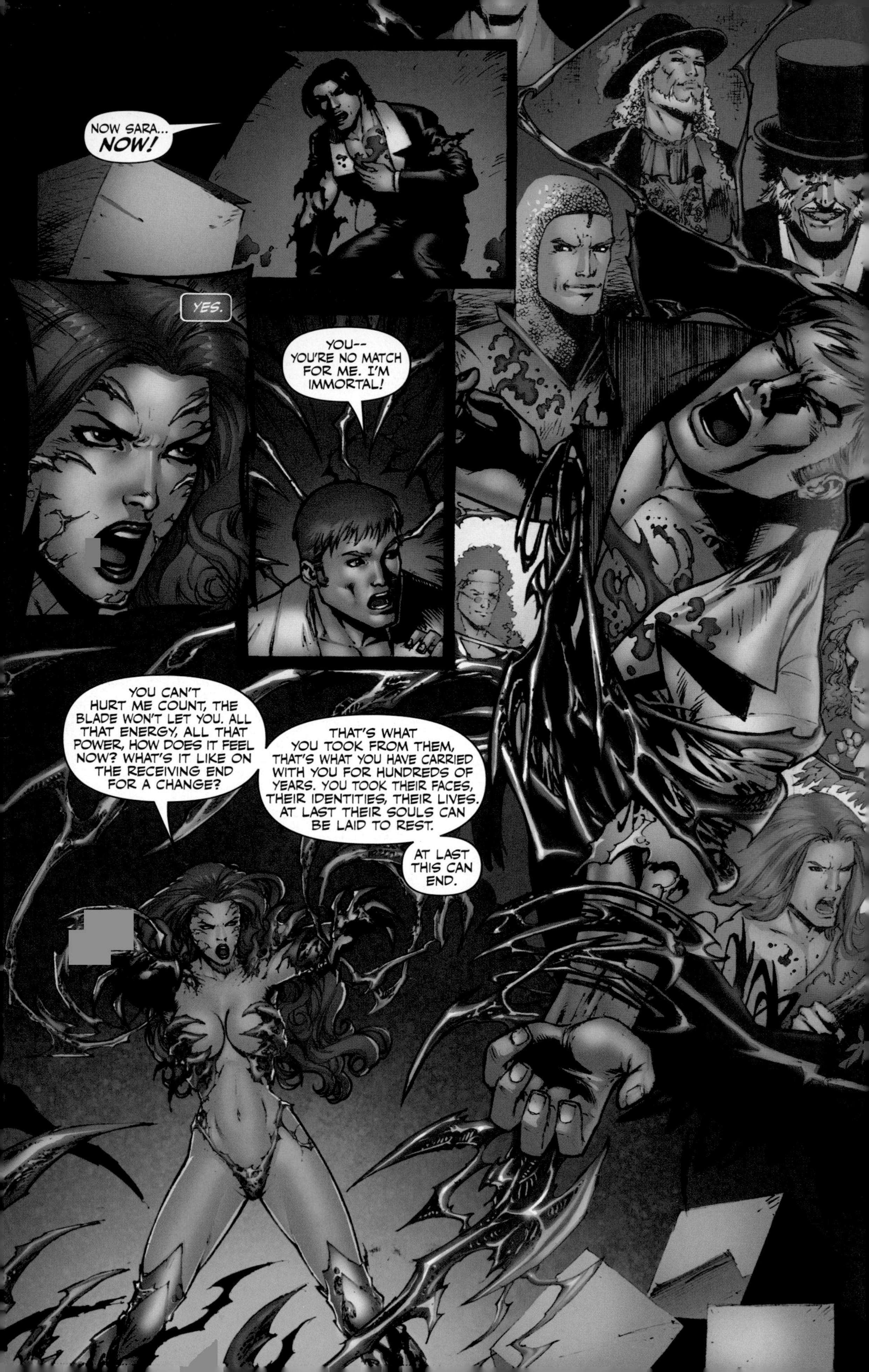
NOW SARA... NOW!
YES.
YOU-- YOU'RE NO MATCH FOR ME. I'M IMMORTAL!
YOU CAN'T HURT ME COUNT, THE BLADE WON'T LET YOU. ALL THAT ENERGY, ALL THAT POWER, HOW DOES IT FEEL NOW? WHAT'S IT LIKE ON THE RECEIVING END FOR A CHANGE?
THAT'S WHAT YOU TOOK FROM THEM, THAT'S WHAT YOU HAVE CARRIED WITH YOU FOR HUNDREDS OF YEARS. YOU TOOK THEIR FACES, THEIR IDENTITIES, THEIR LIVES. AT LAST THEIR SOULS CAN BE LAID TO REST.
AT LAST THIS CAN END.

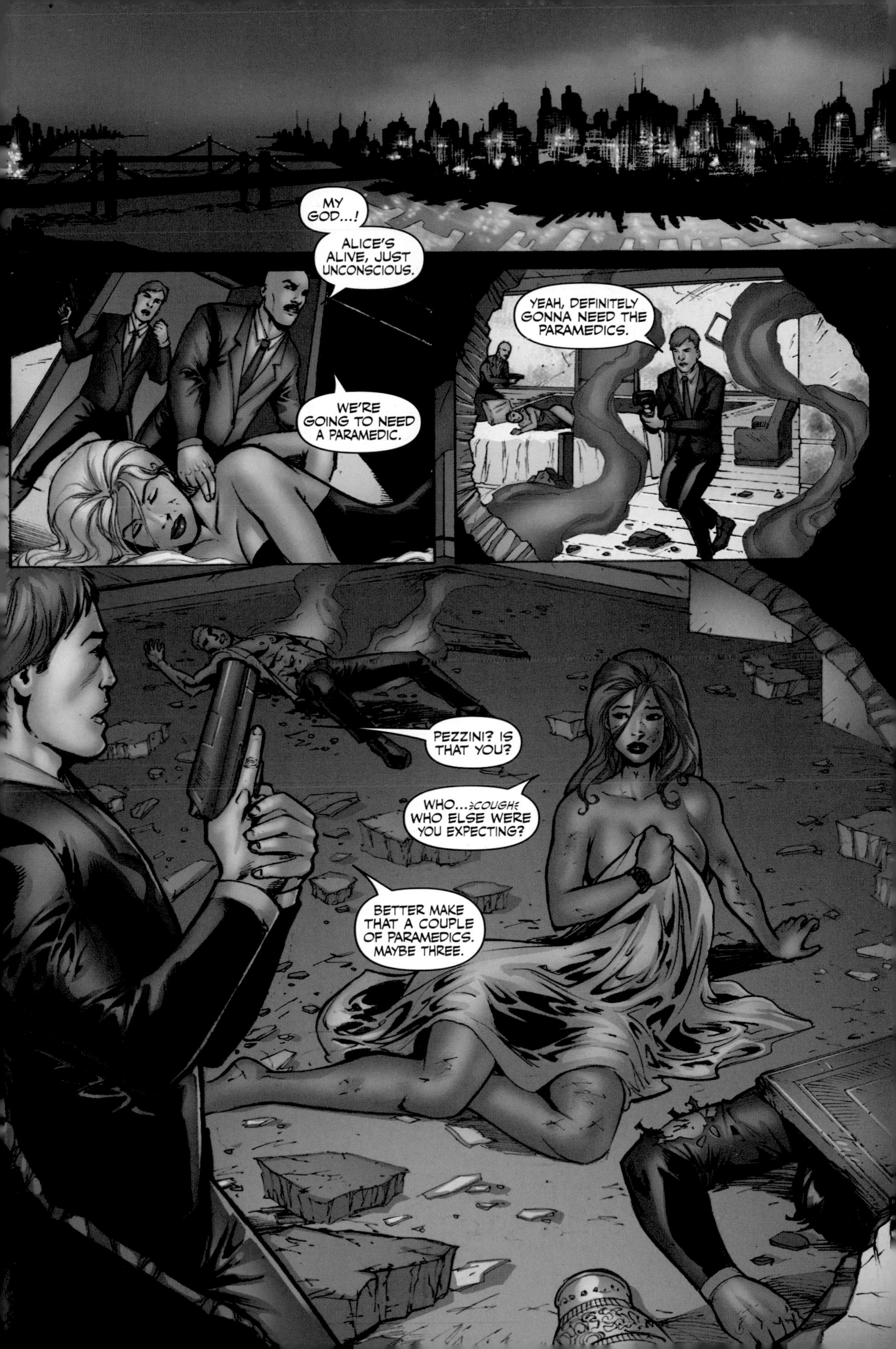
MY GOD...!
ALICE'S ALIVE, JUST UNCONSCIOUS.
WE'RE GOING TO NEED A PARAMEDIC.
YEAH, DEFINITELY GONNA NEED THE PARAMEDICS.
PEZZINI? IS THAT YOU?
WHO... COUGH WHO ELSE WERE YOU EXPECTING?
BETTER MAKE THAT A COUPLE OF PARAMEDICS. MAYBE THREE.

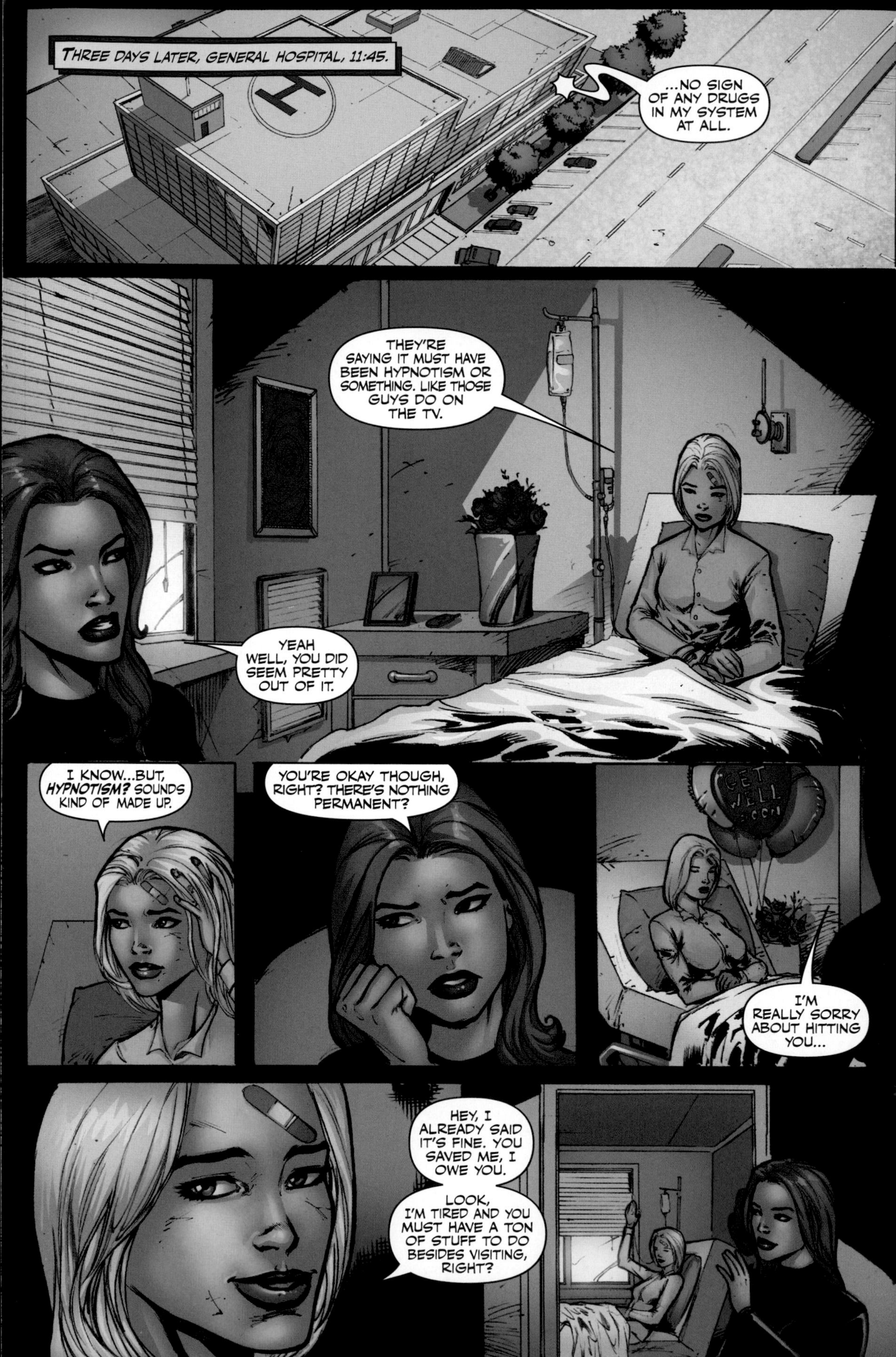
THREE DAYS LATER, GENERAL HOSPITAL, 11:45.
...NO SIGN OF ANY DRUGS IN MY SYSTEM AT ALL.
THEY'RE SAYING IT MUST HAVE BEEN HYPNOTISM OR SOMETHING. LIKE THOSE GUYS DO ON THE TV.
YEAH WELL, YOU DID SEEM PRETTY OUT OF IT.
I KNOW...BUT, *HYPNOTISM?* SOUNDS KIND OF MADE UP.
YOU'RE OKAY THOUGH, RIGHT? THERE'S NOTHING PERMANENT?
GET WELL
I'M REALLY SORRY ABOUT HITTING YOU...
HEY, I ALREADY SAID IT'S FINE. YOU SAVED ME, I OWE YOU.
LOOK, I'M TIRED AND YOU MUST HAVE A TON OF STUFF TO DO BESIDES VISITING, RIGHT?

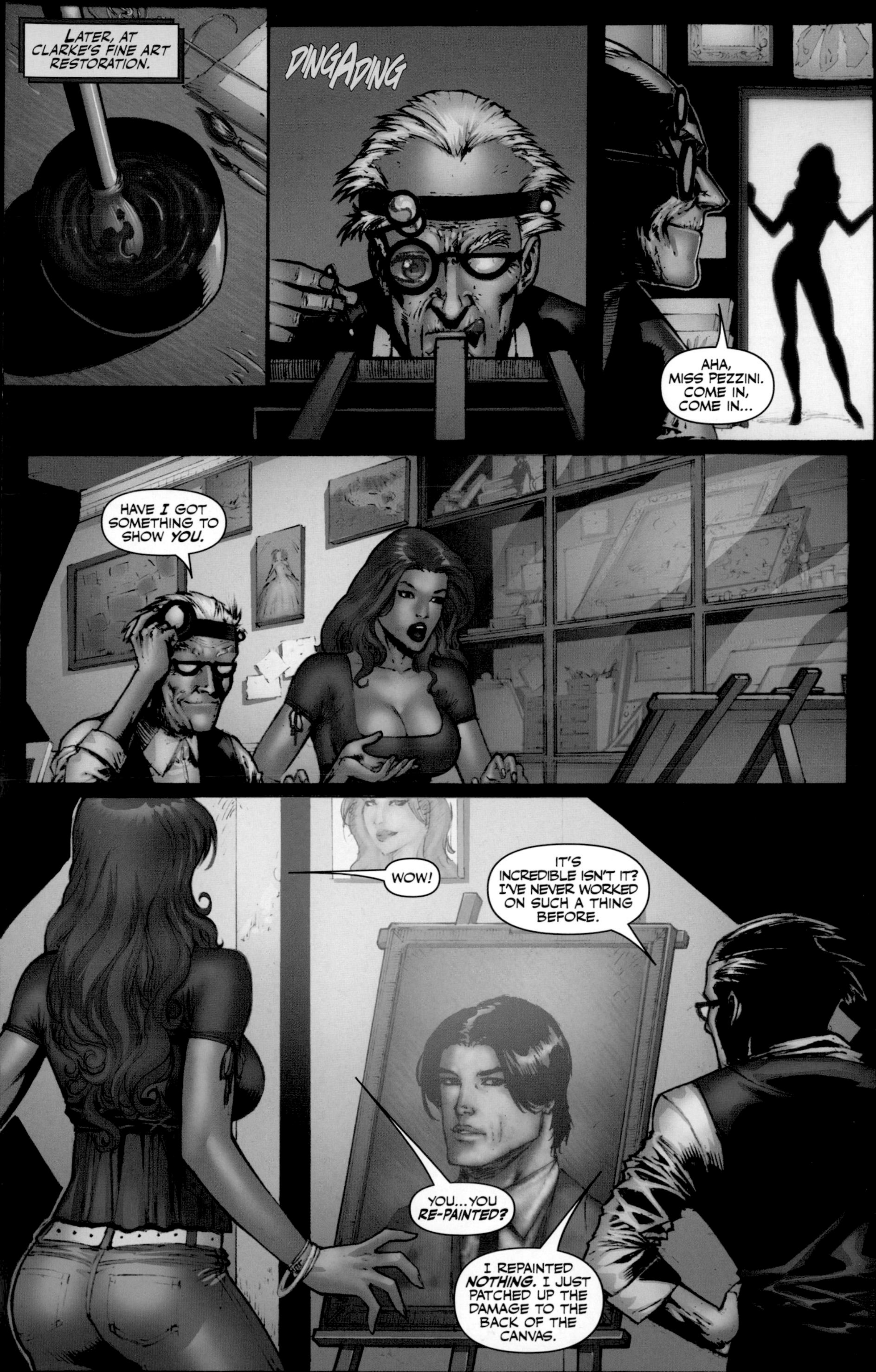
LATER, AT CLARKE'S FINE ART RESTORATION.
DINGADING
AHA, MISS PEZZINI. COME IN, COME IN...
HAVE I GOT SOMETHING TO SHOW YOU.
WOW!
IT'S INCREDIBLE ISN'T IT? I'VE NEVER WORKED ON SUCH A THING BEFORE.
YOU...YOU RE-PAINTED?
I REPAINTED NOTHING. I JUST PATCHED UP THE DAMAGE TO THE BACK OF THE CANVAS.

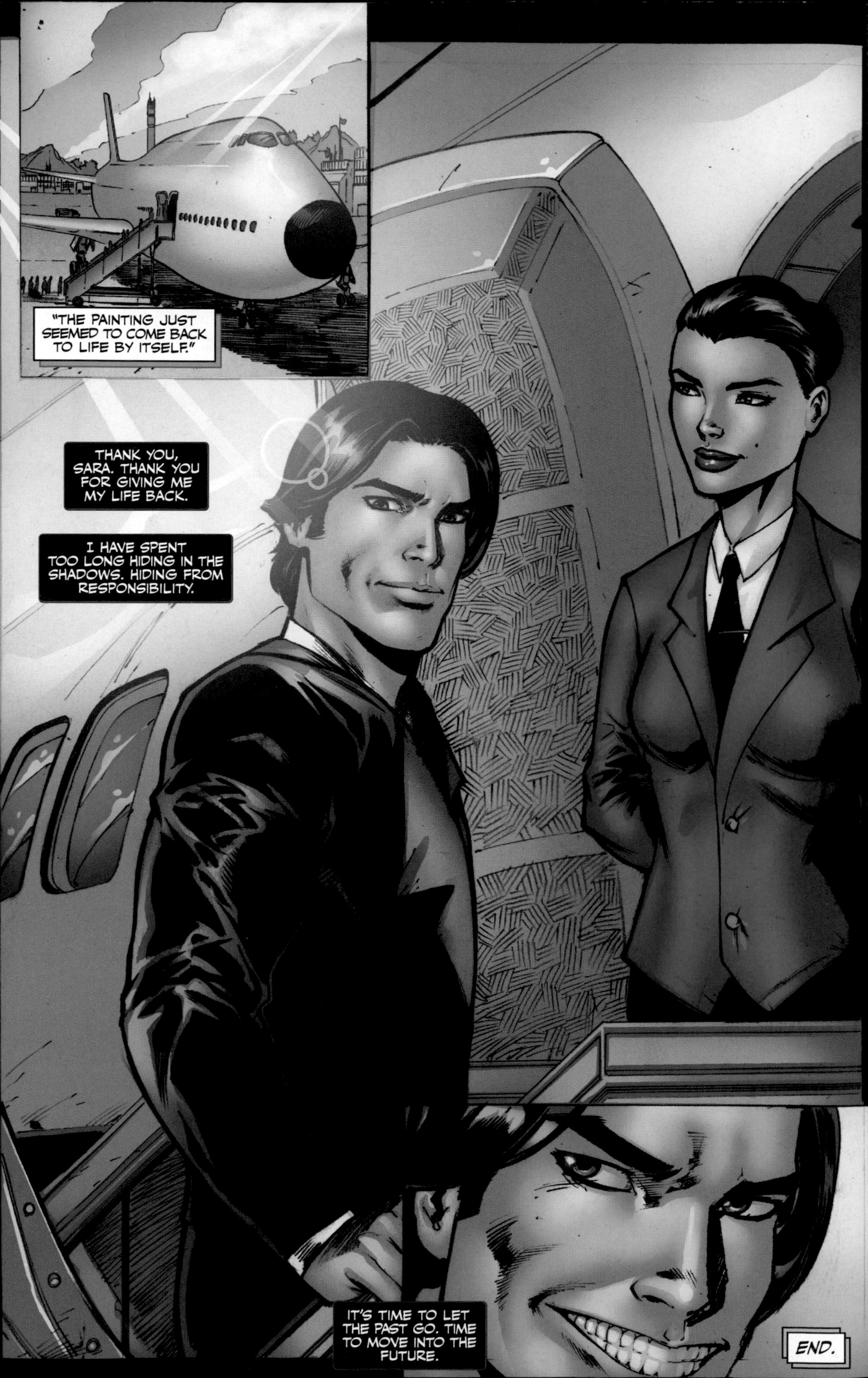
"THE PAINTING JUST SEEMED TO COME BACK TO LIFE BY ITSELF."
THANK YOU, SARA. THANK YOU FOR GIVING ME MY LIFE BACK.
I HAVE SPENT TOO LONG HIDING IN THE SHADOWS. HIDING FROM RESPONSIBILITY.
IT'S TIME TO LET THE PAST GO. TIME TO MOVE INTO THE FUTURE.
END.

COVER GALLERY

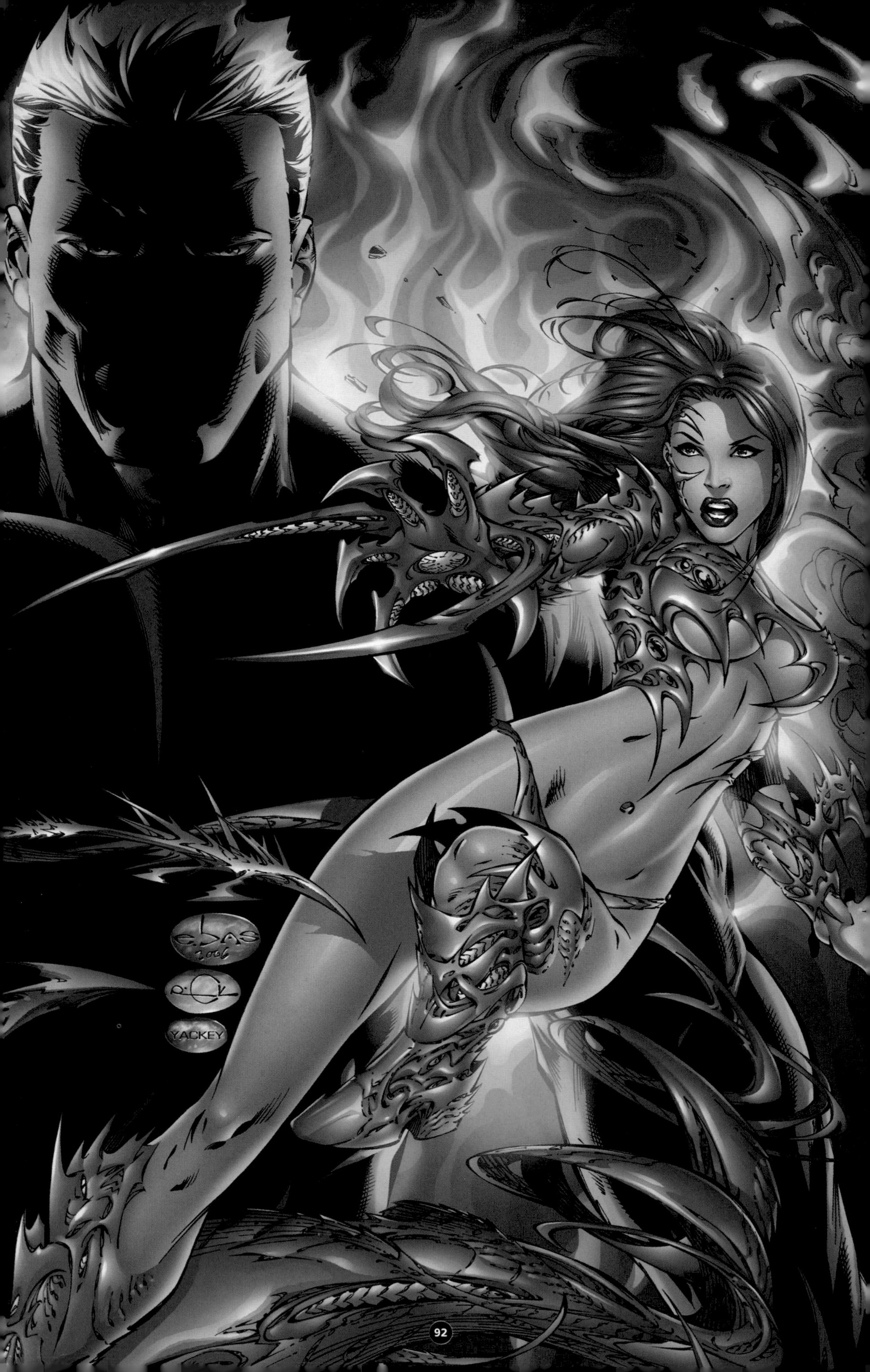
YACKEY

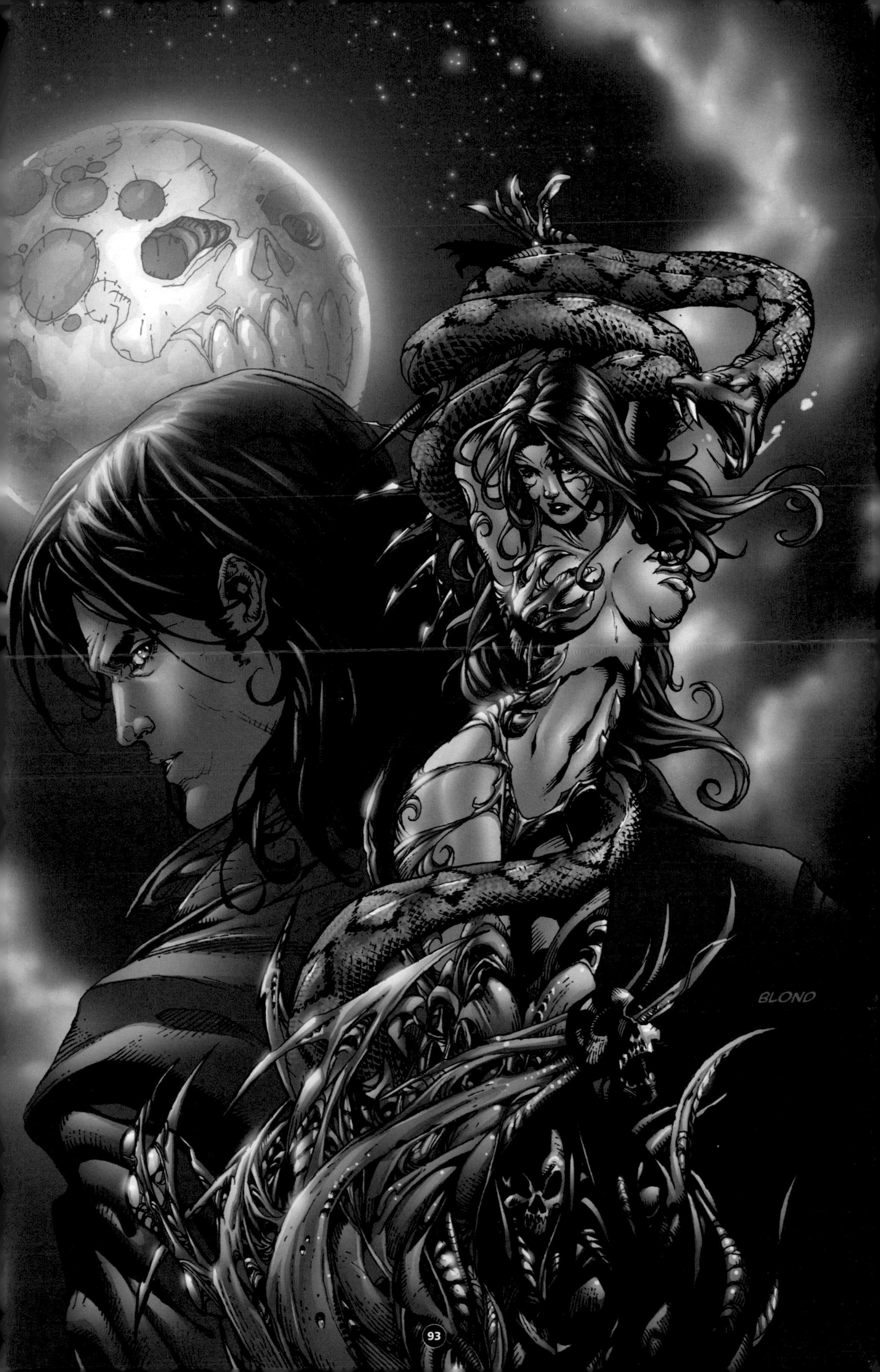
BLOND

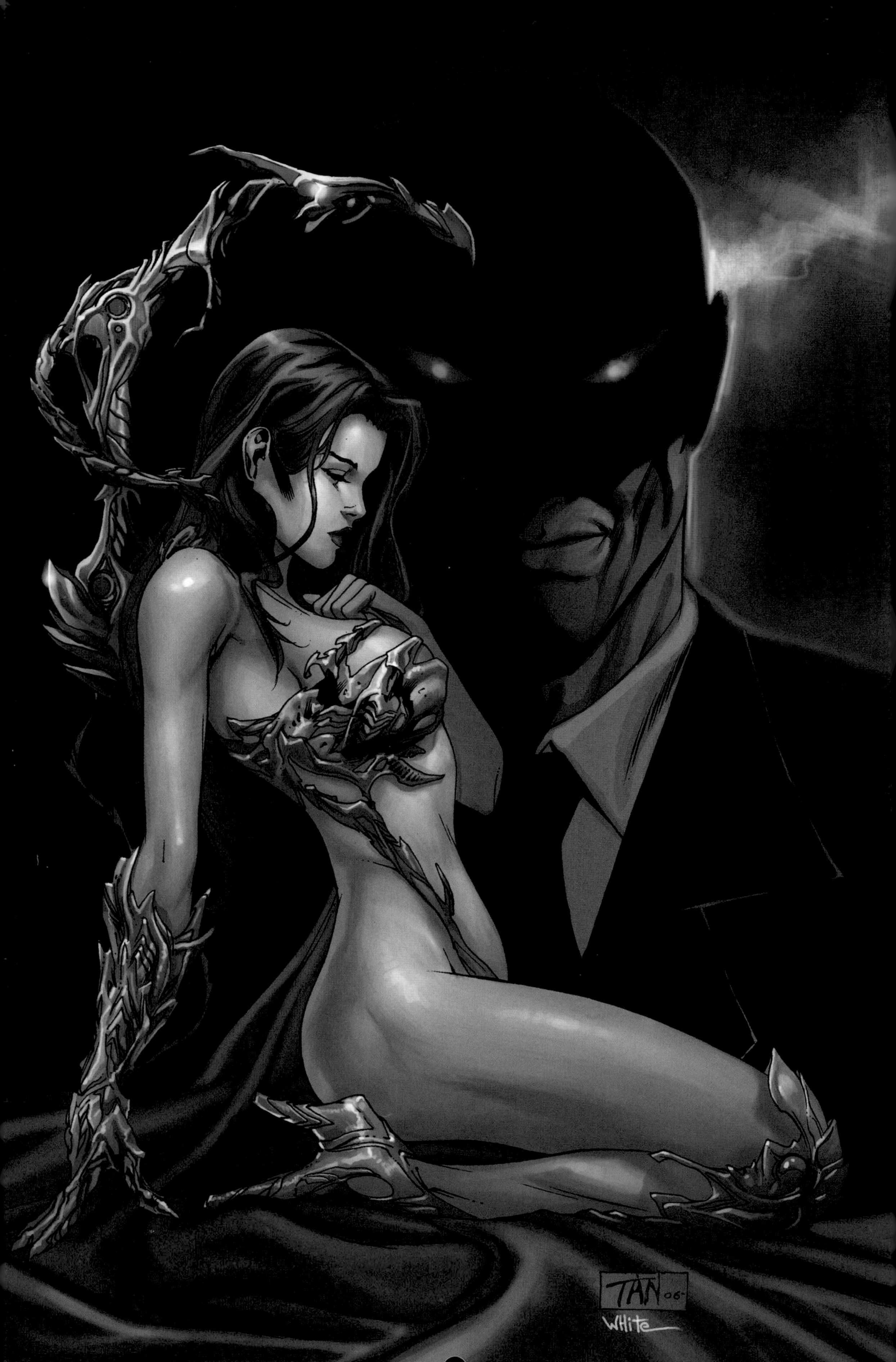
TAN 06
White

e.bas
'06

CÆSAR

95

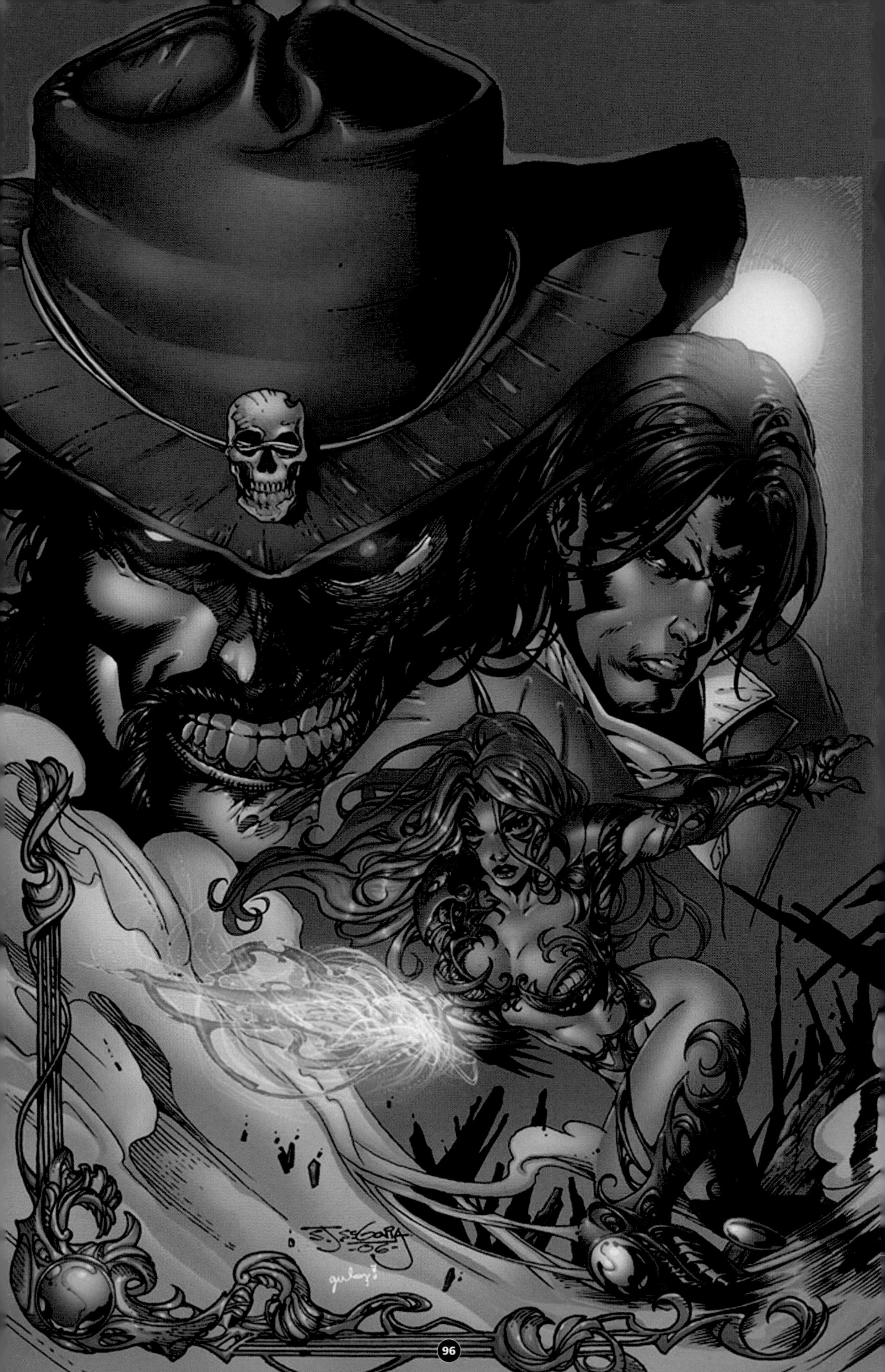

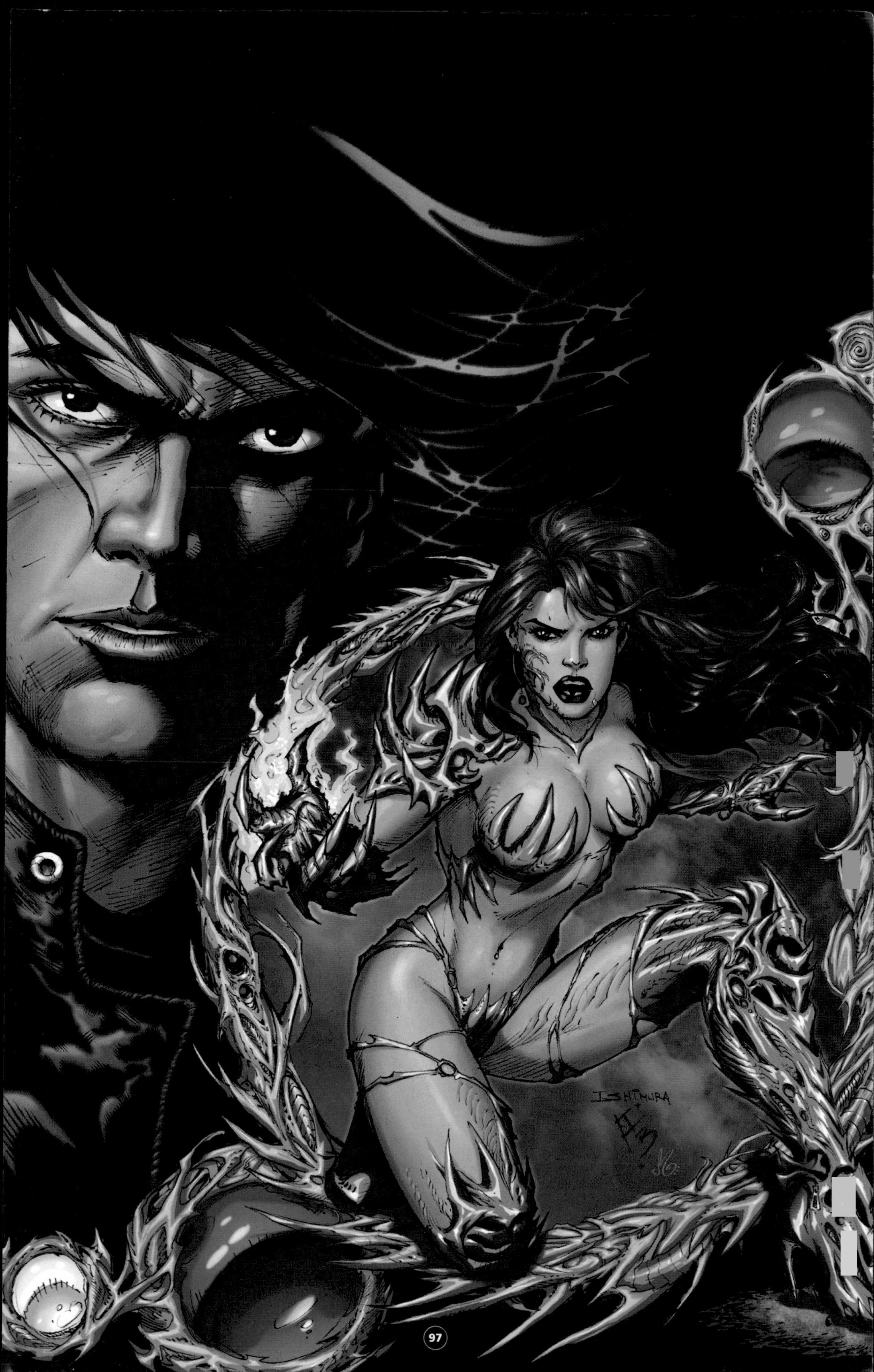
ISHIMURA

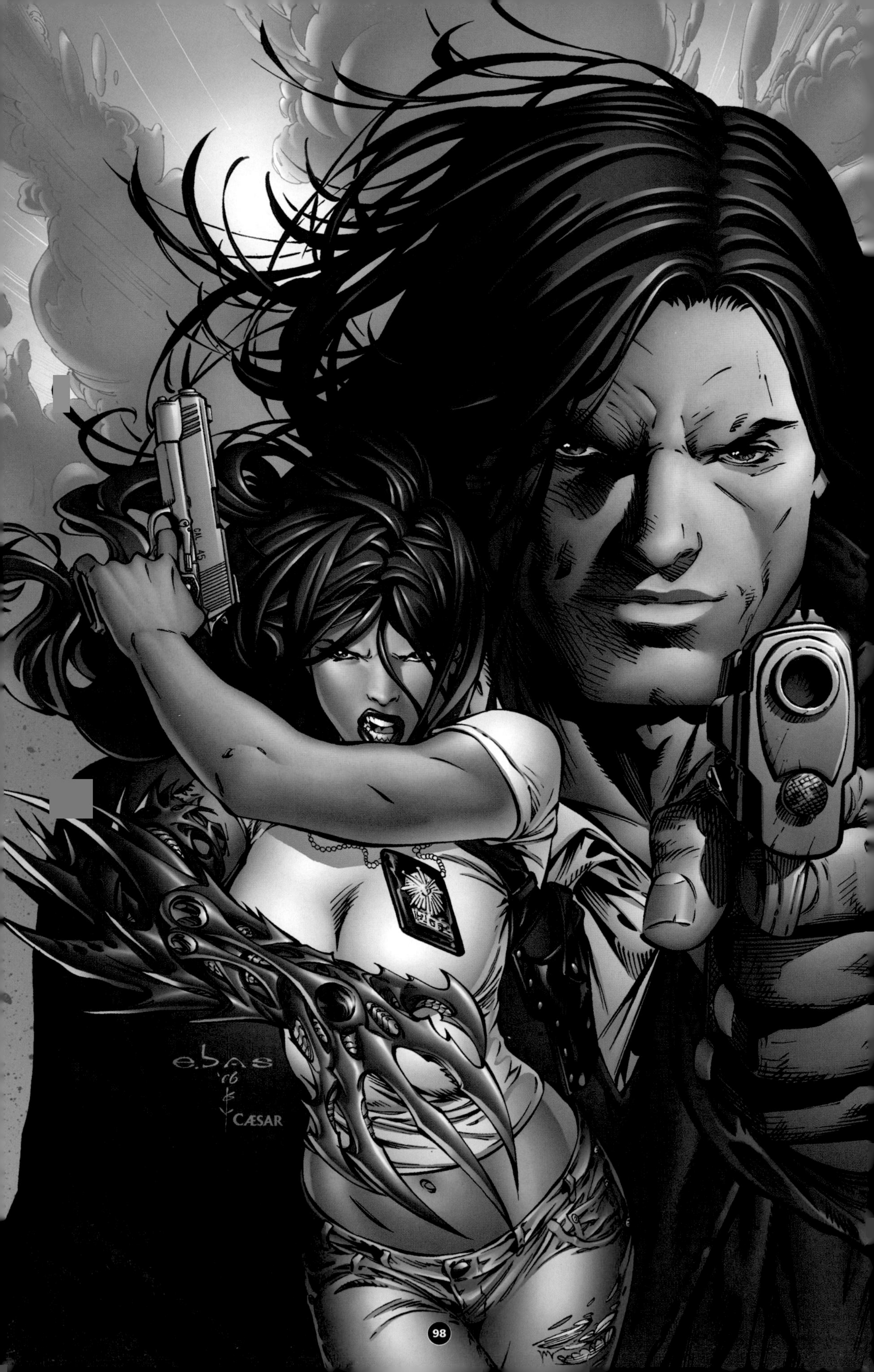
CAL. 45
e.bas
'06
CÆSAR

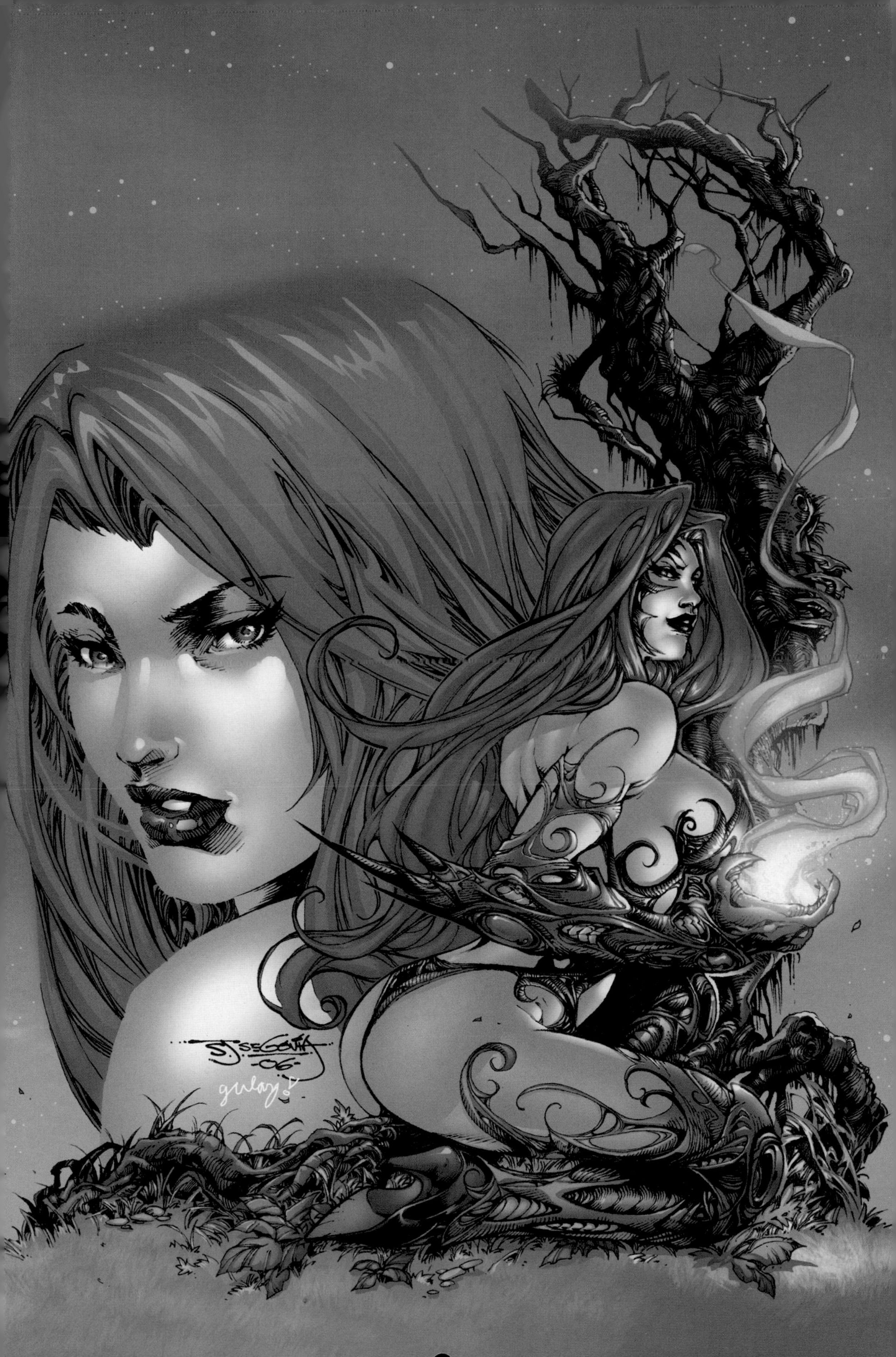

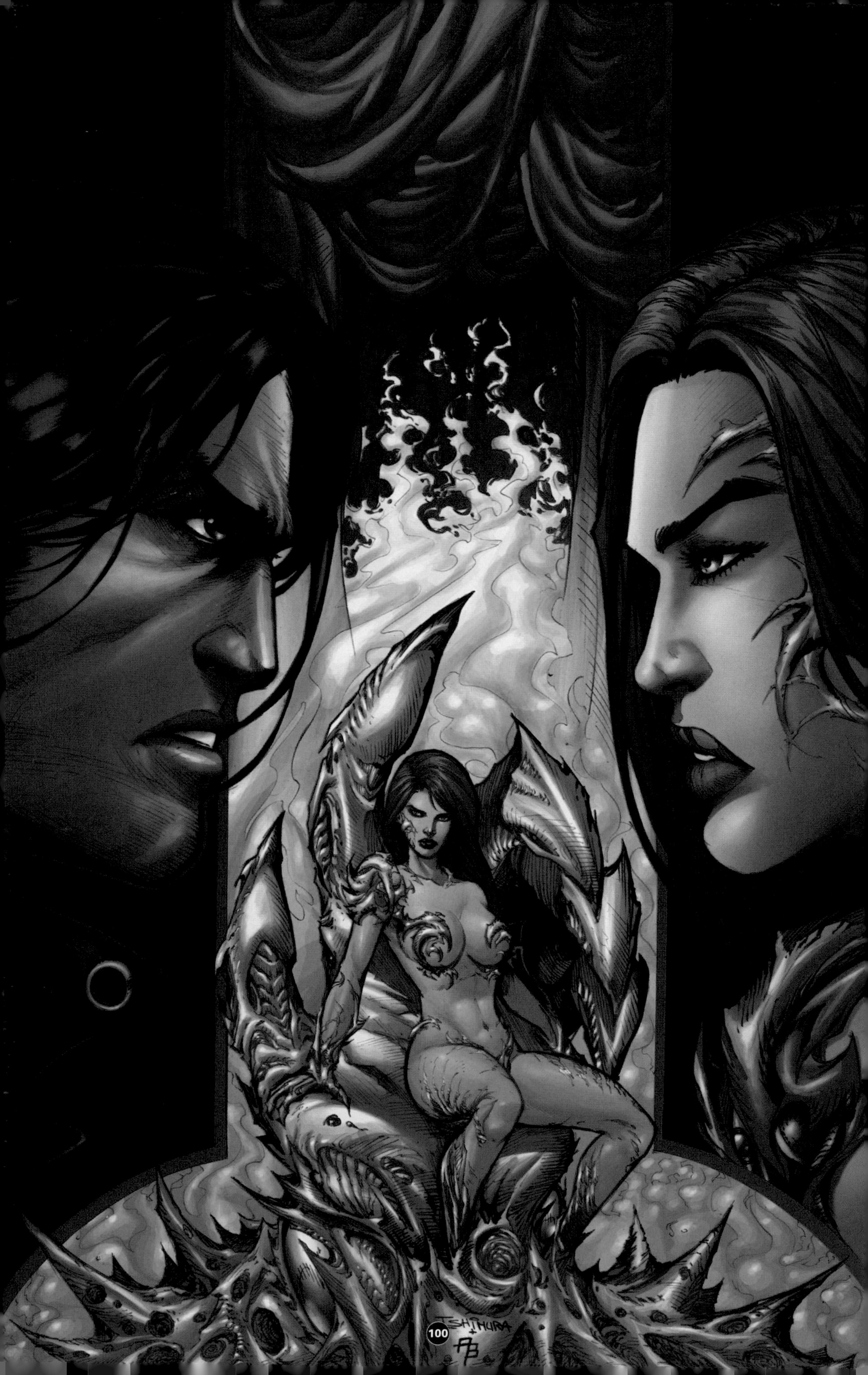

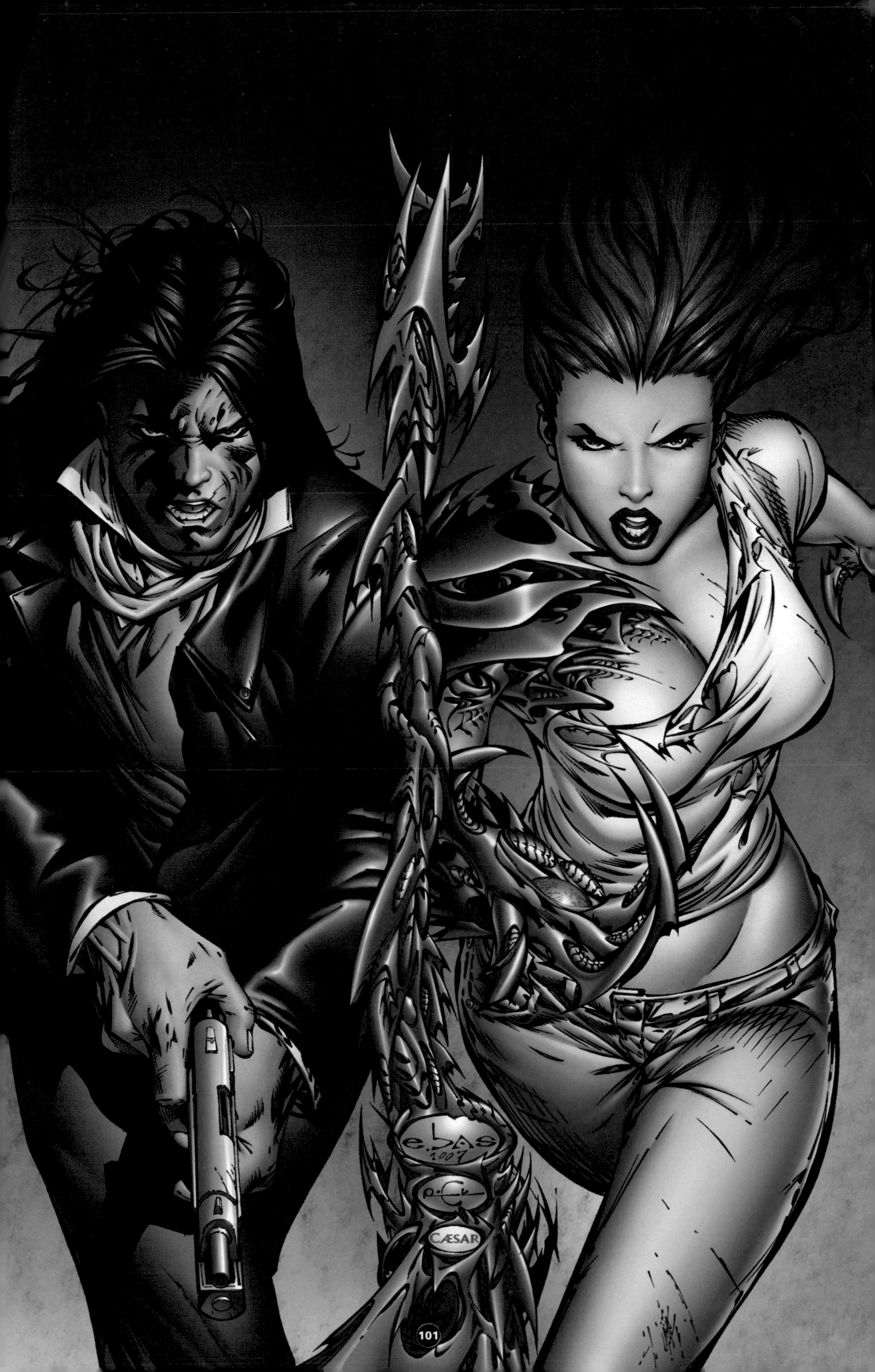
CÆSAR

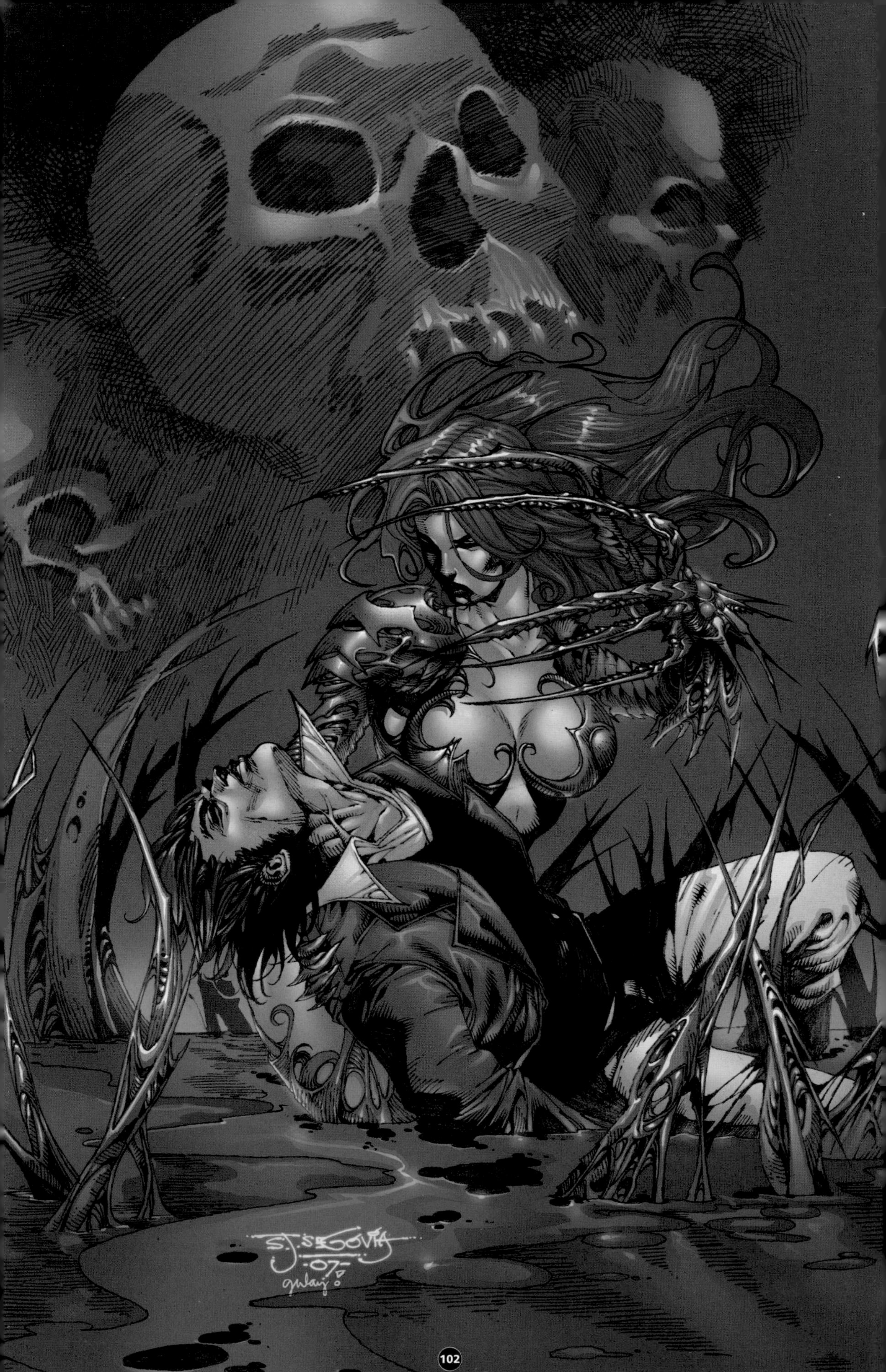
S.J. SEGOVIA
07

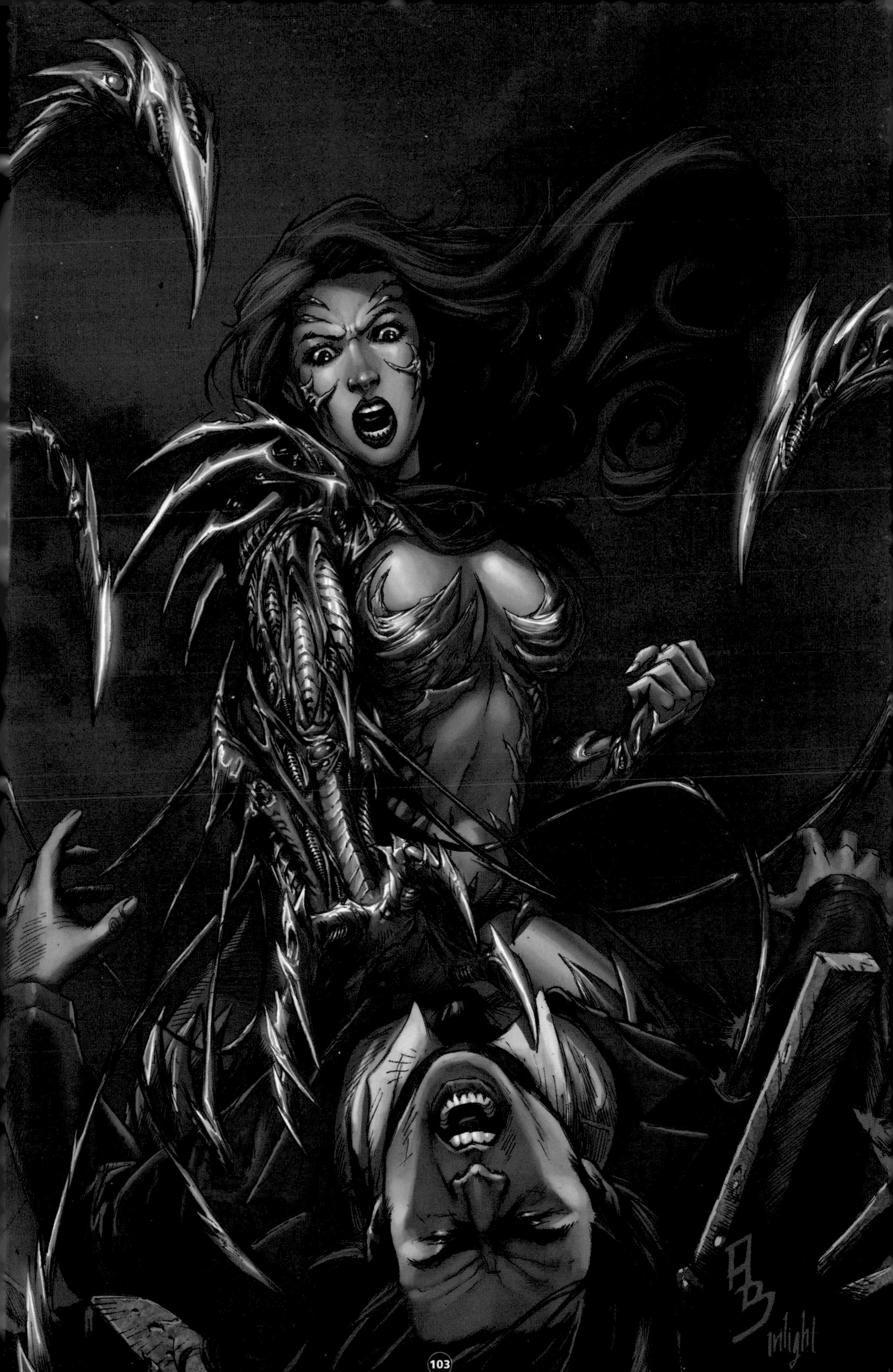

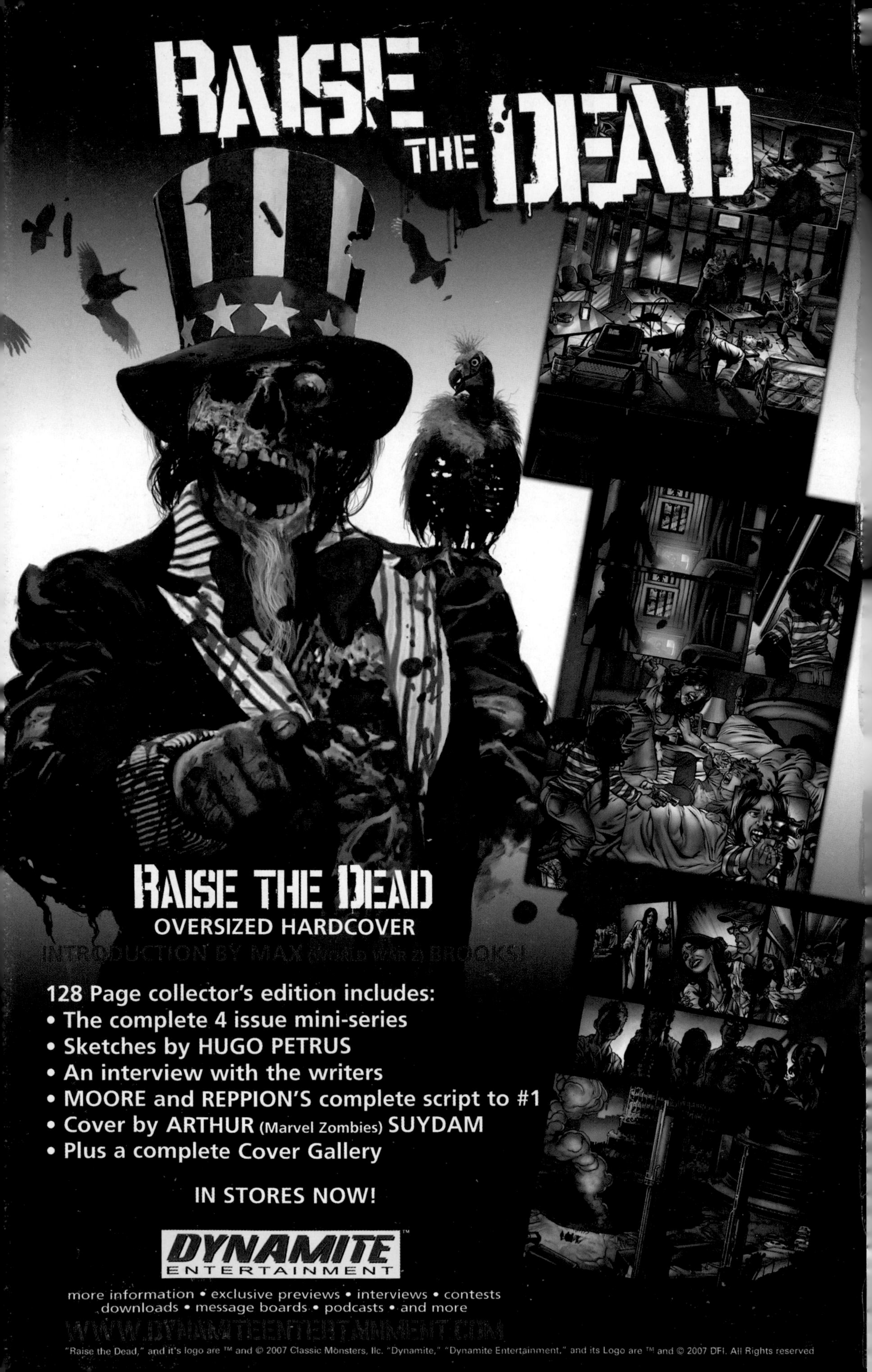
RAISE THE DEAD™
RAISE THE DEAD
OVERSIZED HARDCOVER
INTRODUCTION BY MAX (World War Z) BROOKS!
128 Page collector's edition includes:
• The complete 4 issue mini-series
• Sketches by HUGO PETRUS
• An interview with the writers
• MOORE and REPPION'S complete script to #1
• Cover by ARTHUR (Marvel Zombies) SUYDAM
• Plus a complete Cover Gallery
IN STORES NOW!
DYNAMITE ENTERTAINMENT™
more information • exclusive previews • interviews • contests
downloads • message boards • podcasts • and more
WWW.DYNAMITEENTERTAINMENT.COM
"Raise the Dead," and it's logo are ™ and © 2007 Classic Monsters, llc. "Dynamite," "Dynamite Entertainment," and its Logo are ™ and © 2007 DFI. All Rights reserved